THE SIMON AND SCHUSTER
STEP-BY-STEP ENCYCLOPEDIA
OF PRACTICAL GARDENING
Published in Cooperation with the Royal Horticultural Society

Vegetables

by Tony Biggs

Editor-in-chief Christopher Brickell
Technical editor Kenneth A. Beckett

Editor Margaret Mulvihill
Art Editor Tony Spalding
Assistant Art Editor Janet Carrod
Assistant Editor Lloyd Lindo
Designers Valerie Hill, Sean Keogh
   Winnie Malcolm, Michael Nawrocki
Editorial Assistant Helen Buttery
Executive Editor Chris Foulkes

Published by Simon and Schuster
A Division of Gulf & Western Corporation
Simon & Schuster Building, Rockefeller Center,
1230 Avenue of the Americas, New York,
New York 10020

ISBN 0 671 24833 2
Library of Congress Catalog Card Number 79 195 82

Vegetables was edited and designed by
Mitchell Beazley Publishers Limited, Mill House,
87–89 Shaftesbury Avenue, London W1V 7AD

Typesetting by Tradespools Ltd, Frome, Somerset
Origination by Culver Graphics Ltd,
High Wycombe, Buckinghamshire
Printed in Spain by Printer industria gráfica sa.,
Sant Vicenç dels Horts, Barcelona
Depósito Legal B. 1399—1980

Contents

Introduction

The rewards of vegetable gardening have been justifiably proclaimed many times before. Ecologists, gourmets, health enthusiasts and consumer conscious people agree that growing vegetables is a worthwhile pursuit; it can also be extremely enjoyable. This book has been written and designed to ensure that, in addition, it is a successful one. *Vegetables* assumes no prior knowledge and cuts no corners; it reveals what the experts do and, also, why they do it. Practical and theoretical information is contained in the introductory sections on gardening practices. Then, each vegetable is dealt with in clear detail from the moment when you step outside with a spade to the moment, so many weeks or months later, when you return with a basket of succulent produce.

Flavor and freshness
A major incentive for the home grower must be the vastly superior flavor of fresh vegetables that have been personally selected and tended. Understandably enough, the commercial grower is principally concerned with high yields, uniformity of appearance, the ability of a vegetable to be stored or transported long distances and remain in an acceptable condition, and other marketing factors. Varieties are selected to meet these requirements and, unfortunately, flavor often has to be a lesser consideration.

The home grower need not be so restricted. Varieties can be chosen to suit personal tastes, and the incomparable flavour of fresh produce can be recaptured to provide a new pleasure for young people and revitalize a distant memory for older generations.

The benefits of science
The advances made in commercial growing over the past 25 years have not, however, been ignored in this book. *Vegetables* has an unashamedly scientific approach. This has not meant a rejection of the accumulated wisdom of practical vegetable gardeners; but such experience has been reinforced, and only occasionally modified, to take account of modern research.

During the last two decades tremendous strides have been made in the development of highly efficient systems of vegetable production, and there is no reason why the home grower should not take advantage of the progress made. An understanding of how plants grow and respond to various conditions and techniques can increase the satisfaction and profit to be gained from tending a vegetable plot. In this connection the work of the National Vegetable Research Station at Wellesbourne, England, has been gratefully incorporated. The plant spacings recommended throughout the book and the introductory sections on watering and sowing are influenced by NVRS research.

Reading the pictures
The illustrations in this book are not mere embellishments of the text. They provide a step-by-step guide to the main stages in growing a particular vegetable. And each illustration has been painstakingly researched to visually amplify the information in the accompanying captions. In this respect the resources of the Royal Horticultural Society Garden at Wisley, which is renowned throughout the world as a center of horticultural practice, were invaluable in obtaining information for illustrating each operation.

Throughout the book the main text about each vegetable describes crop management from sowing to harvesting, and it explains in greater detail the reasons behind the brief instructions in the step-by-step captions. Often, special or alternative procedures have been "boxed" for greater clarity.

Climate and local conditions
Despite the helpful conclusions of modern research and the step-by-step approach, the successful vegetable gardener must also be sensitive to and be able to interpret local conditions. *Vegetables* has been written for growers who live in cool temperate climates and, where possible, the range of climatic variations within this category has been accommodated. Sowings can take place earlier in a mild and favourable location such as South Carolina than they can in North Dakota, for example. The section on cloches and cold frames demonstrates how plants can be protected against adverse climatic conditions.

Again, bird damage is something which many gardeners will never have to contend with because it varies from district to district and depends to a large extent on the incidence of particular bird populations. In each situation the grower should be observant and ready to take action according to an informed interpretation of local conditions. It is always a good idea to talk to other local gardeners to find out what does well and benefit from the community's many years of experience.

Pests and diseases
Throughout *Vegetables* great emphasis has been laid on the importance of preventative gardening. Factors such as thinning, watering and the selection of varieties are stressed as the keys to healthy vegetable production. However, the causes, symptoms and control of common pests and diseases are mentioned under each vegetable. An introductory section provides more information about the chemicals involved, their methods of application and the operations suggested throughout the book. **Remember to keep all chemicals out of the reach of children; label the containers carefully; and always follow the manufacturer's instructions.** The authority for recommending or banning garden chemicals is vested in the Federal Government's EPA (Environmental Protection Agency). Most States have also formed their own regulatory agencies such as DEP (Department of Environmental Protection), which have put even more drastic regulations into effect. As a result, some chemicals for control of a specific disease or pest are approved by one State and banned by the DEP in an adjoining State.

New regulations to approve or ban a given pesticide are frequently issued by the EPA and the State regulatory agencies. For this reason, readers are advised to check with their own State Agricultural Experiment Stations for advice on the control of the diseases, pests and weeds in their area.

All chemicals should be handled and stored carefully, and package directions should always be followed.

For the gardener who is seriously plagued by pests and diseases perhaps as a result of inheriting a neglected plot, there is another volume in this series with more comprehensive information on this subject.

The less common vegetables
Many vegetable growers are motivated to start a plot by the desire to produce less common vegetables, which are often difficult to obtain commercially. For example, okra can be bought in the street markets of large cities but is a rare commodity in the cooler North. A section of the book is specially devoted to these more unusual vegetables and it includes 14 of the most popular herbs—the essential complement to fresh vegetables. Throughout, the less well-known relatives of familiar vegetables, and more interesting ways of growing those, are also included.

Glossary

Aeration The incorporation of air into the soil.

Annual A plant that completes its life cycle within one season.

Bare-root plant A plant lifted from the open ground with little or no soil clinging to the roots.

Base-dressing Fertilizer applied immediately before sowing or planting.

Biennial A plant that completes its life cycle over two seasons.

Blanching The exclusion of light from a plant to whiten the stems, shoots or leaves.

Bolting Premature flowering or "running to seed".

Brassica The cabbage, cauliflower and turnip genus of the Cruciferae.

Broadcast sowing A uniform distribution of seed over an entire seedbed, as opposed to sowing in a drill.

Calyx The outer whorl of a flower, consisting of sepals which may be free to the base or partially joined, as in tomato flowers.

Cap A hard crust on the soil surface.

Catch crop A rapidly-maturing crop grown between harvesting one vegetable and sowing or planting the next on the same ground.

Chicon The large, swollen white bud produced from forced chicory roots.

Compost (garden) Rotted organic matter used as an addition to or substitute for manure.

Compound fertilizer One that contains all three major constituents needed for healthy growth, ie nitrogen, phosphorus and potassium.

Crown The part of a plant at or close to ground level that normally produces stems; also the whole rootstock, especially when it is planted to produce a crop such as rhubarb.

Cucurbit A member of the cucumber, squash and melon family.

Cultivar see Variety.

Cutting A separated piece of stem, root or leaf taken in order to propagate a new plant.

Dibble A tool that is pushed into the soil to make a hole in which to plant a seedling, cutting or small plant.

Dormant Asleep. A dormant seed or plant is one that is in a temporary resting state during adverse climatic conditions.

Drill A furrow into which seeds are sown.

Eye A bud.

Fertilizer Material that provides plant food. It can be organic, ie derived from decayed plant or animal matter, or inorganic, ie made from chemicals.

F₁ hybrid A plant that is the result of a cross between two parent strains, usually with the best features of each. It does not breed true in further generations.

Foliar feed A solution of plant nutrients sprayed on to and absorbed through the leaves.

Forcing The hastening of growth by providing warmth and/or excluding light.

Friable Describes a fine and crumbly soil with no hard or wet lumps.

Frost-lifting The loosening and lifting of plants in the soil after hard frost.

Fungicide A chemical that kills molds and fungi.

Genus A group of closely related species.

Germination The sprouting of seeds.

Growing point The extreme tip of roots or shoots, sometimes removed to encourage growth. See Pinching out.

Growing season The period from planting to maturity of a particular crop during one season. Also, generally, the number of frost-free days per year in a given area.

Half-hardy A plant unable to survive the winter without protection.

Harden off To acclimatize gradually plants grown under glass to colder conditions outside; usually done in a cold frame, by exposing the plants to more air daily.

Hardy A plant capable of surviving winter conditions in the open without protection.

Heel cutting see page 89.

Heeling in The storing of plant material, upright or inclined, in a trench which is then filled in with soil and firmed.

Herbicide A chemical used to kill or control weeds.

Hill A point at which plants are grouped together.

Hilling up Mounding earth around the base and stems of a plant.

Humus Fertile, decomposed organic matter added to or already in the soil.

Hybrid A plant produced by the cross fertilization of two species or variants of a species.

Inhibit To suppress a particular growth or

developmental pattern (eg, by pinching).

Insecticide A chemical that kills insects.

Lateral A side growth that develops at an angle to the main axis. Lateral shoots are side-shoots which grow from lateral buds on a main or leading stem.

Legumes Vegetables of the family Leguminosae that produce pods, such as peas or beans.

Light The glass or plastic covering of a cold frame.

Manure Bulky material of animal origin added to soil to improve its structure and fertility.

Mature Capable of bearing flowers and reproduction.

Mulch A layer of material, such as straw, peat or polyethylene, spread on the soil to conserve moisture and suppress weeds.

Mutant or sport A plant that differs genetically, usually in one characteristic, from the typical growth of the plant that produced it.

Offsets Small bulbs produced at the base of the parent bulb; also a young plant developing beside the parent from a runner.

Pan A hard layer beneath the soil surface.

Pelleted seeds Small seeds coated to make them easier to handle for space sowing.

Perennial A plant that goes on living year after year.

Pesticide A chemical used to kill or deter pests.

Pinching out or pinching The removal of the growing tip of a shoot to prevent further terminal growth and to encourage the production of side-shoots.

pH The degree of acidity or alkalinity. Below 7.0 on the pH scale is acid; above it is alkaline.

Pricking out The transplanting of a seedling from a seed tray to a pot or another tray.

Rhizome A lateral-growing, usually food-storing stem, that grows on or just below the soil surface.

Root cuttings Pieces of root that are used to propagate new plants.

Rootstock The underground part of a plant from which roots and shoots are produced; also the root system and stem on which a scion is grafted.

Seed leaves The first leaf or leaves produced by a germinated seed.

Sets Whole or part bulbs or tubers used for propagation.

Seedcoat The tough, protective layer around

a seed which swells and bursts to release the seedling at the time of germination.

Side-dress To apply fertilizer next to a plant and work it in.

Soil-borne Present in the soil.

Space sowing or station sowing The sowing of seeds individually at a set spacing in the site in which they will grow until pricking out or harvesting.

Spit depth The depth of a blade on a normal digging spade; about 10 in.

Sport see Mutant.

Station Individual positions at which seeds are sown along a row.

Stopping see Pinching out.

Strike To take root; usually of cuttings.

Sucker A secondary shoot that develops from a stem or root below ground level.

Systemic insecticide A chemical which permeates a plant's sap stream and kills biting or sucking insects.

Tilth The cultivated surface of the soil. Good tilth is fine and crumbly with no large stones or lumps of earth.

Tine The prong of a fork, hoe or rake.

Top-dressing A fertilizer applied to established crops, usually more effective if hoed or watered into the surface of the soil.

Transpiration The loss of water through the leaves of plants as water vapor.

True leaves Leaves typical of the mature plant as opposed to the usually simpler seed leaves, which are the first to appear.

Truss The collective name for a group of flowers, such as those on tomatoes, that develop into fruit.

Tuber A swollen underground stem modified for food storage; the edible portion of plants such as potatoes.

Turgid Plant material that contains its full complement of water and is not therefore under stress.

Variety A distinct variant of a species, either arising in cultivation (a cultivar) or occurring naturally.

Virus Disease-causing organism not visible to the naked eye, that may live in plants and less often in the soil.

Weed Any plant growing where the gardener does not want it to grow.

Wind-rock The loosening of a plant's root system by strong winds.

Tools

Always choose tools to match height and build, and when buying a spade or fork, pick up several different types and go through the motions of digging to make certain that the balance and weight suit and that they are comfortable to use. A 30 in handle on a spade or fork is about right for the person of average height who likes to dig with a straight back; a 28 in handle often suits those who bend their backs slightly when digging.

Design and materials

Avoid flimsy, poorly made tools however cheap they may be. Badly designed tools made of materials that bend after a little use or with a rough finish or narrow spaces between the tines, where the soil clogs, are worthless. Conventional good quality steel tools with a smooth finish should be used to obtain the best results with the least physical effort. Stainless steel tools are durable and require only minor maintenance, but they are expensive and sometimes heavy and exhausting to use. If the weight and balance are suitable, however, they are undoubtedly the "best buy" because cleaning and oiling is minimal and they will last for many years.

Specially designed tools are available for the elderly and disabled, and some of these may be useful for gardeners who suffer from back trouble or who find that conventional tools do not suit them for some other reason.

Maintenance

Always clean garden tools and oil the metal parts as soon as possible after use. Store them in a dry shed or garage. This is not simply an aesthetic consideration because rusty tools mean harder work and they need replacement more quickly than tools cared for by washing, drying and rubbing over with an oily rag.

Mechanization

If a large area of land is to be used for vegetables, powered garden cultivators with rotating tines or blades that churn up the soil may save hand-digging. Their use is neither practical nor economical on small plots, however, because to use them efficiently for inter-row cultivation, widely spaced rows at least 30 ft long are required as well as sufficient room to turn the machine at each end of the plot. This wastes valuable growing space and ultimately reduces the crop-yield.

The illustrations show the basic tools needed for successful vegetable growing, although some gardeners may find other tools not illustrated here to be useful.

Spade (a) Good quality steel or stainless steel with a strong thin blade for digging.

Garden fork (b) Good quality steel or stainless steel with four well-spaced, rounded or angled prongs for breaking up soil. A flat-pronged fork (c) may also be useful for lifting root crops.

Dutch hoe (d) With its 4 in flat blade, the ideal tool for inter-row cultivation, loosening the soil and uprooting weeds.

Draw hoe (e) Valuable for taking out seed drills and hilling up crops such as potatoes and celery.

Onion hoe (f) With a 3 in wide blade good for inter-row cultivation, particularly at the seedling stage.

Hand cultivator (g) With three (or sometimes five) tines, useful for inter-row cultivation to loosen the soil and dislodge weeds.

Rake (h) Essential for seedbed preparation, the rake's head is also useful as a measuring device for the 12 in distance between certain crop rows.

Trowel (i) With a short handle for planting out seedlings.

Hand-fork (j) Useful for inter-row cultivation.

Watering can (k) Made of strong galvanized steel with a fine brass nozzle, or rose (l) with screw fittings. Strong plastic cans, if well-balanced when full, are as good. Avoid push-on roses because these may become loose and fall off when a full can is tilted suddenly. A perforated dribble bar (m) is useful for accurately applying liquid fertilizers or weedkillers.

Dibble (n) With a steel point to make holes for seedlings and deep-sown seeds. An old spade or fork handle, suitably tapered at the end, is equally useful.

Garden line (o) On a strong reel for accurate and symmetrical row alignment.

Wheelbarrow (p) A strongly constructed and maneuvrable barrow, either of wood or galvanized steel, with a pneumatic or hard rubber tire. When full it should be well balanced and easily pushed.

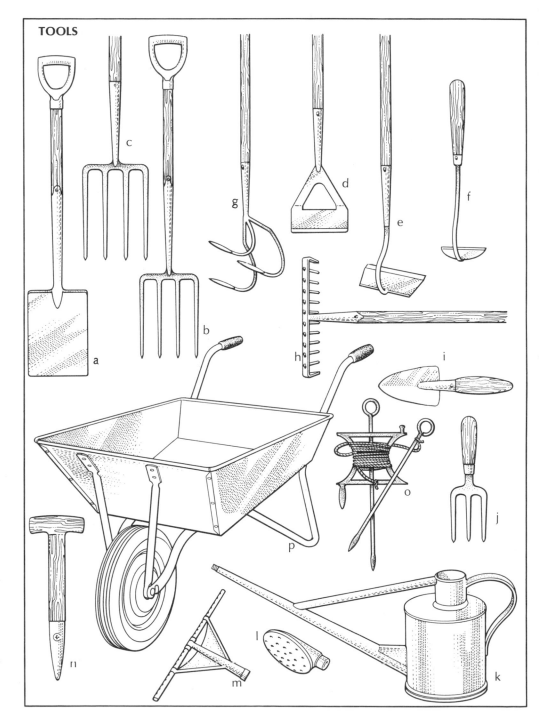

TOOLS

Preparing the ground 1

Not always the most popular chore in the gardener's calendar, digging is done for three reasons: to ensure that annual weeds are buried; to introduce manure or compost into the ground; and to aerate the soil. Fortunately this is only a once-a-year task, best tackled in autumn or early winter, leaving rough soil exposed to be broken down by the winter frosts. By the spring, soil that has been well dug should merely need superficial attention—raking or a light touch with the fork—in readiness for sowing or planting.

Properly carried out, digging should not be an unduly strenuous exercise. Once a good working rhythm has been established, digging a raw patch should be an enjoyable experience. Exhausted diggers are usually those who rush into the garden and proceed to attack their unruly earth without regard for some simple guidelines. Start off gradually and do a little at a time—half an hour the first day to get accustomed to the exercise should be sufficient. When the feel of the spade has been gauged, digging efficiently without too much physical effort becomes easier. Digging is a skill but it does not take long to learn and once acquired it gives the satisfaction of a well-prepared vegetable plot as well as the mastery of a new skill. As indicated on page 4, the choice of tools is also important, so be careful to select a spade and fork to suit your height. Remember that good quality steel tools are perfectly adequate and the more expensive stainless steel tools will not in themselves improve the digging. In preparing the ground, the garden line also comes into its own because the very first task is to stretch the line down the middle of the plot to divide it into two.

Single digging and double digging

As a rule it is sufficient to dig to a spade's depth (known as a spit deep). However, double digging may sometimes be required—for example to enrich deeper beds for permanent plants or to enhance the drainage of heavy soils. Either way, whether single or double digging, on cultivated soils or grassland, there are simple techniques to be followed to guarantee the best results.

The most efficient way of digging over soil is by the use of the trench method. This involves working across the plot in orderly trenches, each about 12–15 in wide or a spade's width, and then back-filling with soil. This way, only the soil heaped on the surface—that removed from the first trench dug—is used to fill in the final trench.

Working across the plot in this way, manure or compost can be introduced simultaneously as each successive trench is filled in. This should be done by spreading the manure on the surface first, if it is to be mixed in well. Otherwise the manure can end up in a lump at the bottom of each trench. Always check the requirements of each intended crop before doing this, however, as for some (such as carrots and parsnips) the incorporation of manure or compost is not beneficial.

If the ground requires an application of lime, this should never be dug in. Instead, lime is scattered on the surface, to be washed into the soil by rain. Lime should never be applied to ground freshly dug with manure, because the chemical constituents of the two tend to react with each other.

The key to successful digging is to keep the spade vertical. A slanting thrust, which achieves less depth, merely means that the work takes longer. Also, it is good technique to drive the spade in at right angles across the trench to free the clod of earth to be moved, enabling it to be lifted away cleanly.

The practice of growing vegetable crops without digging at all is often advocated. Adherents of the organic school of non-digging simply sow and plant on compost that has been laid over the surface of the soil. Underlying this practice—and it is a perfectly feasible one—is the theory of primeval forest regeneration in which bacteria work to convert layers of decaying matter into humus. Non-diggers argue that, while digging does indeed bury weeds, it also has the effect of reactivating weed seeds that have been lying dormant in the soil.

The non-digging method is technically a viable one: considerable fertility develops in the soil over a period of years and vegetables will grow successfully. The labor saved in not digging must be offset by the cost of the compost, however, and experimental work has proved that the yield and quality of vegetables from dug plots is far superior.

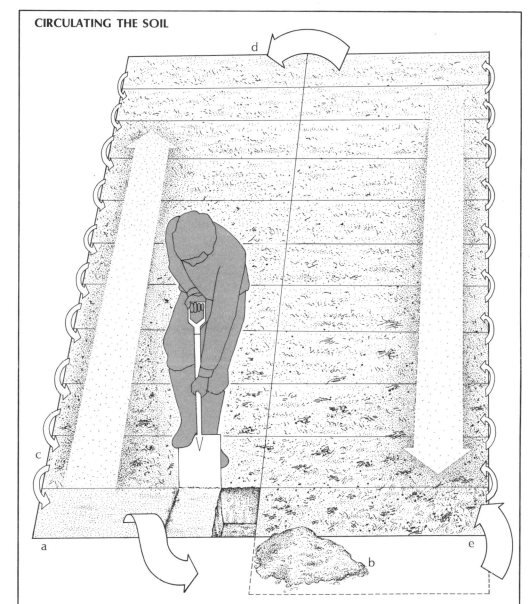

CIRCULATING THE SOIL

The plot is divided down the middle. Excavated soil from the first trench (a) is placed at the same end of the plot opposite the other half (b). The first trench is filled with soil from the second trench (c) and so on. The soil from the first trench in the second half fills in the last trench in the first half (d) and the last trench in the second half takes the soil removed from the first trench (e).

Preparing the ground 2

Single digging

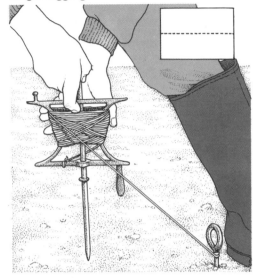

1 Autumn or early winter. Divide the plot down the middle with a garden line.

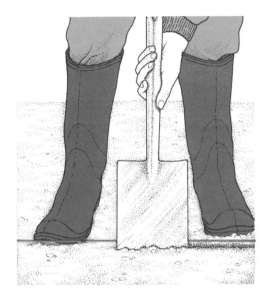

2 Nick out a shallow furrow along the division's length and remove the line.

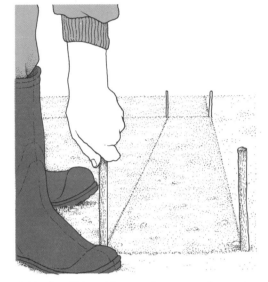

3 Mark a 12 in wide trench area at the end of one half of the plot.

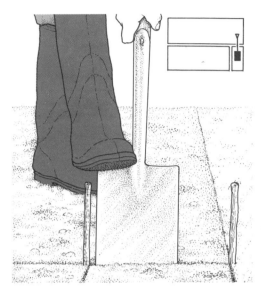

4 Thrust the spade vertically into the trench area and lift a spadeful of soil.

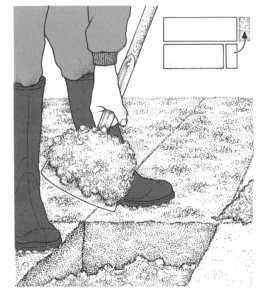

5 Put the excavated soil in a heap at the same end of the plot opposite the other half.

6 Dig at right angles to slice off the next spadeful of soil, and repeat the process.

7 Incorporate manure or well-rotted compost, if desired, by digging it into the bottom of each trench before it is filled in with the excavated soil.

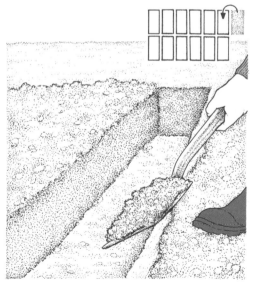

8 Proceed down the first half of the plot and fill the last trench with the soil removed from the first trench at the same end of the second half of the plot. This procedure should leave the plot level.

Preparing the ground 3

Double digging

Double digging, sometimes known as "bastard trenching", is an extra thorough way of preparing the ground. Because it improves drainage, double digging is an especially valuable exercise on heavy soils which may be waterlogged. Root crops, such as carrots and parsnips, grow deep into the ground in search of nutrients and water and if they encounter a hard layer of soil beneath a spit's depth, their growth is arrested. Such a hard layer may develop as a result of single digging over a number of years; compacted ground is a poor growing medium in any case and double digging may be the answer. Divide the plot down the middle and proceed around it as for single digging but take out trenches 24 in wide (instead of 12 in). Because the trenches are wider it is advisable to mark them out with sticks and a garden line. Dig the first trench to a spade's depth. Then loosen up the sub-soil at the bottom of the trench with a garden fork. The fork will penetrate a further spit of soil because its depth is about the same as that of the spade. Make sure you break up the soil all around the trench and not just the area in the middle. If incorporating manure, dig it into the broken-up sub-soil.

Double digging grassland If the plot is a grass-covered area that has not been cultivated for some time, tame it for vegetable growing by adopting a different digging strategy. Divide the plot down the middle with a garden line. Nick out a shallow furrow along the division's length and remove the line. Mark out the first 24 in wide trench. First of all, skim off 2 in of turf with the spade and place it, with the right side up, opposite the other half of the plot at the same end (as with excavated soil in single digging). Dig the exposed soil to a spade's depth and place it in a separate heap near the sliced off turf. Then break up the sub-soil to a 12 in depth.

Chop up the skimmed off turf from the second trench and place it with the grassy part downwards, on top of the loosened up soil in the first trench; the excavated soil is placed on top, and so on. The turf sliced off the first trench is used to fill in the last trench.

If manure or compost is to be applied to grassland, mix it up with the broken-up soil before filling in with the chopped sods.

Double digging

1 Autumn or early winter. Mark out the first 24 in trench with a garden line and dig it to a spade's depth, placing the excavated soil at the same end of the plot but opposite the other half.

2 Fork up the sub-soil to a spit's depth and, if appropriate, in both grassland and cultivated plots, fork well-rotted compost or manure into the broken-up soil.

3 Fill in the first trench of a cultivated plot with the soil removed from the second trench. Repeat the operation until the plot is dug completely.

Double digging grassland

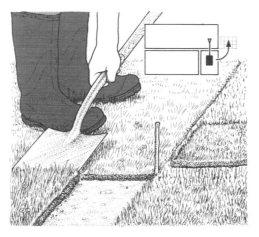

1 Skim off 2 in of turf from the first 24 in trench. Place this turf, grassy side upwards, at the same end of the plot opposite the other half.

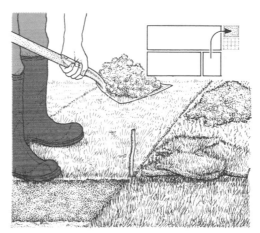

2 Dig the exposed soil to a spade's depth, placing the excavated soil in a separate heap near the removed turf.

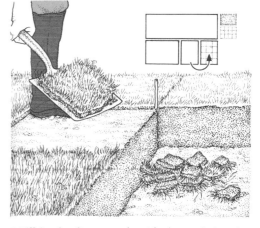

3 Fill in the first trench with the turf sliced off the second trench by placing it, grassy side downwards, on top of the loosened soil and chopping it up. Place the excavated soil on top of this, and so on.

Watering

Vegetables depend on water in the soil to absorb the nutrients required for growth, and if insufficient water is available they cannot manufacture food. Water is also constantly lost through the leaves by transpiration and once the amount of water lost exceeds the amount taken in by the roots, wilting with reduction in growth and yield results.

Water also evaporates from the soil surface around plants and in temperate climates the total loss for leafy crops may be as much as 1 gal per square yard on a sunny day. It is obvious, therefore, that an adequate supply of water is essential to obtain the best growth, quality and yield possible. However, this does not mean drenching the vegetables every day, because an excess of water may well discourage root and shoot growth by inhibiting soil aeration and leaching away nutrients. It may also affect the flavor of some crops adversely.

Seeds and transplanted seedlings require plenty of water to aid germination and growth but research has shown that the need for water varies markedly with different vegetable crops. Leafy crops, such as cabbages and cauliflowers, in which the foliage or shoots are eaten, benefit from frequent, regular supplies of water from the seedling stage onwards, provided that adequate nutrients

are available. An application of 2–3 gal of water per square yard each week in dry periods during the growing season produces the best growth and yield.

In pod-producing vegetables, such as peas and some beans, too much water during the early life of the plants increases leafy growth at the expense of flowers and fruit. No artificial watering is necessary after the seedling stage (except in a drought), but give 1–2 gal of water per square yard weekly at flowering time and as the pods develop. This increases the size and quality of crops.

The timing of additional applications of water to certain vegetables is critical and will be described under the crop concerned. Always try to water crops in the evening or early morning when evaporation by the sun is low and apply it in reasonable quantities so that it penetrates deeply into the soil around the roots. Sprinkling water on the soil surface merely results in much of the water evaporating without reaching the roots where it is needed. Watering in the evening sometimes favors the spread of disease if the foliage remains wet overnight.

To avoid the need for constant watering of the vegetable plot it is important to make sure the soil is able to provide adequate supplies of water. On soils that do not retain

moisture naturally, deep digging increases the volume of soil for the roots of the crops to penetrate in search of moisture. But the maximum benefit comes from regular applications of organic matter such as manure, compost, leaf-mold or moist peat. This should be thoroughly mixed into the soil as the plot is dug, not merely placed in a lump at the bottom of a trench.

Competition between the roots of neighboring plants is another factor affecting water intake. Weed competition should be eliminated at a very early stage and the distance between crop rows and the spacing of individual plants in the rows should be based partly on the water required by the crop concerned. Experimental work has provided information on the best spacing distances for various vegetables and these are given for each crop described.

Mulching crops with compost, leaf-mold or grass clippings is useful in cutting down water loss from the soil surface and it also provides a certain amount of additional food for the plants. The organic material used for mulching should be applied after rainfall or artificial watering as soon as the young plants have become well established. Cultivate the soil surface before mulching so that it is not too compacted. Mulching helps to suppress

weeds and any weeds that develop on the mulch from windblown seed are easily pulled out of the loose surface.

Seeds require adequate water to germinate and, preferably, they should be sown when the soil is naturally moist. If the soil is dry, artificial watering is necessary. The whole area may be watered thoroughly a day or two before preparing the seedbed so that a good tilth can be obtained and the soil is sufficiently moist for germination to occur. Alternatively, water can be dribbled into the seed drill before sowing at a rate of about 1 gal to 20–25 ft length of the drill. Both methods are preferable to watering after sowing, which in some soils "caps" the soil surface so that seedlings may have difficulty in pushing their way through.

Seedlings transplanted to their permanent positions require frequent watering. Each seedling needs approximately $\frac{1}{4}$ pt of water daily until it becomes re-established and it is better to apply the water around the base of the seedling than to spread it generally over the soil surface. In large areas this is not practical and a thorough daily soaking from a sprinkler is needed; although wasteful of water it does save time. In sunny weather seedlings may be covered with paper to reduce water loss.

Water loss

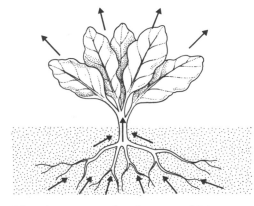

The plant's roots absorb water which passes up the stem and into the leaves. The water is then lost by the plant through its leaves by a process called transpiration.

Mulching

Reduce water loss by mulching the crop with well-rotted compost immediately after rain or artificial watering as soon as the plants are established.

Watering transplanted seedlings

Use a coarse nozzle on the watering can to apply $\frac{1}{4}$ pt of water around the base of transplanted seedlings daily in the morning or evening, until they are re-established.

Protecting transplanted seedlings

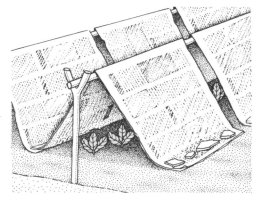

Cover transplanted seedlings with newspaper on sunny days to cut down water loss from the plants and soil. Replace the newspaper each morning if necessary.

Manure and compost

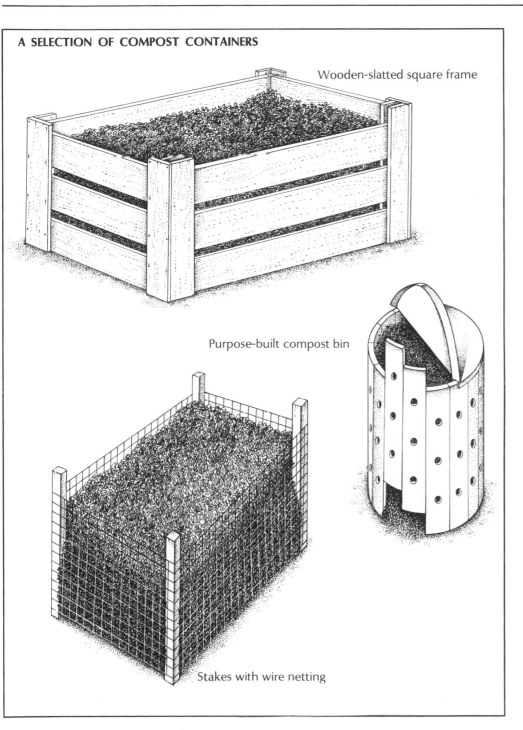

Wooden-slatted square frame

Purpose-built compost bin

Stakes with wire netting

The fertility of a vegetable garden can be compared with a current bank account which is never allowed to become overdrawn. Growing vegetables every year quickly reduces soil fertility unless positive measures are taken to replace the losses. Manure and garden compost are used as soil conditioning agents. They maintain soil structure, provide the materials for bacterial action and improve the soil's moisture-holding capacity. They supply some of the nutrients required but usually not enough to maintain healthy growth, and so fertilizers (see page 10) are used to replenish the supply of plant nutrients in the soil.

Farmyard manure
Adding bulky organic material helps to maintain fertility, although farmyard manure is a luxury which most gardeners have to do without today. If there is a local supply available take advantage of it, however, because well-made, well-rotted farmyard manure is still invaluable material with which to maintain a vegetable garden's fertility. Other locally available materials, such as spent mushroom compost or peat, can also help to condition the soil.

Garden compost
For most gardeners, however, good compost making is the key to fertility maintenance. Any healthy and uncontaminated green vegetation can be used to make compost. Never use woody material and avoid using vegetation which is seriously affected by pests and diseases, because some of these can survive the composting process. Similarly, plant material that has been sprayed with persistent, hormone weedkillers, such as brush killer, should not be used. Do not use brassicas affected by club-root, onions suffering from white rot, potato foliage affected by blight or potato tubers from eelworm-attacked plants. This kind of unhealthy material is best burned immediately and added to the compost heap as ash.

Building the compost heap
Build the heap directly on the soil. Waste materials are decomposed by bacteria which require air, moisture and nitrogen. Therefore the compost heap should be well aerated, moist (but not soaking wet) and of a size to allow heat to be generated and thus speed up the natural process of decomposition. A compost heap with a yard square base and a final height of 3–4 ft is very suitable. A circle of 1 in mesh wire netting, a purpose-built plastic compost bin or a wooden-slatted square frame keeps the heap tidy and less obtrusive in the garden. Without some such device to hold the heap together, birds can pull the sides to pieces.

Build up the heap in 6–9 in layers of waste vegetation. Do not use thick layers of any one material, such as grass cuttings, because this slows down the rotting process. Mix the materials well—the more they are mixed the better. When the first layer is finished and well packed, but not unduly compacted, apply a 1 in layer of garden soil and sprinkle this with lime if the soil is acid. Repeat the application after each subsequent 6–9 in layer. Garden soil supplies the soil bacteria which rapidly multiply and cause decomposition, and the lime keeps the heap sweet (see page 11). When the heap is completed cover the top with a thin layer of soil and cover this with old polyethylene sheeting to retain heat and encourage decomposition. The time taken before the composted material becomes friable and ready for use depends on the time of the year and the nature of the materials in the heap, but six months can be taken as a rough guide. A compost heap completed in October should be ready for use the following April. When green composting material is in short supply the soil layers can be sprinkled with ammonium sulfate or fresh manure to provide the nitrogen required, but never apply lime to the same layer as these activators.

Fertilizers
Short-term, major plant nutrient requirements are supplied by fertilizers. Nitrogen, phosphorus and potassium (NPK) are the main elements required by plants; calcium and magnesium are also of considerable importance. Sodium, iron, molybdenum, copper, boron, manganese and zinc are essential but only in small amounts.

Nitrogen fertilizers encourage vegetative

Manure and compost/Fertilizers

1 Select an area with a yard square base and start the heap with the first 6–9 in of vegetation. Mix the materials well.

2 Apply a 1 in layer of soil. Sprinkle each soil layer with lime if the soil is acid.

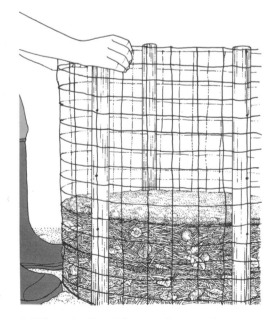

3 When the first 2 layers of vegetation have been prepared protect the heap with a circle of 1 in mesh wire netting.

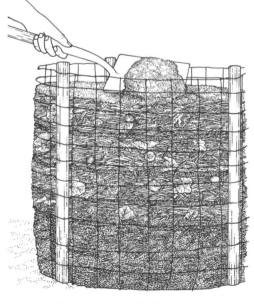

4 When the heap is 3–4 ft high, cover it with a final 1 in layer of soil and then with polyethylene sheeting.

growth and are particularly important for leafy vegetables and for top dressing to promote rapid growth in the spring and summer. Phosphates are necessary for good root growth; they also encourage fruit ripening. Potash fertilizers balance the effects of nitrogenous materials and make the plant less soft, more cold-tolerant and more disease-resistant. The main effects of NPK are shown in the table below. Too much of one element may cancel the effects of others and the most important requirement is to provide a balanced mixture of the nutrients necessary for a particular crop.

Organic and inorganic fertilizers

Fertilizers may be organic or inorganic. Organic fertilizers are derived from animal or plant remains and include materials such as dried blood, meat and fish meal, and bonemeal. They tend to release their nutrients more slowly than do inorganic fertilizers, such as sulfate of ammonia, superphosphate of lime and sulfate of potash, which are produced by industrial processes.

Simple and compound fertilizers

Fertilizers may be simple or compound. Simple materials supply a major plant food only, for example, sulfate of ammonia supplies nitrogen, whereas compound fertilizers supply a mixture of plant foods. A fertilizer labeled 10-10-10 or 5-8-7, for example, is a compound fertilizer which supplies balanced amounts of nitrogen, phosphorus and potassium. Compound fertilizers are generally used to provide the basic requirements of vegetables, and simple fertilizers—usually nitrogenous ones—are used as top-dressing.

Applying fertilizers

Crops normally receive most of their fertilizer requirements as a base dressing which is applied during the final soil preparations before the vegetables are planted or sown. For crops such as spring-sown onions, potatoes and most root crops no more fertilizer applications are usually necessary. Other crops need further feeding, however, especially if rapid and continuing vegetative growth is needed over a long period. For

IMPORTANT PLANT FOODS

FOOD	EFFECTS	DEFICIENCY SYMPTOMS	MAIN FERTILIZERS
Nitrogen	Encourages leafy growth An excess delays flowering and fruiting An excess encourages soft growth which is easily damaged by cold and diseases	Stunted growth Pale yellow leaves Premature ripening, often with improved flavour	Sulphate of ammonia Calcium nitrate Nitrate of soda
Phosphorus	Necessary for good root development Encourages crop ripening Useful for strong seedling development	Poor, stunted growth Purple coloration of leaves and stems Poor seedling growth Fruits ripen very slowly	Superphosphate (placed close to the roots) Bonemeal
Potassium	Prevents soft growth Makes plants more winter hardy and disease-resistant Enables plants to withstand drought better	Generally slow growth High disease incidence Bronzing of leaves on some crops	Sulphate of potash Muriate of potash (more likely to cause damage to young plants)

Fertilizers/Garden lime

example, early summer cabbage should receive a balanced base-dressing of a compound or balanced fertilizer but also benefits greatly from top-dressings of nitrogenous materials, such as nitrate of soda when in growth. With some crops, such as directly sown lettuce, there is a danger of putting too much nitrogen fertilizer in as a base dressing because seed germination may be inhibited.

Base-dressing crops
Base-dressing fertilizers are applied during the final stages of soil preparation before sowing or planting. Rates of application usually range from 1–4 oz per square yard, and the material must be spread evenly. Divide the fertilizer into two lots and rake one lot up and down the area, and the other lot from side to side. This helps with even distribution. Very small quantities can be mixed up with soil, sand or sawdust to make distribution easier, but such materials must be thoroughly mixed in with the fertilizers if the method is to be successful.

Top-dressing crops
Top-dressings are most commonly applied in solid form around the base of plants. Most fertilizers are formulated as fairly coarse granules but care is needed to ensure that they do not land in the middle of developing plants and cause burning and scorching of the young tissues. This is particularly important with nitrogen and potassium fertilizers. Phosphates, however, are best placed close to seeds or the roots of young plants. Scatter top-dressings directly on the ground, rake or hoe them in lightly and water them immediately. This ensures that the top-dressing has a rapid effect on plant growth.

Foliar feeding
A number of proprietary foliar feed materials are available, some of which are of organic origin. Foliar feeding is a convenient way of top-dressing plants but the effects are rarely as rapid and dramatic as those achieved with more conventional materials where the major elements of NPK are required. Foliar applications are very effective for correcting deficiency symptoms, however, particularly of magnesium and various minor elements.

Garden lime
Soils are derived from a wide variety of natural materials that may be alkaline (limestone soils) or acid (peaty soils), in reaction. An alkaline soil contains an abundance of calcium—an element required in small quantities by all plants. In very acid soils there is a shortage of calcium salts. The acidity or alkalinity of a soil is measured by the pH scale which ranges from 0 to 14. Chemically pure water has a pH value of 7, the neutral point. Acid soils have pH values lower than 7, and the pH value of alkaline soils exceeds 7.

Equally important is the level of acidity or alkalinity best suited to various vegetable crops. It is obviously impractical to try to adjust the soil to provide the best level of acidity or alkalinity for each group, so a compromise is needed. Luckily, most vegetables grow well at a pH value between 6.0 and 7.0, and if the soil pH can be adjusted to and maintained at pH 6.0–6.5, even crops such as potatoes, which prefer a more acid soil, should thrive.

If the soil has a low pH the use of lime is advocated to neutralize the acidity if vegetables are to be grown. However, this cannot be achieved quickly and it may take a few years to obtain the desirable pH balance, particularly on light soils where there is leaching of nutrients by heavy rain.

An annual dressing of lime, regarded as obligatory for the vegetable plot by some gardeners, should never be given without first checking whether the soil is acid or alkaline.

Soil testing kits
The soil's pH value can be tested with one of the simple soil testing kits that are available from most garden centers. Take small random samples of the soil and shake them up with the solution provided in the kit. Allow the soil to settle and then compare the color of the liquid with the range of colors on the chart, also provided, which indicates the pH value by depth of color. This can then be translated, according to the directions on the package, into the amount of lime needed.

Alternatively, for about $2, send a pint sample of soil to your state agricultural extension service and obtain a more accurate determination of the pH of your soil, and also what nutrients the soil needs.

Types of lime
It is always preferable to use ground limestone, which is safe and easy to apply. Other forms of lime (quicklime and hydrated, or slaked, lime) are available but they require careful application to avoid damaging plants in the vicinity. The rate of application varies from $\frac{1}{2}$–$1\frac{1}{2}$ lb per square yard, depending on the pH value, the soil type, and the crops.

Applying garden lime
Apply lime in autumn or after winter digging so that the rains wash it in slowly. The best time for an application is a winter day when there is frost on the ground and therefore less chance of it blowing into the eyes. Seek a physician's attention in the event of a mishap and always wash both face and hands immediately afterwards. Never use lime at the same time as manure, compost or fertilizers because they may react adversely.

Using a soil testing kit

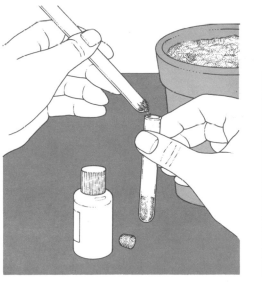

1 Take small, random samples of soil and mix them with the solution provided in the testing kit.

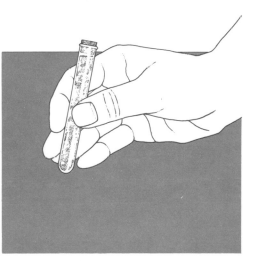

2 Shake the soil in the solution well and allow it to settle.

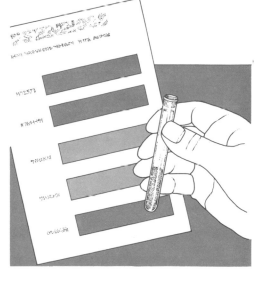

3 Compare the color with the range of colors on the chart provided, which indicates the soil pH value.

Preparing a seedbed

After the ground has been dug in the fall or winter the rough soil is exposed to the weathering effects of freezing, thawing and wetting (see pages 5–7). Drying spring winds then begin to break down the large clods of earth and form a friable crumb structure on the surface of the soil.

Preparing the tilth
A seedbed is prepared by cultivating this crumb structure to produce a tilth into which seeds can be sown or seedlings can be transplanted.

Cultivating First use a hand cultivator to work the top 6–8 in of soil only, because it is important not to bring up large quantities of cloddy, unweathered soil, or buried weeds and organic manure from deep down. Cultivate thoroughly in both directions (ie at right angles to each other) to break down the surface clods and roughly level the surface. Do not over-work the soil at this stage because the tilth may become too fine for subsequent operations

Applying fertilizer Base dressings of fertilizer are applied at this stage and any surface weeds or stones should be removed. Use a pronged cultivator to roughly incorporate fertilizer into the top 4–6 in of soil. Even application is important and where very small quantities are to be incorporated, sand can be used to bulk it up, but the sand must be very well mixed.

Producing the final tilth
Traditionally any further consolidation of the soil required is by treading, shuffling the feet along or across the seedbed to break down the remaining lumps and fill depressions. However, this practice can seriously harm the soil structure, particularly that of a heavy soil. Whenever possible it is far better not to tread seedbeds but to use the head of a rake to break down any remaining clods, to firm any loose areas and to fill any depressions. On light "fluffy" soils treading may be necessary to produce a satisfactory seedbed. In these cases it is essential to tread very lightly and only when the soil is not wet so as to avoid damaging its structure.

Then use the rake with a rhythmic "forward-and-backward" motion, and do not use it too

Cultivating

1 March to April. With a hand cultivator cultivate the top 6–8 in of soil, using a "backward-and-forward" motion.

Consolidating

3 If necessary consolidate the soil by breaking up any remaining clods with the head of the rake and fill any depressions with soil.

Applying fertilizer

2 Roughly incorporate a base dressing of fertilizer into the top 4–6 in of soil and remove any surface weeds or stones.

Leveling

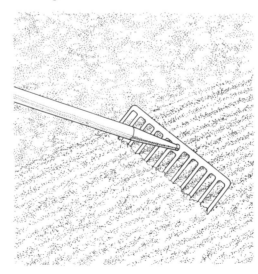

4 Rake to produce the final, level tilth. Move backward and forward with as little soil movement as possible, keeping the teeth of the rake only just in the soil surface.

deeply. If the initial cultivation has been done correctly it should not be necessary to move large quantities of soil.

The fineness of tilth
The type of soil and the kind of seed to be sown determine the fineness of tilth required. A finer tilth is needed for seed sowing than for transplanting and small seeds, such as lettuce, require a finer surface than do large seeds, such as peas and beans. Virtually any degree of fineness can be prepared on sandy or loamy soils, but silty and clayey soils must be treated much more carefully. Very fine silt or clay particles stick together in rainy conditions and then dry into a hard surface crust or cap through which it may be difficult for fine seedlings to penetrate.

Do not prepare very fine tilths on these kinds of soils. As a general rule it is best to prepare the coarsest sowing tilth that the particular seed tolerates, because the surface then remains more stable without "capping." Clayey soils eventually become less prone to capping as the proportion of compost in the soil builds up through repeated manuring.

Sowing vegetable seeds
Vegetable seeds can be sown directly outside or they can be transplanted after raising indoors or after purchasing from a grower or garden center.

Direct sowing Small seeds, such as those of lettuce and carrots, are usually sown in drills and subsequently thinned out to the required spacing. Always sow the seed very thinly in rows. Apart from saving seed, this cuts down competition for food between seedlings and it also produces sturdier plants—crowded seedlings are very much more prone to disease. Mark out the position of the row with a stake at each end and stretch a garden line tightly between them. Use a draw hoe against the line to take out the drill, the depth of which should relate to the size of the seed—small seeds need shallow drills whereas larger ones can be sown deeper. After watering the bottom of the drill, the soil should be carefully raked back over the seeds and lightly tapped down with the back of the rake. Then tag each row with the name and variety of the vegetable and the sowing date.

Sowing

Yields
Vegetable crop yields cannot be estimated with absolute accuracy. Much depends on weather and soil, variety, time of harvesting, spacing and weakening through pest, disease and weed competition. In the following list average yields are given, where relevant, as the output from a 33 ft row.

Asparagus, established crowns 20 bundles 1 lb per bundle	Cabbage 1 head per plant
Beans, broad 44 lb	Carrots, main crop 26½ lb
Beans, bush 26½ lb	Broccoli, all types 1 curd per plant
Beans, pole 55 lb	
climbing French 55 lb	Celeriac 35 lb
Beets 35 lb	Celery 1 lb per stick
Broccoli, sprouting 20 lb	Chicory 40 roots
Brussels sprouts 22 lb	Endive 33 heads
	Florence fennel 10 lb

Space sowing Large seeds, such as beans, squash and sweet corn, can be space sown to their final spacings. Take out a drill as described above—obviously to a greater depth—or use a dibble or trowel to make a hole for each seed or group of seeds. It is impossible to be certain that each seed will germinate so it is better to sow two or three seeds at each station and thin out to one plant later if necessary.

Pelleted seed
Space sowing is a much more economical way of using large natural seeds but small seeds, such as those of lettuce, parsnip and carrot, can also be handled individually and space sown if pelleted seeds are used. These are seeds that are surrounded with a coat of clay-like material to facilitate more accurate sowing. Pelleted seed is expensive, however, and in some cases the results are unpredictable. Some vegetable seeds are also sold in plastic tapes which are stretched out along the ground. The seeds are neatly spaced within the tape, which soon disintegrates to free the seeds. But tapes, like pelleted seeds, are expensive.

Pre-germinating seeds
Seed suppliers must provide a minimum percentage germination figure for dry, natural seed, but it is still impossible to know just how many will come up. Consequently, more seeds must be sown and then thinned out to produce the required number of plants and the right spacing. But it is possible to pre-germinate seeds before putting them in the ground. Then only those that have started to germinate are sown and seed can be used more economically. Pre-germination of seed can be carried out in a plastic container.

Fluid drilling A technique known as fluid drilling allows pre-germinated seeds to be sown in a stream of fluid gel, such as fairly liquid wallpaper paste without fungicide, in a polyethylene bag from which the mixture of gel plus seeds is piped into the previously prepared and watered drill. The gel protects the germinating seeds.

PRE-GERMINATION

The seeds are sprinkled on moistened kitchen tissue in a container which is then covered and kept in a warm place (21°C/70°F) until they germinate.

Watering and thinning
Water is crucial for germination and it should be applied as a routine part of all seed sowing operations. Generous applications of water are particularly important for pelleted and taped seeds because the material encasing the seed must be dissolved before the seed can emerge. In each seed sowing operation, however, in drills or holes and with natural, pre-germinated, pelleted or taped seeds, water the soil beforehand and keep the rows constantly moist until the seedlings emerge. Whenever possible water should be applied before sowing because watering seed drills after sowing can result in a "capped" soil surface which inhibits the growth of germinating seedlings. If this does happen keep the soil surface damp to soften the hard crust. Even thinly sown seeds produce more seedlings than will be needed and they must be thinned out. This is best done at the earliest possible stage because prolonged overcrowding encourages weak, leggy seedlings which are readily attacked by damping-off fungi. Remove unwanted seedlings by hand.

Taking out a drill

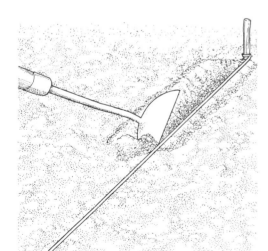

1 Stretch a garden line tightly between stakes at each end of the intended row. Keep the corner of the hoe tightly against the line to make a V-shaped drill.

Direct sowing

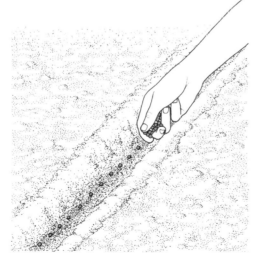

2 Water the bottom of the drill. Allow the water to drain before sprinkling seeds very thinly and regularly along it. Then cover the seeds with soil.

Thinning

3 Remove unwanted seedlings as soon as possible, leaving the strongest plant at each station. Water the row of seedlings, and if necessary, firm afterwards.

Space sowing

Put 2–3 large or pelleted seeds at each position in the drill, then cover them and water. Later thin to 1 seedling per station if necessary.

13

Globe artichokes 12–15 large heads	Peas, main crop 22 lb	Spinach beet 35 lb
Kale 30–35 lb	Potatoes, early 22 lb	Squashes 3–4 fruits (bush)
Kohlrabi 20–30 lb	Potatoes, second early 35 lb	6–8 fruits (trailing)
Leeks 40 lb	Potatoes, main crop 40 lb	Sweetcorn 25 cobs
Lettuce 33 heads	Radishes 25 lb	Tomatoes, outdoor
Onions, bulb 22 lb	Rhubarb, outdoor 35 lb	4–5 lb per plant
Parsnips 33 lb	Salsify 12½ lb	Turnips 20 lb
Peas, early 15½ lb	Shallots 20 lb	Zucchinis
	Spinach 20 lb	12–18 fruits per plant

Spacing/Purchasing seed

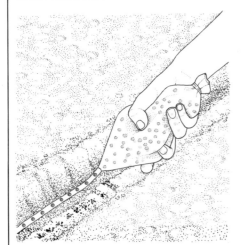

FLUID DRILLING

By this technique pre-germinated seeds are piped from a polyethylene bag in a stream of fluid gel, such as a fairly liquid wallpaper paste without fungicide.

Transplanting
Always plant vegetables to a line and use a measuring rod to mark the correct in-the-row spacings. Plant with a dibble, a hand fork, or a trowel depending on the type of transplant being handled. Plants raised in pots, soil blocks or seed trays have quite large root systems and the holes are probably best made with a trowel. Make the holes large enough for the roots and plant at the same depth that they were in their container or seedbed. Dibbles can be used for transplanting leek and brassica plants raised in outdoor seedbeds because they have smaller root systems. On heavy, wet soils take care when using the dibble not to compress the soil at the sides of the hole because this can inhibit root spread and the establishment of transplants. It is also important to achieve the correct planting depth with a dibble and the soil must be firmed tightly around the plant roots of brassicas.

Water plants immediately after transplanting and again at regular intervals until they are established. Transplants are particularly liable to attack from birds (see page 15).

The principles of spacing
Most of the spacings used in the home vegetable garden are used for traditional and historical reasons, but as new varieties are introduced (particularly F_1 hybrids) and requirements in vegetable size change, spacings may need to be reconsidered.

Plants develop most uniformly if the spacings between the rows are more or less the same as the spacings between plants in the row. This is not always practical, however, because a wider between-row spacing may be needed to allow for weed control, inter-row cultivations and access to other rows.

Growing plants closer together results in smaller plants, for example, cabbage or cauliflower, but the plants also mature more evenly. This is also true of Brussels sprouts where close spacings result in smaller sprout buttons maturing evenly up the stems.

Close spacings put particular pressure on soil moisture and plant foods and if the soil dries out rapidly or has low reserves of organic matter they increase the likelihood of drought stress. Under these conditions—or if it is not possible to water the plants sufficiently regularly—it is better to place the plants farther apart and give the roots a larger volume of soil from which to draw their supplies of water.

Pest and disease spread is likely to be more rapid in closely spaced plants, and if rows of different vegetables are close together there is a danger of insecticide or fungicide spray drift on to adjoining rows.

Closely spaced plants exert a greater competitive effect against weeds, particularly if the crop plants have a spreading habit and can shade out the weeds. On the other hand, control of weeds may be more difficult in closely spaced plants because there is less space in which to use a hoe, and the danger of damaging the crops is increased.

Home vegetable gardens are generally highly productive areas of land. The range and quantity of vegetables produced from a small area is very great indeed and there are great pressures on the space available. The choice of crop spacings therefore depends on a careful consideration of all the factors outlined above in relation to the time and effort involved.

Purchasing seeds and plants
Planning the next season's cropping in the vegetable garden begins in the winter with the arrival of the new editions of seed catalogs. Many seed firms produce excellent catalogs which contain interesting and valuable information.

Seed for the vegetable garden is relatively cheap and so it is worth while selecting and buying good quality seed. Buy from a reliable firm and use previous experience to choose varieties of proven performance. Be prepared to try something new but always grow a small quantity initially alongside the standard varieties. It is a good idea to consult other gardeners in the area to find out what does well in the locality. In the U.S., seed firms must state the purity and minimum germination percentages of their seed so there is a high degree of protection for the gardener.

F_1 hybrids
By a complex process in which two true-breeding plants are crossed to produce a hybrid generation (the first filial or F_1 generation), an increasing number of F_1 hybrids are appearing in the catalogs. The advantage of these hybrids is that they are often more vigorous than their parents, and they tend to have more uniform characteristics of height, form and color, as well as maturing at the same time. F_1 hybrids are produced only after a considerable amount of selection and careful crossing over a number of years and they are invariably more expensive than conventional varieties. Never save seed from F_1 hybrids because the next generation of plants will have lost its uniformity.

F_1 hybrids do not suit everyone's vegetable requirements but they are ideal for those who want uniformly maturing produce to put into household freezers.

Conventional varieties
Conventional varieties mature over a longer period and they are preferred by many gardeners. One advantage is that seed can be saved from them, but it must be selected from healthy, true-to-type plants only.

Storing seeds
Seeds should be stored dry in paper bags or packs rather than in plastic bags because these tend to conserve dampness, if it is present, and reduce the viability of the seeds. Store seeds in a cool, dry place, such as a cellar or a refrigerator, and keep all the packages clearly labeled.

If they have been stored correctly most vegetable seeds remain viable for at least two years. But because there are some exceptions—parsnip seed, for example, rapidly loses the ability to germinate once a pack has been opened—it is wise to buy several small-sized packs of seed and sow all the contents of one pack once it has been opened.

Buying vegetable plants
Some vegetable plants are purchased from nurseries or garden centers. This is probably most convenient for tomatoes, peppers, eggplants, celery and celeriac, but care is needed when purchases are made. Trust and goodwill between the nursery owner and the customer are essential so always return to purchase seeds where good service has been received before. In any event, it is wise to buy from a recognized grower.

Be certain of the varieties being purchased. Take great care when buying plants that could introduce a persistent disease to the garden. This is particularly true for club-root on brassica plants and white rot on onion or leek plants, and the warning is even more applicable to plants which friendly gardening neighbors may provide.

With such acquisitions it is very important to know about the origins of the plants because it is almost impossible to eradicate disease once it spreads throughout the vegetable garden.

Buying perennial vegetables
Perennial vegetables such as rhubarb, artichokes and asparagus are purchased as plants rather than as seed. Again, they could be infected with virus diseases which gradually reduce the vigor and productivity of the plants, and so only virus-free or tested material should be purchased.

This is also true of "seed" potatoes which are likely to be bought every year. Virus-free seed tubers are produced in areas where aphids that spread viruses are no problem.

Pests and diseases 1

Strong, healthy plants are less susceptible to disease and better able to withstand damage from pests. However, despite correct cultivation, vigilant weed control, crop rotation and the increasing availability of disease-resistant varieties, damage due to pests and diseases occurs even in the most carefully managed vegetable gardens. It is therefore important to be able to make a rapid and accurate diagnosis of each problem so that the right action, often involving the use of chemicals, can be taken as soon as possible.

The use of chemicals
Always follow the manufacturer's instructions precisely, especially concerning dilution, the time of application and the period which must elapse between the final application and harvesting. Always store chemicals, sealed and labeled, out of the reach of children, pets and wild animals. Never transfer them to soft drinks bottles. Do not spray on windy days and do not allow spray to drift on to other crops or neighboring gardens, ponds, rivers, ditches or water sources. Never use containers previously used for weedkillers when mixing or applying other sprays and do not mix up more material than is required because it is difficult to dispose of the excess safely. Wash hands and all equipment thoroughly after spraying.

Some chemicals must be treated with extra caution. For example, calomel dust is poisonous and protective gloves should be worn. Captan, dinocap, maneb, thiram and zineb may irritate skin, eyes, nose and mouth: wear gloves, mask and goggles if susceptible to allergic reactions.

Not all insects and animals in the garden are harmful to vegetables and some are beneficial. They can be killed by the chemicals used to control pests so never use pesticides indiscriminately or excessively.

Types of pesticides and fungicides
Fungicides are used to prevent infections, and pesticides to treat infestations. There are various kinds of pesticides and they act in different ways. Contact types such as derris affect the insect itself and it is important to cover all the plant's surfaces for maximum kill. They remain effective for a relatively short period after application. Systemic types such as formothion and dimethoate are absorbed into the plant and spread through the sap. They are very effective against sap-sucking insects. Complete coverage of the plant is not essential and most systemics can be applied as a root drench. Most fungicides only check or prevent disease and should therefore be applied before signs of disease are seen. A few partially systemic fungicides such as benomyl are now available. These are absorbed slightly into the plant's tissues and are effective for a short period even after disease symptoms are visible.

Methods of application Chemicals are available as dusts, sprays, pastes, pellets, wettable powders and aerosols. Not all chemicals are in all forms, however, and not all forms of a chemical are effective against the same range of pests or diseases.

Most of the materials are listed in this book according to their active chemical ingredient and not by their trade name. Use products that contain the appropriate active ingredient which is given on the label or in the instructions issued by the manufacturer.

DISEASES
In the following section the main diseases are briefly described and appropriate control methods are recommended.

Bacterial blight is a seed-borne bacterial disease which appears as spots on the leaves of beans. The spots are surrounded by a light-colored ring or halo. There is no adequate control and the plants should be burnt once the crop has been picked.

Blackleg of potatoes is caused by the bacterium *Erwinia carotovora* var. *atroseptica*. Early in the season the foliage of an affected plant turns yellow and the shoots collapse because of blackening and rotting of the stem bases, although occasionally one or two healthy stems develop. The plant may die before any tubers form but any which have already developed show a brown or gray slimy rot inside starting at the heel end. Destroy affected plants. If severely infected tubers are stored they will decay, but those only slightly infected may show no symptoms and, if planted, will introduce the infection the following season.

Chocolate spot disease (a form of botrytis) causes discoloration on the leaves and stems of broad beans and can seriously affect over-wintered crops. Plants grown in acid soils or which have become soft through excessive applications of nitrogenous fertilizers are more susceptible to attack. Sowing the seeds thinly, applications of potash at $\frac{1}{2}$ oz per square yard before sowing and the maintenance of a pH of 6.5–7.0 will cut down the likelihood of infection. Where the disease is endemic spray the young foliage with a copper fungicide before any symptoms are seen.

Club-root distorts the roots and badly affects the growth of all brassicas. The disease is more prevalent in acid soils so where necessary raise the pH to 6.5–7.5 by applying limestone at 14 oz per square yard and maintain the pH level with smaller dressings as required in subsequent years. Four per cent calomel dust raked into the soil before sowing at $1\frac{1}{2}$ oz per square yard helps to control club-root, and also have some combative function against cabbage maggot (see page 17). Seedlings may also be dipped in calomel paste or a solution of benomyl to protect them from attack. In soils where club-root of brassicas is a major problem sterilization with SMDC (Vapam) or DMTT (Mylone) may be needed.

Common scab of potatoes occurs most frequently in dry soils lacking in humus and is also prevalent on alkaline soils. A soil pH of 5.0–6.0 and improvement of the soil humus content will cut down the incidence of the disease. Potatoes should also be kept well watered, particularly during dry spells. No available chemical control measures are effective against it.

Damping off diseases of seedlings are encouraged by overcrowded, stagnant conditions and the use of garden soil rather than sterilized soils or compost for raising seedlings under glass. Affected seedlings rot and collapse at ground level. Thin sowing in sterilized soil will cut down the incidence of damping off. Slight attacks may be checked by watering with captan or zineb after removing dead seedlings.

Downy mildews may affect lettuce, onions, spinach and young brassicas. Thin sowing and early thinning of seedlings will cut down incidence of these mildews but if seedlings are attacked, remove the affected leaves and spray with zineb. Bordeaux mixture on brassicas, onions and spinach and thiram on lettuce are also effective.

Foot and root rot is caused by several different fungi which kill the roots and bases of the stems of young plants. A seed dressing of captan may help to avoid this trouble but at the first signs of this disease, water the crop with a solution of captan or zineb. Mound sterile compost around the bases of affected tomatoes. Burn badly affected plants.

Gray mold (*Botrytis cinerea*) may affect most vegetables at some stage in their lives. It is encouraged by overcrowded, stagnant conditions and affected stems, leaves or fruits rapidly rot and become covered with a gray-brown fungal growth. To cut down attacks sow seeds thinly and keep seedlings and plants well spaced. Provide good ventilation under glass and make sure that dead or dying material is removed and burnt. Terraclor or dicloran (both only available in commercial packs) raked into the soil prior to sowing or planting helps to protect lettuces. Spray over-wintering plants with thiram.

Leaf spots Several fungal diseases (antracnose is among the best known) cause spots on vegetable leaves and on fruits. The spots vary in color and, often, have pronounced centers. Brassicas, spinach beet and beets are among those crops susceptible to leaf-spot fungi, which usually affect older leaves. Affected tissue sometimes fall away, leaving holes. Leaf spots are most troublesome in wet seasons, particularly among overcrowded plants and on brassicas grown too soft as a result of heavy dressings of nitrogenous fertilizers. Burn infected parts, and spray with zineb or maneb at the first sign of infection.

Neck rot fungus (*Botrytis allii*) can cause considerable loss of stored onions. A gray moldy growth develops on or near the neck of an affected bulb, which subsequently becomes soft and rotten. Later, large black resting bodies of the fungus develop on the rotting tissues. Store only hard, well-dried bulbs in a cool, dry place where there is free circulation of air around them. Examine bulbs frequently and remove rotting onions as they are seen. The disease can be seed-borne, therefore buy good quality seed which has been treated

Pests and diseases 2

against neck rot, or sets from a reputable grower, and dust seeds and sets with dry benomyl before sowing or planting.

Parsnip canker causes rotting of the shoulder tissues of parsnips. There are no satisfactory control measures although the incidence of the disease can be reduced by growing parsnips on a fresh site each year in deep well-worked soil of pH 5.5–7.0. Some varieties are resistant to parsnip canker.

Potato blight is a serious disease of potatoes and is also liable to infect tomatoes. Foliage, stems and tubers of potatoes can be affected and destroyed. Deep planting of healthy tubers in drills at least 5 in deep and timely hilling up minimize infection. Main crop potatoes should also be sprayed from July onwards with maneb, zineb or bordeaux mixture to control the disease. Cut off and remove the stems before lifting. A few varieties are resistant to potato blight and can be grown in areas where this disease is prevalent. Potato blight can be controlled on tomatoes by spraying each season with one of the chemicals recommended for potatoes, as soon as the tops have been pinched out of most of the plants in midsummer. In cool wet seasons the spray should be repeated every 2–3 weeks.

Powdery mildews occur on squashes, cucumbers and some other vegetable crops, particularly if they become dry at the roots. The leaves and stems become covered with a white powdery coating. Control by spraying with benomyl or dinocap as soon as the first symptoms appear, and repeat if necessary.

Sclerotinia disease can attack the roots or stem bases of several vegetables including carrots, cucumbers, Jerusalem artichokes and roots or tubers in storage. Any infected plants must be burnt to avoid further soil contamination from the large resting bodies that form if diseased plants are allowed to remain. There is no practical chemical control. Good hygiene and rotation of affected crops are the only practical methods of control.

Smut is characterized by large, gray and black fungus growths on corn ears and other parts of the plant. Cut off and burn the infected parts. Rotate crops annually.

Violet root rot of asparagus is caused by the soil-borne fungus, *Helicobasidium pur-*

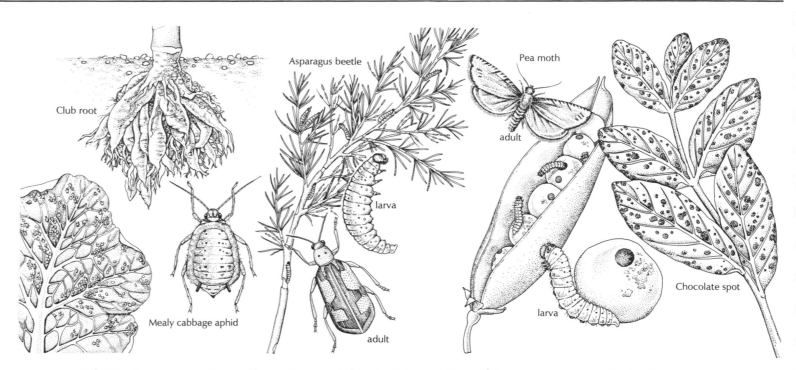

Club root

Mealy cabbage aphid

Asparagus beetle

larva

adult

Pea moth

adult

larva

Chocolate spot

pureum, which kills the crown and roots. It grows on them as violet web-like strands. Small round masses of fungal threads may also appear. With the death of the roots the top growth turns yellow and dies, and a gap develops in the asparagus bed as the disease gradually spreads outward. Where only slight infection has occurred, isolate the diseased area by sinking sheets of thick polyethylene into the soil to form a vertical cylinder to a depth of 12 in. In severe cases abandon the infected bed.

Viruses causing leaf mottling and distortion and often stunting of the plants can affect squashes in particular, celery, cucumbers, tomatoes and several other vegetables. They are spread by aphids or eelworms and so control of these pests and removal of weeds that may act as hosts for both the viruses and their vectors is important. There is no cure for virus-affected plants, which should be burnt once the trouble has been diagnosed. Always wash hands and tools after handling virus-infected plants.

White rot of onions appears as a fluffy white growth at the bases of onions and quickly

affects and kills the foliage. Affected plants should be burnt as soon as the disease is seen. Control may be obtained by applying four per cent calomel dust or benomyl to the drills prior to sowing, or spraying with the recommended rate of benomyl when the plants are approximately 7–8 in tall.

Wilt Fusarium wilt occurs in hot weather; verticillium wilt occurs in cool weather. Both diseases cause wilting, yellowing and death of tomatoes, peppers and other vegetables. Control is to plant resistant varieties.

PESTS

In the following section the main pests are briefly described and appropriate control methods are recommended.

Aphids (greenfly and blackfly) will infest most vegetable crops. Apart from the damage caused by the aphids themselves, they are carriers of virus diseases and vegetables should be checked regularly for their presence. Infestations should be dealt with at an early stage by spraying with dimethoate, derris or malathion. If the plants are to be harvested within one week of applying the

spray use derris. Cucurbits are also best sprayed with derris or a pyrethroid compound to avoid damage.

Root aphids may also be troublesome on beans, lettuce and artichokes. Attacks are not usually noticed until the plants are infested. A malathion drench may check heavy infestations but soil treatment with diazinon granules prior to sowing or planting should prevent attack. Some lettuce varieties are resistant to root aphids.

Asparagus beetle Small yellow and black beetles and their gray-black grubs can defoliate the plants during the summer. Control by spraying with derris or lindane as soon as these pests are seen. Rotenone, malathion and carbaryl also are recommended chemicals for the control of asparagus beetle.

Bean seed fly maggots can prevent germination of all types of bean seed and they can also damage onions. Damage usually occurs in cold, wet seasons when germination is slow. The use of cloches to warm the soil early in the year encourages germination and cuts down attacks. Treating the seed row with diazinon gives some protection.

Pests and diseases 3

Birds Damage to vegetable crops by birds, can occur throughout the year. Scaring devices and bird repellent sprays are of limited value in deterring birds. In some instances they may be effective for short periods, but where birds are a persistent problem some form of cage or netting is essential to produce worthwhile crops.

Cabbage maggots (*Hylemya brassica*) can devastate many brassica seedlings and young plants. The seed rows and transplanting sites should be treated with diazinon prior to sowing or planting. Attacks on established plants can be checked with trichlorphon.

Cabbage worms Several green worms riddle the leaves of cabbages, broccoli, cauliflower and related plants with holes. Regular weekly dusting with rotenone from the time the worms first appear in the spring gives control.

Carrot rust fly (*Psila rosae*) is one of the most damaging pests of carrots and also attacks parsley, parsnip and celery. Growth is stunted and secondary rots may develop in the damaged carrots. Careful spacing of pelleted seed or very thin sowing to cut down the need to thin carrots will help to minimize damage because the female carrot rust flies are strongly attracted by the aroma of carrot foliage bruised when thinning. Sowings made after the end of May normally miss the first generation of maggots but carrot rust fly is such a widespread pest that treatment of the seed drills with diazinon is advisable to give protection for 6–8 weeks. Carrots that are not to be lifted until fall should also be sprayed with trichlorphon in late August.

Caterpillars are troublesome on cabbages and should be controlled before they penetrate the hearts, where they are difficult to reach. Hand picking with a small number of plants or treatment with carbaryl, lindane, fenitrothion or trichlorphon is effective.

Celery leaf miner lives in the leaves of celery, parsnip and some herbs. Heavy attacks can be controlled by spraying with trichlorphon or dimethoate. Light infestations of celery leaf miner can be overcome by hand picking and burning affected leaves.

Colorado potato beetles are wide beetles with yellow and black stripes and black spots on the head. They lay clusters of orange eggs, from which red grubs emerge in the spring.

Both the larvae and adults feed on the leaves of potatoes, tomatoes, eggplants and peppers. Spray, or dust, with carbaryl.

Corn earworms are 2-in caterpillars with a yellow head and several body colors. They eat the silks and top kernels of corn, and also attack tomatoes and lima beans. Dusting or spraying with carbaryl when the silks start to appear usually controls them, but a repeat application may be necessary.

Cucumber beetles are of two kinds: one with black spots on a yellow background; the other with black stripes on yellow. Both eat the leaves of cucumbers and all related vegetables, and the grubs attack the stems. Dust young plants frequently with rotenone.

Cutworms are large, smooth, fat, soil-dwelling caterpillars, most often brown in color. They chew through the stems of cabbages and related vegetables, tomatoes and other seedling plants. Loosely wrap the stems of plants when set out with aluminum foil or kraft paper. The collars should extend from just below the soil to 4 in above.

Deer, rabbits, raccoons and woodchucks do extensive damage to suburban and country gardens. Repellents are not effective, and should not be applied to vegetables anyway. Control deer by erecting 8 ft high mesh fences around the garden. Rabbits can be controlled by fences that are buried 6 in below ground and extend 2 ft above ground. Trapping is the best control for raccoons and woodchucks.

Eelworms attack mainly members of the onion family but can also damage carrots, parsnips and beans. They are microscopic, worm-like creatures that live inside the stem and leaves. They cause the tissues to become soft and swollen, and infested plants usually rot off and die. There are no chemical controls available to amateur gardeners and infested plants should be burnt. Host plants, which include some weeds, should not be grown in ground infested by onion eelworms for at least two years.

European corn borers are whitish, 1-in caterpillars that eat corn tassels and tunnel into the ears. They may attack beans, too. Spray or dust with carbaryl when tassels appear and four times thereafter at five-day intervals.

Flea beetles Heavy infestation of these tiny

beetles, which eat small holes in the leaves of brassica seedlings, can be controlled with derris or lindane. Damage seldom occurs once the plants have developed beyond the seedling stage.

Gophers are burrowing rodents that eat roots, tubers and underground stems. They can be controlled by the use of traps and poisoned baits in the runs.

Hornworms are enormous green caterpillars that feed on tomato plants and, to some extend, on peppers, potatoes and eggplants. They are not easily seen, despite their large size, but partly eaten leaves are an indication that they are present. Look for them at night with a flashlight and pick them off by hand.

Leafhoppers are small, hopping insects that feed on beans, carrots, cucumbers, melons and potatoes. They stunt the plants and cause leaves to turn brown. Spraying with carbaryl or methoxychlor at weekly intervals controls them effectively.

Mexican bean beetles have yellow and black stripes and lay clusters of yellow eggs under bean leaves. Yellow grubs emerge from the eggs to feed on the foliage. Dust the undersides of beans with rotenone or carbaryl.

Mice In rural areas, mice can be troublesome, eating peas, beans and corn seeds. Chemical deterrents are seldom effective. Covering seeds with holly or other spiky leaves, or dipping seeds in kerosene and dusting them with alum prior to sowing may deter mice, but persistent trapping is the only long-term solution. Traps should be covered to prevent birds and pets being harmed.

Moles can be a considerable nuisance. Trapping in the runs is the only effective method of control.

Nematodes are microscopic soil insects that cause general sickness of many vegetables. Plants are stunted; leaves turn yellow; warty growths appear on roots and stems. Rotate crops annually wherever the insects are present. If they are a serious problem, fumigate the soil before planting. Growing marigold in the vegetable garden also helps.

Onion maggot (*Hylemya antiqua*) attacks all members of the onion family. Young plants may be killed by the maggots, and the bulbs of older onions are tunneled and made useless for consumption. Soil treatment with

diazinon or chlorpyrifos granules when sowing or planting will control this pest during the vulnerable early stages.

Pea and bean weevils feed by eating notches from the leaf margins of pea and broad bean plants. Control measures, using HCH are necessary only if seedlings are being attacked.

Pea moth caterpillars badly damage peas, eating the green peas and spoiling the crop, particularly of late-maturing varieties. Early-maturing crops usually escape damage because they flower before the pea moth lays its eggs. Peas that flower between mid-June and mid-August should be sprayed with fenitrothion 7–10 days after flowering starts.

Slugs, snails, woodlice and millipedes can destroy seedlings and attack many developing vegetable crops. Slugs can be controlled by using metaldehyde pellets along the rows. Lindane controls woodlice and millipedes.

Squash bugs are dark-brown insects which are also known as stink bugs because they have a bad smell when crushed. By sucking the sap of squashes and related plants, they cause leaves to wilt and die. Spray with carbaryl or malathion at the first appearance of the bugs and later when you find brown egg masses on the undersides of the leaves.

Squash vine borers are 1-in white caterpillars with brown heads that tunnel through the stems of squashes and related plants. The parents are red and orange, wasplike moths. Apply carbaryl or methoxychlor to 8 in plants and repeat at weekly intervals for a month.

Whitefly Brassicas, cucurbits, tomatoes and other vegetables are attacked by various whitefly species that may cause a black deposit of sooty mold on the leaves. Cabbage whitefly is a distinct species from the glasshouse whitefly that affects tomatoes and cucurbits, but both may be controlled by three or four sprays with pyrethroid compounds at seven day intervals. Under glass biological control with the wasp *Encarsia formosa* avoids the problems of pesticide residues and resistance.

Wireworms may occur in large numbers in grassland or weed infested areas. They attack the roots of a wide variety of vegetables and may seriously affect the quality of crops such as potatoes. Soil dressings of diazinon at planting or sowing will control infestations.

Weed control

ANNUAL WEEDS
Annual meadow grass
(*Poa annua*)
Fat hen (*Chenopodium album*)
Shepherd's purse
(*Capsella bursa-pastoris*)
Chickweed (*Stellaria media*)
Mayweeds (*Matricaria* spp)
Groundsel (*Senecio vulgaris*)

Annual nettle (*Utrica urens*)
Speedwells (*Veronica* spp)

PERENNIAL WEEDS
Docks (*Rumex* spp)
Couch grass (*Agropyron repens*)
Creeping thistle
(*Cirsium arvense*)
Bindweed (*Convolvulus* spp)

A weed is a plant growing where it is not wanted. Thus one of last year's potatoes which comes up in this year's carrots is a weed. Weeds compete with crops for light, water and nutrients and they also create a micro-environment around plants in which gray mold (*Botrytis cinerea*) and damping-off diseases flourish. Weeds also act as hosts for pests, such as aphids and whitefly, and diseases, such as club-root of brassicas.

Annual weeds and perennial weeds
Annuals are plants that complete their life-cycle within a growing season, and they are often able to undergo more than one life-cycle in a season. Annuals are also character-ized by the production of very many seeds so that the weed seed population in the soil is constantly replenished. Perennial plants live from year to year and usually have underground organs—stems or roots—which enable them to survive through the winter. Thus docks (*Rumex* spp) have thick, fleshy tap roots and couch grass (*Agropyron repens*) has underground stems or rhizomes.

Controlling perennial weeds
Weed control begins with winter digging prior to growing the first crops. Cut down any woody perennials, such as brambles (*Rubus* spp), and dig out all the roots. Double dig the whole vegetable garden in the first instance and remove all perennial weed roots and rhizomes. Burn them all and never use them for compost making. Once the land has been cleared of perennial weeds, they should never be a problem again, unless, of course, they are imported with organic materials such as farmyard manure.

Controlling annual weeds
Annual weeds continually reappear, how-ever, and all vegetable growing soils have a large reservoir of weed seeds. Weed seeds are also blown in on the wind and carried by birds and by man.

When winter digging, the gardener should skim off annual weeds and dig them into the bottom of each trench along with organic manure or garden compost. Digging brings up annual weed seeds which were buried in previous seasons. Many will germinate, but subsequent cultivations should kill the young weed seedlings that emerge. They will have appeared by the time cultivations take place to prepare the land for sowing or planting. Remove these and the next flush of weed seedlings will appear with the sown or planted vegetables.

Hoeing against weeds
Hoeing is the main method of weed control in the growing crop. It is largely a matter of personal preference which type of hoe to use, but in every case the blade must be kept constantly sharpened so that the weeds are severed from their roots rather than pulled up with them.

Choose a warm, drying day so that the weeds wilt and die quickly after hoeing. Care is needed when hoeing closely around crop plants because any damage caused is quickly colonized by disease organisms. Keep the hoe in the upper, surface layers of the soil so as not to bring up more weed seeds to germinate and grow. The dry soil produced by surface hoeing acts as a mulch which in itself inhibits weed growth.

Mulching against weeds
Weeds can also be controlled by using mulches. The use of dry soil as a mulch has already been mentioned but materials such as black polyethylene, well-prepared com-post, or peat can also be used. Black poly-ethylene forms a complete physical barrier to weed growth; it also warms up the soil and conserves moisture. It is usually necessary to bury the edges of the polyethylene to prevent it blowing away and holes must be cut in it through which vegetables can be planted or sown. As well as eliminating weeds, a black polyethylene mulch can bring crops forward and hasten their maturity by as much as three weeks but, unfortunately, pests can thrive in the moist conditions produced. Organic mulches, such as peat, perform similar func-tions but have the advantage that they can be dug into the soil at the end of the season, thus improving its structure and fertility. Straw is not recommended as a mulch material because the bacterial action re-quired to break it down can lead to a nitrogen deficiency in certain soils.

Using chemicals against weeds
The amateur's vegetable garden is extremely productive and a large number of crops are grown in a very small area. The danger of spray drift and persistence from chemical weedkillers is therefore considerable. Against annual weeds non-persistent contact weed-killers such as paraquat or diquat, do have a place, however, but they must be applied at low level with a dribble bar when there is no wind and, therefore, no danger of drift. These materials are inactivated rapidly on contact with the soil but they kill any green tissues with which they come into contact.

More toxic and persistent weedkillers should not be used in the home vegetable garden because the risks involved are too great. Whenever using chemicals always follow the manufacturer's instructions.

Hoeing

Carefully hoe annual weeds, keeping the blade level with the surface layers of the soil. Choose a warm, drying day for hoeing and keep the blade sharp.

Digging perennial weeds

During winter digging remove all perennial roots and rhizomes and burn them.

Mulching

Use black polyethylene (or organic mulches) to act as a barrier against weed growth, to conserve moisture and to warm up the soil.

Chemical weed control

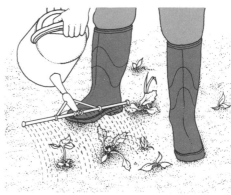

Use a dribble bar to deliver herbicides at ground level just on top of each weed. Never apply herbicides on a windy day and follow the manufacturer's instructions.

Cloches, tunnels and frames

Cloches are the gardener's allies because they raise the temperature of the soil and air around plants and protect crops against unfavorable weather. This makes it possible to grow a wider range of vegetables successfully and in many cases to harvest them much earlier. Lettuces, for example, can be grown throughout the year in mild climates and melons are a possibility in the north. At the sowing stage of many crops cloches are extremely helpful. If they are placed over a seedbed a couple of weeks before sowing, the soil is warmed up and speedy germination is encouraged. Various crops, such as onions, can be placed under cloches at harvesting time to dry and ripen before storing.

The old type of cloche was bell-shaped and made of very thick glass. Today's protective structures come in a variety of shapes and sizes and are made of glass, polyethylene or semi-rigid or clear plastic. Each type has its advantages, but when selecting a cloche certain points should always be considered. It is essential to have ready access to plants under cloches for weeding, training, spraying and harvesting. Except when they are covering small seedlings (see page 8), cloches need not be removed for watering. Water can be applied overhead; it runs down the sides of the cloches, is absorbed into the soil and reaches the roots of the plants, which grow naturally towards sources of food and water.

Heat and light A cloche must retain heat and transmit light. But the retention of heat should not preclude adequate ventilation, and cloches should never be completely airtight. Stagnant air building up underneath them encourages disease. If there is no built-in ventilation, small gaps should be left between individual cloches in rows. However, too much draft and consequent heat loss must also be avoided and it should be possible to close securely the ends of individual cloches or of rows of cloches. Some cloches have end-pieces designed for this purpose.

A cloche must conserve heat and glass types are the best at retaining warmth, although plastic is perfectly adequate in this respect. Glass is also the best transmitter of light, but because it becomes dirty easily, glass cloches should be easy to dismantle for cleaning.

Size and stability Glass cloches are obviously less likely to be upset by wind than plastic structures but all types of cloche should have fittings to anchor them securely into the ground if they are exposed to strong winds. Plastic cloches, besides being relatively cheap and comparable in performance to glass, have the advantage of being more easily moved around the vegetable garden and they are probably safer when there are children in the vicinity.

Cloches are available in a variety of shapes and sizes to suit the circumstances and the preferred crops of vegetable growers. Many modern types can be adjusted to several widths and they have side extensions to increase height. The glass or plastic covering of some cloches can be replaced by netting as a protective device against birds.

Polyethylene tunnels

Polyethylene sheeting stretched over wire hoops and secured with string or wire is a good, cheap alternative to cloches. It transmits light and retains heat well but it needs replacing as it becomes yellow or torn. The tunnels are simple to erect and transport to different parts of the garden. They can be ventilated by leaving the ends open or by rolling up the sides.

Cold frames

Frames provide virtually the same protection as cloches, although heat is retained better and wind has less effect, making them ideal for hardening off plants initially raised indoors or in a greenhouse. However, they are less flexible to use, although portable types can be obtained. Modern frames usually have steel or aluminum frames and glass all round. The glass roof, known as a "light", can be hinged or designed to slide back. To retain the most heat a solid-sided frame should be used, whereas for more light glass-to-ground frames are the better. Regular ventilation is more important than for cloches because frames are almost airtight, so prop the lights open and remove them altogether in summer. Poor ventilation may encourage the spread of disease. If the weather is very cold the frames may be covered with burlap, straw or similar material at night.

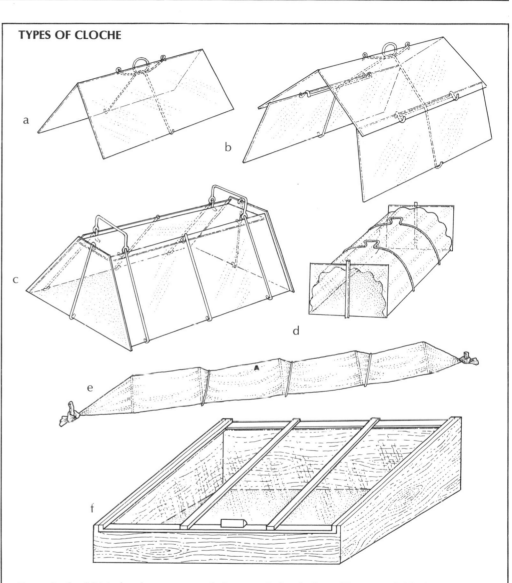

TYPES OF CLOCHE

Tent cloche (a) Made of two panes of glass held together with a wire frame.
Barn cloche (b) Shaped as the name suggests, using four panes of glass.
Utility or tomato cloche (c) Flat-topped with three panes of glass.
Corrugated PVC sheeting (d) A strong, long-lasting rigid material which transmits plenty of light and retains heat well.

Polyethylene film tunnel (e) The cheapest and most satisfactory form of protection. The sheeting is stretched over wire hoops and fixed with strings or wires. It is ventilated by leaving the ends open or by rolling up the sides. A polyethylene tunnel is easily dismantled and stored.
Cold frame (f) Home-made with a wooden framework and a Dutch "light".

Crop rotation

Growing the same vegetables in the same piece of ground each year eventually results in a build-up of soil-borne pests or diseases. Such continuous growing of brassicas, for example, favors club-root, and successive crops of onions are likely to cause a build-up of stem eelworm.

Different types of vegetables require different ground preparation and cultivation procedures. Potatoes need a deeply cultivated soil which is continually moved during hilling up. On the other hand, root crops—such as carrots, parsnips and beets—need a firm, level soil with a fine tilth which is disturbed very little during the growing season.

Fertilizer, lime and manure requirements also vary. Potatoes respond to large applications of organic manure and fertilizer but they should not be limed. Brassica crops also respond to applications of manure and fertilizer but they require a soil between pH 6.5 and 7.5.

These are the major reasons for practicing crop rotation in the vegetable garden. It must be said that rotations are easier to effect on paper than they are on the ground.

Grouping the crops

It is useful to put vegetables together in groups which have similar crop protection, cultivation, manure, fertilizer and liming requirements. Groups are then moved sequentially around the vegetable plot so that, over a period of years, a particular piece of ground grows all the crops. In theory it is better to leave as large an interval as possible between growing a crop again on the same site, but it is rarely possible to leave more than three or four years. Thus three and four year rotations have been devised and a three year plan is considered here. A certain amount of compromise is necessary in order to simplify the rotation. Potatoes are grouped with root crops, even though they benefit from applications of organic manure and root crops do not.

Having divided the vegetables in this way, the groups are moved sequentially around the plot over a three year period. The plot is roughly divided into three equal sized units, but an area should be left at one end on which perennial vegetables, such as asparagus and artichokes are grown permanently.

In year one the potato and root crop unit receives no manure or lime but moderately heavy quantities of fertilizer. The legume and onion unit receives heavy dressings of manure and little fertilizer or lime. The brassicas receive average amounts of manure and fertilizer but heavy applications of lime. Crop rotation therefore ensures that all parts of the plot receive manure, fertilizer and lime regularly while the dangers of pest and disease build-up are minimized.

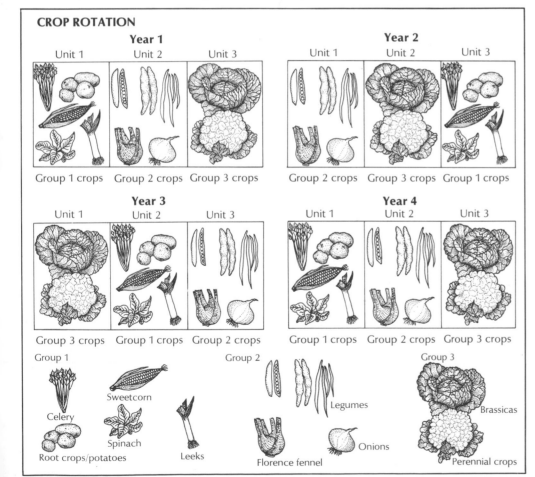

CROP ROTATION

Year 1
Unit 1 — Group 1 crops
Unit 2 — Group 2 crops
Unit 3 — Group 3 crops

Year 2
Unit 1 — Group 2 crops
Unit 2 — Group 3 crops
Unit 3 — Group 1 crops

Year 3
Unit 1 — Group 3 crops
Unit 2 — Group 1 crops
Unit 3 — Group 2 crops

Year 4
Unit 1 — Group 1 crops
Unit 2 — Group 2 crops
Unit 3 — Group 3 crops

Group 1
Celery
Sweetcorn
Spinach
Root crops/potatoes
Leeks

Group 2
Legumes
Florence fennel
Onions

Group 3
Brassicas
Perennial crops

CATCH CROPPING AND INTERCROPPING

Some vegetables grow and mature more quickly than others so there are times of the year when gaps appear in the vegetable plot. These gaps can be used to grow—or catch—a crop of rapidly maturing vegetables. Thus the ground occupied by peas in Unit 2 of the crop rotation plan may not be needed for brassicas until the following spring and can be used for crops such as radishes or endive.

Intercropping Rapidly maturing crops can also be intercropped or grown between slower maturing crops. Spinach can be grown between rows of slow-growing leeks, for example.

Lettuces 1

OUTDOOR LETTUCE
Head types (butterheads)
'Arctic King', 'Buttercrunch',
'Cobham Green', 'Fortune',
'Mildura' (mildew resistant),
'Suzan'.

Head types (crispheads)
'Avoncrisp' (resistant to mildew
and root aphids), 'Great Lakes',
'Webbs Wonderful',
'Windermere'.
Cos types:
'Little Gem', 'Lobjoits Green Cos',
'Winter Density'.

Lettuce is the salad plant for all seasons. Although an annual that matures naturally during the early summer, the use of suitable varieties, cloches or heated frames, and the correct growing conditions make it possible to harvest lettuce throughout all but the very coldest months.

Types of lettuce
Several different types of lettuce have been bred and they vary considerably in size, form and texture. Three main groups may be recognized although there are intermediates.
Head lettuce These include the butterheads with globular soft-leaved heads, and the crispheads, also round-headed but with crinkly, crisped leaves. They will usually tolerate poorer and drier soils than the other groups.
Cos lettuce The lettuces of this group are upright in growth with more or less oblong heads of crisp leaves. They grow best in rich, moist soils. Modern varieties do not need to be tied to produce a compact head.
Leaf lettuce These non-heading lettuces produce masses of curled foliage but no true head. The leaves can be picked a few at a time and the plants will continue to grow and produce further leaves for later picking. Some varieties of cos lettuce will continue growing in the same way if closely spaced.

Cultivation
Many modern varieties of lettuce have been specially bred to mature at particular seasons and it is important to select those suitable for the crops required. Depending on the weather and the region, summer- and autumn-maturing lettuce is sown successively from late March to early August to mature from June to October. In warm regions, heat-resistant varieties should be grown during summer months because lettuce germinate and thrive best in a cool climate. Lettuce sown outdoors in August will mature in November to December if kept under cloches from just before the first frost. Mildew-resistant and forcing varieties should be used at this time of year. For eating from January to March, lettuce must be sown and raised in a heated (7°C/45°F) greenhouse from November to January. Small varieties can also be grown indoors under fluorescent lights. In mild areas, early spring lettuce is obtained from seeds sown in September or October and grown under cloches to mature in April.
Soil and situation All lettuce varieties prefer an open position in a well-drained and fairly rich soil of pH 6.5–7.5. Lettuces require considerable quantities of water during the growing period and the soil must be humus-rich so that it is able to retain and supply moisture for the rapidly growing plants. A soil well manured for a previous crop is ideal, but on poor, thin soils dig in a further dressing of well-rotted compost at a rate of 10–15 lb per square yard when the site is prepared. Apply a balanced general fertilizer at 20 oz per square yard, and before sowing rake the soil to produce a fine tilth.
Sowing To reduce the amount of thinning later, always sow lettuce seed very thinly. Sow in drills $\frac{1}{4}$ in deep at a rate of no more than 10–12 seeds for each 12 in run of drill—head lettuces will have a final spacing of 9–12 in apart in the row. Alternatively, lettuce can be sown in boxes or in a seedbed and then transplanted when the seedlings are no taller than 1 in. Extreme care is needed when handling the delicate seedlings. Take care not to sow too deeply as this inhibits germination, which should occur within 6–12 days. It is sensible to maintain a regular supply by making frequent sowings with short intervals between, because lettuces, once headed, do not stand in good condition for very long and soon "bolt", or run to seed.

Spacing
Various spacings and planting patterns are recommended for heading varieties. The most efficient is to stagger the plants in adjacent rows in a triangular pattern so that the maximum use is made of the land available. Place the plants at 12 in intervals in rows 10 in apart. For dwarf varieties and cloche-grown lettuce spacings of 9 in between the plants and 8 in between the rows may be used. This triangular pattern is particularly valuable for cloche-grown lettuces. If the familiar square pattern with plants opposite one another in adjacent rows is used, the spacings should be 12 in × 12 in, or 9 in × 9 in for dwarf varieties. With conventional leaf-

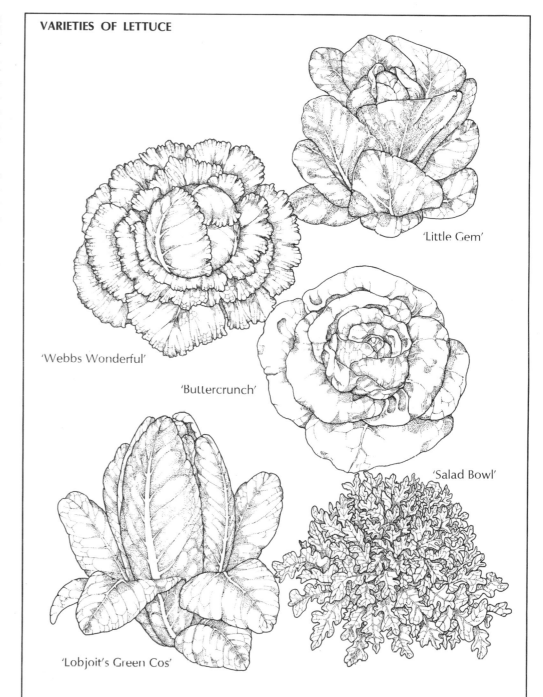

VARIETIES OF LETTUCE

'Little Gem'

'Webbs Wonderful'

'Buttercrunch'

'Salad Bowl'

'Lobjoit's Green Cos'

LEAF LETTUCE
'Salad Bowl', 'Lobjoits Green
Cos', 'Paris White' (cos),
'Valmaine' (cos).

PROTECTED LETTUCE
Head types
'Amanda Plus', 'Avondefiance'
(mildew resistant), 'Delta',
'Knap', 'Kwiek' (mildew resistant).

Lettuces 2

lettuce of the 'Salad Bowl' type, spacings are similar to those given for heading varieties. Some cos lettuces, however, will produce well during spring and summer with only 5–6 in between the rows and 1 in between individual plants.

Thinning and transplanting Direct-sown crops should be thinned as soon as the seedlings are large enough to handle. Never let the seedlings become overcrowded as this will check growth. There is a tendency to grow more lettuce than can be consumed and this is particularly true with sown crops. Transplanting allows more control. The method of plant raising is critical however, since any check to growth at transplanting may easily lead to "bolting"—premature running to flower, induced by high temperatures (over 21°C/70°F) and dry conditions. Lettuce transplants for outside should always be raised in small individual peat pots or blocks and never grown in a seedbed for bare-root planting. Sow lettuce seed in a 3½ in pot every ten days and prick out as many seedlings as necessary into pots or blocks. Do this at the first true leaf stage.

Keep the seedlings cool to produce short, sturdy plants and transplant them when they have four or five true leaves.

Watering The best crops are produced when there has been no check to growth. The quality and size of the crop will be improved greatly by weekly applications of 3–4 gal of water per square yard in dry weather. If this is not possible, a single application at the same rate 7–10 days before they are due to mature will increase the size of the lettuce heads markedly in spring and summer. Overwintered lettuce should not normally need additional watering.

Try to water in the morning, and on sunny, drying days if possible, so that the leaves are dry by nightfall. Lettuces that are wet overnight are vulnerable to disease.

Pests and diseases

Birds, slugs and cutworms may be troublesome but can be controlled by the methods described on page 17. Leaf aphids may be controlled by the use of systemic aphicides such as dimethoate or by applying derris as the plants near maturity. Some varieties are resistant to lettuce root aphids but applications of diazinon during the summer may be necessary for other varieties. Zineb or thiram sprays may be used against downy mildew, which is encouraged by overcrowding.

Botrytis cinerea or gray mold may be a problem on lettuce in damp, cool weather. Affected plants should be destroyed and a preventive spray of thiram or benomyl applied to the remaining plants.

Lettuce viruses show up either as a mosaic or pronounced vein network on the leaves. Burn infected plants because there is no really effective method of control once the symptoms appear. Remove weeds, which may harbor viruses, by completely uprooting them and control any aphids that appear. For control of aphids see page 16.

LEAF LETTUCE

'Salad Bowl', 'Grand Rapids' and 'Oak Leaf' are the conventional leaf lettuces but certain cos varieties can also be grown successfully for leafing. Closely spaced, leaf lettuces can produce good leaf in 40–50 days compared with the 60–80 days required for other lettuces. They also have the advantage of growing again from the base to provide a second crop. Grown this way, one square yard of leaf lettuce sown each week from April to late May, and again from mid-July to the end of August, will produce lettuce leaves throughout summer and early fall.

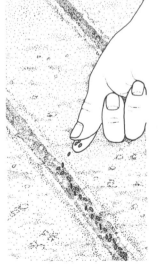 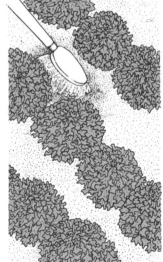 

1 April to mid-May. At weekly intervals sow the seed in ½ in drills, 4–5 in apart in the prepared seedbed, allowing 10–15 plants per 12 in of drill.

2 Early May to June. Allow the seedlings to develop unchecked without thinning. Water in dry weather. Spray aphids and diseases as required.

3 Late May to late June. Harvest the leaves by cutting them off near ground level. Leave stumps to re-grow.

Protected lettuce

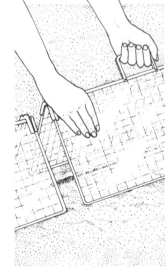 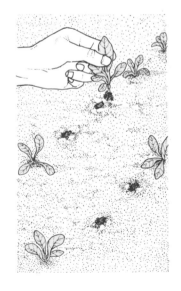

1 Sow 3–4 seeds ½ in deep at 3 in intervals in drills 8 in apart in the prepared seedbed, and place cloches over the drills.

2 When the seedlings are ½ in high, thin each group, leaving the strongest plant at each position. Ventilate on mild days.

3 As growth accelerates, thin to 9 in (6 in for dwarf varieties). In dry weather, water the plants 7–10 days before harvesting.

Lettuces 3

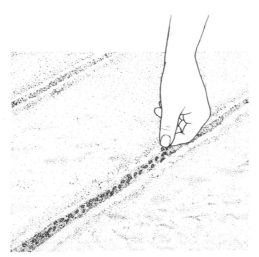

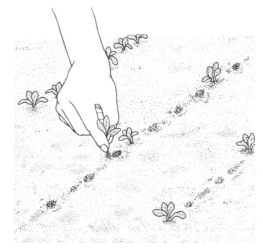

1 In the prepared seedbed take out $\frac{1}{2}$ in drills 10 in apart (8 in for dwarf varieties) and sow the seed thinly. Cover the drill.

2 Sow the seed thinly in $\frac{1}{2}$ in drills 10 in apart in the prepared seedbed. Cover the drills with fine soil.

3 When the seedlings are $\frac{1}{2}$–1 in high, thin to 12 in (9 in for dwarf varieties). Alternate the seedlings in adjacent rows.

4 Hoe between the rows to keep down weeds which compete with the seedlings.

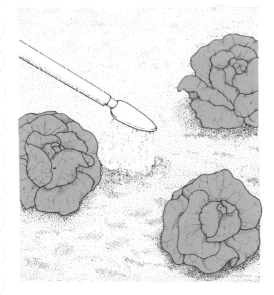

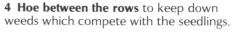

5 In dry weather apply 3–4 gal of water per square yard each week. Direct the water on to the soil and keep it away from the leaves. Damp encourages mildew.

6 Spray the developing plants with insecticides against aphids and fungicides against diseases as necessary.

7 Push heading lettuces gently with the back of the hand to test for firmness. Squeezing between the fingers damages the heads.

8 When firm, harvest by cutting the plants below the lower leaves. Alternatively, pull up whole plants and trim off roots. Harvest every second lettuce when young, allowing the remaining plants to grow larger. Place debris on the compost heap.

Endive/Celtuce

ENDIVE
SUMMER
'Exquisite Curled', 'Moss Curled'.
WINTER
'Broad-leaved Batavian'.

CELTUCE
No named varieties available.

Endive—also called escarole—is a hardy annual plant of the same genus as chicory. It is grown for the use of its leaves in salads and it requires blanching to be palatable. Endive can be grown over a long season and it is most valuable as an autumn and winter vegetable.

Cultivation

Endive needs a good medium to light soil that has been deeply winter dug and, preferably, manured for a previous crop. Choose an open position except for spring-sown crops, which may bolt unless grown in partial shade.

Sowing For successional blanchings sow batches of seed every two or three weeks in the spring and late summer. Sow the seed in $\frac{1}{2}$ in deep drills 12 in apart. As soon as the first true leaves appear, thin the seedlings, leaving the curly-leaved varieties 9 in apart and the broad-leaved varieties 12 in apart. Water the growing plants regularly, as for lettuce, especially during dry hot weather, because drought encourages endive to run to seed. When the plants are fully grown about 12 weeks after sowing, make sure they are dry and tie them loosely with raffia to keep the lower leaves off the ground and lessen the risk of rotting. Then begin to blanch two or three plants at a time to provide a convenient supply over a longer period. Place a large plastic pot over each plant to exclude light completely. Remember to cover the pots' drainage holes with a tile or stones and leave a slight gap between the rims and the soil for ventilation. The blanched leaves should be edible within 2–3 weeks, although they take twice as long in the fall.

Winter endive In mild climates, hardy broad-leaved varieties of endive can be sown under glass in late August or early September for winter use until March or April.

Harvesting

Cut the plants with a sharp knife just above soil level when the leaves are a creamy-white color. Use blanched endive immediately because it does not keep well.

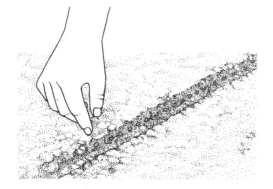

1 Late March and August. Sow the seed very thinly in $\frac{1}{2}$ in drills 12 in apart.

2 When the first true leaves appear, thin the seedlings until they are 9–12 in apart.

3 July and October. Loosely tie the fully grown plants with raffia.

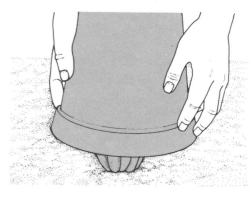

4 At the same time, select some plants for blanching. Place plastic pots over them.

CELTUCE

Celtuce is a mutant of lettuce which grows on a short stem. As its name suggests it combines two vegetables in one. The stems are used in the same way as celery and the leaves can be substituted for lettuce.

Celtuce requires a humus-rich soil of pH 6.5–7.5 and, to ensure this, compost or manure should be incorporated during winter digging. Sow the seed from late March until May at two week intervals and in August in shallow $\frac{1}{4}$ in drills that are 12 in apart. When the seedlings are about 7 in high thin them until they are 9 in apart. Celtuce needs to be well watered because otherwise the leaves become tough. In hot dry weather celtuce resists bolting better than most ordinary lettuce.

Pick celtuce leaves as soon as they form on the plants, but never pick the plants completely bare because this severely weakens them. The stems are ready within three months of the sowing date. Cut the stalks when they are about 1 in thick at the plant's base.

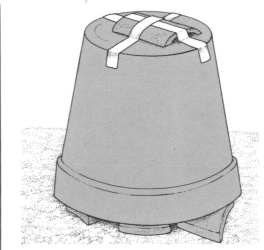

5 Cover the pots' drainage holes to exclude all light. Leave a slight gap between each pot's rim and the soil for ventilation.

6 After 2-3 weeks when the leaves are creamy-white, cut the plants off just above soil level with a sharp knife.

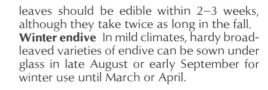

Chicory

Witloof chicory—also called French endive—is a hardy perennial plant related to the dandelion. It is sown in early May, lifted in October and then grown in complete darkness to produce the blanched chicons (tightly bunched groups of leaves) which may be used for salads throughout the winter. Ground, dried chicory roots are also used as a substitute or additive for coffee, especially in New Orleans and France. Blanching is usually required to make the leaves palatable but some varieties of chicory, such as 'Sugar Loaf', need no blanching. Chicory is seldom troubled by pests and diseases.

Cultivation
Chicory grows best in a medium to light soil that is moderately rich. Soil manured for a previous crop is ideal. Do not incorporate any manure or compost into the ground just before sowing, however, because this encourages forked roots which are less suitable for forcing. The seedbed should be in an open position. A few days before sowing apply a general, balanced fertilizer at 1 oz per square yard and then rake the soil to a fine tilth.

Sowing In May or June sow the seed thinly in ½ in drills that are 9–12 in apart. When the first true leaves appear thin the seedlings until they are 8 in apart in the row and hoe regularly to keep down weeds.

Storing From late September to November when the foliage has died down lift the parsnip-like roots for storing prior to forcing.

Discard any thin or forked roots and retain those that are 1–1½ in in diameter at the top because these are most suitable for forcing. Cut off any remaining leaves to within ½ in of the crown and trim the root ends and side roots, leaving a length of 9 in. Pack the roots in boxes of dry sand in a cool frost-free place.

Blanching
Stored chicory roots need to be forced in complete darkness to produce creamy-white chicons. From mid-November onwards remove a few roots for blanching at weekly intervals to provide a continual supply throughout winter until the end of March. Plant them in big, deep plastic pots or wooden boxes filled with sand or light garden soil, making sure that ½ in of crown is above the surface. Water them sparingly and then completely cover them with black polyethylene to exclude all light. Alternatively, the light can be excluded by completely covering the roots to a depth of 6 in. Keep the sand or soil moist but never wet it, and keep the pots well-ventilated at 7°–13°C/45°–55°F.

Harvesting
The blanched chicons should be ready for cutting within four weeks. Cut or snap them off just above soil level and use them immediately. After the chicons have been harvested, the roots will produce several smaller shoots that are very acceptable for salads if blanched in the same way.

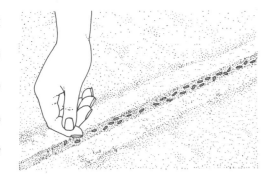

1 Early May. Sow the seed thinly in ½ in drills that are 9–12 in apart.

2 When the first true leaves appear thin the seedlings until they are 8 in apart.

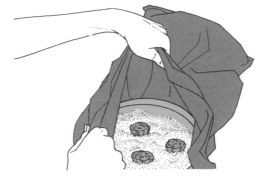

3 October to November. When the leaves are dying lift the roots with a fork.

4 Cut off remaining leaves to ½ in of the crown and discard unsuitable roots. Shorten the roots to 9 in and remove any side roots.

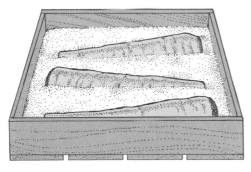

5 Store the prepared roots horizontally in boxes of dry sand in a cool frost-free shed.

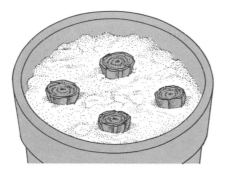

6 Mid-November. At weekly intervals plant three or four roots in a large pot or box of sand, keeping ½ in of each crown above the surface of the soil.

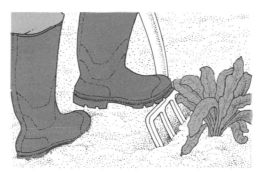

7 Water the roots sparingly and cover the top of the pot with polyethylene to exclude all light. Place in a well-ventilated shed at a temperature of 7°–13°C/45°–55°F.

8 Mid-December to mid-February. Cut or snap off the chicons just above the soil surface about four weeks after planting.

Growing brassicas

Admirably suited to cooler climates, the brassicas, such as cabbages, Brussels sprouts, cauliflowers, broccoli and kale, are key plants in any vegetable grower's plot. Certain general principles apply to their cultivation. Most brassicas, except some varieties of kale and Chinese cabbage, should be raised in a special brassica seedbed and then transplanted, usually 5–7 weeks later, to a permanent bed. This saves space, because the main brassica plots can be used for other vegetables while the seedlings are growing. Alternatively, buy young brassica plants ready for planting out.

Brassicas need a fertile soil and they should not be grown in the same plot more than one year in three. Move them around each year, preferably to ground where peas or beans have been grown the previous year (see page 20). Peas and beans leave nitrogen in the soil at a level which suits brassicas. The other reason for keeping brassicas on the move is the danger of previous infections of club-root lingering on in the soil. Another, resistant, vegetable can be grown in a plot which has suffered from club-root. Brassica crops must not be grown again in an affected plot for at least seven years.

Dig the ground early in winter and leave it to consolidate. All brassicas need firm ground. If the area has been dug shortly before sowing or planting, work it over with a three-pronged hand cultivator and firm it well with the feet. All brassicas need a pH of 6.5–7.5.

The seedbed
The seedbed should be in an open, sunny but sheltered position. Ideally, make a seedbed on soil manured for a previous crop. If this is not possible, in autumn apply well-rotted manure or garden compost (1 bucketful per square yard) and leave the plot to weather over the winter. Before sowing, rake in a balanced general fertilizer at a rate of 2 oz per square yard. At the same time apply diazinon to combat cabbage maggot and club-root. Firm the soil and rake to produce a fine tilth.

Sowing If the seedbed is dry, water thoroughly before sowing. Use a foot-board to avoid compacting the surface of the bed while sowing. Mark out shallow drills 6 in apart and draw out the drills $\frac{3}{4}$–1 in deep. Dust the seed with Captan or thiram before sowing to control damping-off disease. Mark each row with sticks, placing a label with sowing date

and variety, written in indelible ink. Germination takes 7–12 days. Keep the seedlings free from weeds, and water them during dry weather. Thin the seedlings to 1–2 in apart as soon as they can be handled. Firm back the soil after thinning.

The permanent (planting) bed
Double-dig the permanent brassica plot in winter and dress it with 10–15 lb per square yard of well-rotted manure or compost. Experiments have shown that a marked increase in yield can result from preparing soils deeply for brassicas. The roots of Brussels sprouts, for instance, penetrate 36 in or more into deeply dug soils. Although it is seldom practical to dig the plot to this depth, double-dig it if possible to a depth of 18–12 in. Brassicas are greedy for water, and deep digging allows their root systems to develop and extract more water from lower levels in the soil. It also reduces the uptake of water from the upper soil layers, which remain moist for longer than would be the case with shallower digging.

Transplanting
The young brassicas are ready to transplant

5–7 weeks after sowing, when they have 3–4 leaves and are 4–6 in tall. The day before transplanting, water the seedlings thoroughly so that they lift easily with minimum damage to the roots.

Lift the seedlings carefully so that the roots are disturbed as little as possible. Cover them with burlap or polyethylene so that they do not dry out before being planted. Dip the roots of the seedlings in calomel paste to control cabbage maggot and club-root. Plant the seedlings with a trowel or hand fork at the appropriate distance for the brassica concerned. The prepared plot should be watered thoroughly the day before planting takes place. Firm the soil around the roots by hand. Water the plants in, using a nozzle on the can or, if the weather is dry, prepare planting holes and "puddle" in the young plants. Make sure they are firm by tugging the upper leaf gently. Water them until they become established, placing $\frac{1}{4}$ pint of water around the base of each plant daily. In hot, sunny weather protect the transplants by covering them with newspaper during the day to cut down transpiration. Within three days of planting-out apply diazinon to the soil as a further insurance against cabbage maggot.

1 Lift the seedlings carefully, taking care not to damage the roots. Dip the roots in paste made of calomel, available at drugstores.

2 Plant the seedlings at the spacing given for each brassica and check that they are firmly planted by gently tugging a leaf.

3 In dry weather prepare planting holes and puddle in the young plants.

4 Apply diazinon to the soil at each plant's base within 3 days of planting. Water until they are established.

Cabbages 1

SPRING
'April', 'Harbinger',
'Offenham' (very hardy).

SUMMER/FALL
'Golden Acre', 'Hispi',
'May Star', 'Primo'.

Storing varieties
'Decerma', 'Langendijk',
'Winter White'.

WINTER
'Christmas Drumhead', 'January
King', 'Winter Salad'.

Savoys
'Best of All',
'Ormskirk-Rearguard'.

RED CABBAGE
'Blood Red', 'Ruby Ball'.

CHINESE CABBAGE
'Nagaoka—50 days', 'Sampan'.

TYPES OF CABBAGE

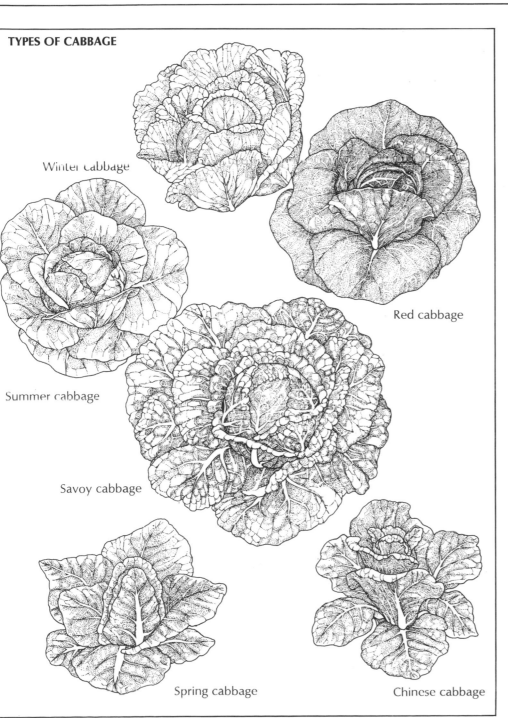

Winter cabbage

Red cabbage

Summer cabbage

Savoy cabbage

Spring cabbage

Chinese cabbage

Cabbage is a biennial plant and the most widely grown brassica. Individual tastes can be satisfied throughout the year with the four types available. Summer cabbage, both early and mid-season varieties, provides a welcome alternative to summer salads. Winter cabbage, including savoys, is easy to grow and is hardy. Apart from its pickling qualities, red cabbage is delicious as a cooked autumn vegetable. The increasingly popular, autumn-harvested Chinese cabbage can be cooked (with little aroma) or used in salads.

Spring cabbage
Spring cabbage is grown from summer varieties that are planted in zones 8 to 10 in late October or November to mature in spring. "Spring greens" are simply closely planted spring cabbages eaten before they head up.

Sowing The seed is sown directly in the garden in rows 12 in apart and thinned to 12 in between the plants in each row if headed cabbages are required.

Spring greens If space is limited and spring greens are required thin to 4 in intervals in the rows. The plants can either be left to produce unheaded greens, or two out of every three plants can be removed and used for greens in early spring while the remaining plants, now spaced at 12 in by 12 in, will head up for use later. Wider row spacings are often recommended but these give a lesser yield.

After plants are well-established it is useful to pull a little soil around the stems to give some additional protection against winter cold. No fertilizer should be given at this stage and, apart from keeping the plot free from weeds, the only attention the plants need until growth starts in late winter is to firm back plants loosened by frost or other adverse weather.

In early March, if the weather is good, apply and water in a dressing of nitrate of soda or sulfate of ammonia at a rate of 2 oz per square yard. This encourages rapid growth as the weather becomes warmer. Alternatively, in nitrogen-rich soils, a balanced fertilizer can be used at the same rate.

Harvesting
The crop may be harvested as required. In mild seasons spring greens are ready in February while in late seasons headed cabbages stand until early June. In some cold areas cloches may be used to protect spring cabbages over winter.

Summer cabbage
Summer cabbage is sown indoors in February and March for harvesting from mid-May until August, depending on the variety. When deciding how much to grow, remember that it matures at the same time as many other vegetables. The permanent plot should be well prepared in late winter. Sowing indoors during February for planting out after last frost provides the earliest crops, but seeds can also be sown in a seedbed shortly before last frost for later crops.

Sowing On a seedbed sow the seed thinly in $\frac{3}{4}$–1 in deep drills 6 in apart. Water the drills beforehand to encourage speedy germination and if the weather is warm and dry, dust along the length of the drills with derris or HCH before the seedlings emerge, as a precaution against flea beetle. Summer cabbages are very vulnerable to cabbage maggot and it is important to apply appropriate control measures against this and club-root at both the sowing and transplanting stages.

If seeds are started indoors in flats, use a prepared sterile planting soil such as Jiffy-Mix and just cover them.

Transplanting From April to May dip the seedlings in calomel paste and plant them in the permanent bed, at 18 in intervals in rows 18 in apart for large-headed varieties or at 14 in intervals in rows 14 in apart for smaller-headed varieties. Firm the seedlings into their holes and water thoroughly.

When the plants are well-established, apply and water in a balanced fertilizer, such as 10-10-10 at 2 oz per square yard. Throughout the growing season, hoe between the rows to keep down weeds and maintain a water-conserving tilth. If necessary spray or dust to control any pests or diseases that occur.

Harvesting
Headed summer cabbages are ready for cutting from late June until fall. Cut with a sharp knife just above soil level.

Cabbages 2

Spring cabbage

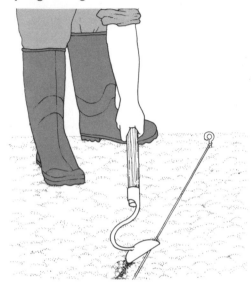

1 October to November. Take out $\frac{3}{4}$–1 in drills, 6 in apart in the garden. Sprinkle diazinon along the drills and water them thoroughly.

2 October to November. Sow the seed thinly and dust with derris along the drills. Cover with fine soil.

3 When seedlings are well-established, thin them to the desired spacing in the rows.

4 Pull up a little soil around the base of each plant to protect against cold. Firm any plants loosened later by adverse weather.

5 Throughout the growing season hoe between the rows regularly to keep them weed-free and maintain a good tilth.

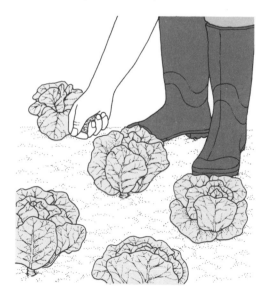

6 February to March. Spread and then hoe in 2 oz of nitrate of soda or sulfate of ammonia to encourage heading.

7 March. To obtain spring greens, remove 2 plants out of 3. Those remaining will head up for later use.

8 April to June. Cut spring cabbages as required. Clear any stumps and roots away.

Cabbages 3

Winter cabbage

Winter cabbages are sown in May or June and harvested from late summer on. They include the savoys, which are easily recognized by their dark green, wrinkled leaves. All the varieties are easy to grow and hardy, succeeding better on poor soils than most other brassicas. Apart from the times of sowing, transplanting and maturing their cultivation differs little from that of summer cabbage.

Sowing In May sow the seed very thinly in $\frac{3}{4}$–1 in drills that are 6 in apart. Water the drills before sowing.

Transplanting In July transplant the seedlings to the permanent bed, which should have been enriched with fertilizer a few weeks before (see page 26). Plant the seedlings at 18 in intervals in rows 18 in apart. If the weather is very dry, pour a little water into each hole before putting the plants down. Remember also to sprinkle diazinon into the holes before setting out the seedlings and firming them in well. When the plants begin to grow apply a nitrogen-rich fertilizer and hoe it in lightly.

Water the growing plants frequently during the summer and hoe lightly between the rows to keep down the weeds.

Harvesting

From September on, cut the individual heads as they mature.

Red cabbage

Red cabbage is sown in the spring at the same time as summer cabbage but it needs a slightly longer growing season. In warm climates it can also be treated like spring cabbage. Before sowing, work out what is needed because a few plants are enough for pickling purposes. Cultivate red cabbage in the same way as summer cabbage. Sow the seed indoors in late winter or outdoors after frost and transplant when the seedlings are 4–6 in tall, and transplant 12–15 in each way.

Harvesting

Red cabbage is ready from mid-July onwards. Be sure to cut the mature heads well before there is any danger of severe frost.

Red cabbage can be stored for several months in a cool, frost-free place.

HARVESTING AND STORING CABBAGE

Some types of cabbage, especially the Danish varieties, can be stored after harvesting in the fall. They will keep until April but should be inspected for blemishes or rot two or three times during the winter.

1 Lift the whole plant up with a fork when the head is firm to the touch.

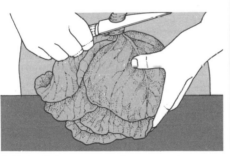

2 Cut off the roots and stem and remove the coarse outer leaves.

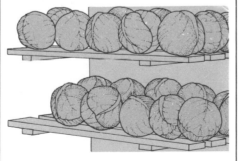

3 Store cabbages on slatted shelving, in heaps if required, in a dark, humid place.

Chinese cabbage

Chinese cabbage is a versatile vegetable that is easier to grow than other vegetables in the brassica group and has a relatively short growing season. The general principles of brassica growing (page 26) apply. It is especially important to have a moisture-retentive, rich seedbed because Chinese cabbage is not transplanted but is matured in the area where it has been sown.

Sowing About three months before first fall frost, sow 2–3 of the large seeds at 8–9 in intervals in $\frac{3}{4}$–1 in deep drills, 12 in apart. Thin the seedlings to one plant per station.

Keep them well watered because they may "bolt" in hot summer weather. Do not water, however, if the weather is wet, as this may cause "splitting" of the heads. When the plants begin to head up in August, tie the leaves together with raffia. This is not necessary with self-heading varieties.

Harvesting

From September to November cut the heads just above soil level with a knife.

2 July. Thin each group of seedlings to leave a single plant at each station. Apply diazinon around the base of each plant.

1 Early July. Dribble water into the $\frac{3}{4}$–1 in deep drills, 12 in apart, and sow 2–3 seeds at 9 in intervals.

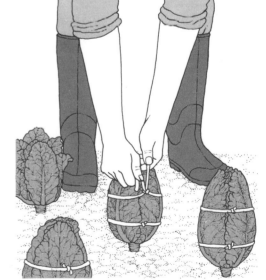

3 August. When the plants begin to head up tie the outer leaves together with raffia. Keep them well watered.

Brussels sprouts 1

F₁ hybrids
'Citadel', 'King Arthur',
'Peer Gynt'.

CONVENTIONAL VARIETIES
'Irish Elegance', 'Market
Rearguard', 'Winter Harvest'.

Brussels sprouts are popular and hardy brassicas, and for many people they are a traditional ingredient of the Christmas dinner. In recent years F₁ hybrids have been bred, mostly of compact growth, that mature all their uniform "button" sprouts at the same time. While these are ideal for the freezer, most gardeners still grow some of the open pollinated, conventional varieties. With these, the sprouts mature a few at a time on individual plants, so picking may be carried out over a period of several months. This is important for growers without freezers, who may require only a pound or two at a time.

The most useful crops are gathered from October to about December, because few other fresh vegetables are available at this time. In mild climates, they can be left standing outdoors for harvest at any time.

Cultivation

The general principles of brassica growing apply to Brussels sprouts (see page 26). An open position, in full sun but sheltered from strong winds, is most suitable although they will tolerate slight shade. A firm soil is important because Brussels sprouts may grow to 3 ft or more and good root anchorage is essential. In light soils hilling up the stems slightly about a month after transplanting helps to anchor them, but in exposed areas staking is sometimes necessary.

Soil and situation Brussels sprouts grow best on fertile soil that has been deeply dug and well manured the previous winter. Like other brassicas, Brussels sprouts need lime. A pH of between 6·5 and 6·8 is ideal. As they are not usually planted out until June or July, another crop is often taken from the same land beforehand. The site should be dug over about a week before planting and a dressing at 2 oz per square yard of a balanced general fertilizer raked in. The seed is sown in the brassica seedbed during May or June and the seedlings are transplanted in four to six weeks later to the prepared site. Nitrogenous fertilizer applied during growth produces weak plants.

Sowing Sow the seed thinly in ¾–1 in drills that are spaced 6 in apart. The seed is sown thinly to prevent overcrowding and to encourage strong plants, which are necessary

for the successful growth of this tall, top-heavy vegetable. Brussels sprouts are vulnerable to club-root and cabbage maggot and the same control measures given for cabbages must be applied at both the sowing and transplanting stages. Seeds sown in cold frames in February for planting out in April will give an earlier crop. This method is useful for producing sprouts in August in addition to the main crop sown in the open to provide fall sprouts, but results are not so reliable.

F₁ hybrids If F₁ hybrids to produce button sprouts for freezing are being grown, spacings of 20 in between the rows and 20 in between plants can be used. This provides a good yield from a relatively small area for picking at one time. Remove the growing point and smaller leaves when the lower sprouts are about ½ in across to encourage most of them to mature at the same time.

For the "cut and come again" requirement of most gardeners, spacings of 36 in × 36 in are used. Grown at these distances most varieties produce an excellent crop while allowing easy access for harvesting. There

1 June. Dig over the planting site and rake in a balanced, general fertilizer, such as 10-10-10, at 2 oz per square yard.

2 Transplant the seedlings from the seedbed into rows 36 in apart with 36 in (20 in for F₁ hybrids) between plants. Plant them firmly with the lowest leaf at soil level.

3 At the same time, puddle in the young plants and check that they are firmly planted by gently tugging each top leaf.

4 June. Apply diazinon to the soil at the base of the plants to combat cabbage maggot.

5 June. Continue to water the young plants until they are well-established.

Brussels sprouts 2

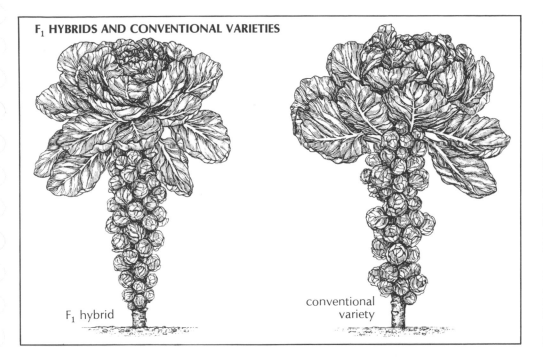

F₁ HYBRIDS AND CONVENTIONAL VARIETIES

F₁ hybrid

conventional variety

appears to be no advantage in closer spacing unless dwarf varieties are used, when spacings of 2½ ft each way are sufficient. Firm planting is essential and the seedlings should be set with the lowest leaves at soil level to help establish a good root system. Water or puddle in the young plants. Check that they are firmly established by tugging gently at the top leaf of each plant.

Although additional watering during the growing season is often beneficial to cabbages, there appears to be no advantage in watering Brussels sprouts regularly unless the weather is very dry. Brussels sprout plants are in the ground for a long period, so regular weeding and hoeing should be carried out and any necessary pest and disease controls should be applied as necessary.

Aphids are often particularly troublesome and if left can spoil the developing sprouts. Aphids must be sprayed as soon as they are spotted, or they will penetrate the sprouts themselves. Sparrows may attack the sprouts. A system of stakes carrying netting will protect the growing crop against birds and help to support the plants. Application of a foliar feed or a high potash fertilizer in July–August is often beneficial, particularly if crops are grown on light soils.

Harvesting

As the sprouts mature, remove any yellowing leaves from the lower part of the stem to improve air circulation. Pick or cut the sprouts when they are still tight and about the size of a walnut. Start picking from the base. When all the sprouts have been picked from a stem, use the Brussels sprout tops as "winter greens".

Aftercare

Surplus leaves can go on the compost heap, but the woody stems should be pulled up with the roots, dried and burned at the end of the season.

Do not leave Brussels sprouts in the ground to flower and seed, because they will continue to draw up nutrients from the soil and leave an unnecessarily large deficit for the crop that follows them.

6 July. In light soils or exposed sites draw up a little soil round the base of each stem. Hoe regularly between the rows to keep the plants free from weeds.

7 July. Apply a foliar feed or water in a high potash fertilizer at a rate of 1oz per square yard. Spray with dimethoate to control aphid attacks.

8 September onwards. Remove yellowing leaves from the stems, and any "blown" (loose and open) sprouts.

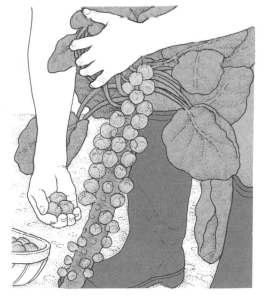

9 As soon as the buttons are firm, gather them as required from the bottom of the stem.

Cauliflowers 1

SUMMER
'Alpha', 'Dominant',
'Predominant', 'Snowball'.

SUMMER/FALL
'All the Year Round',
'Barrier Reef'.

WINTER (HEADING BROCCOLI)
'Late Enterprise', 'Snowball',
'Thanet'.

To American gardeners the word "cauliflower" means a vegetable with a large head of tightly packed, white, immature flowers known as "curds". Broccoli has a flatter, somewhat wider head of little green buds that open into yellow flowers if not picked at the right time. Also listed in most seed catalogs is "Purple Head Cauliflower", which looks and tastes more like broccoli than cauliflower and has a dense head of purplish buds that turn green when cooked.

This understanding of the closely related cauliflower-broccoli tribe is different from the European thinking. In that part of the world, cauliflower is the same vegetable that we know. But broccoli is called calabrese. And Purple Head Cauliflower is known as sprouting broccoli. The Europeans also have a white sprouting broccoli.

Nomenclature to the contrary, the vegetables are the same. But there are fewer American varieties, and they cannot be grown in so many months of the year. Except in warm climates, ours are planted either in early spring for summer use or in mid-summer for fall use. All can be frozen for winter use.

Cauliflowers

A favorite among brassicas, the cauliflower is one of the more difficult vegetables to grow successfully because it is demanding in its soil, moisture and food requirements.

Soil and situation A deeply dug, fertile soil rich in humus is essential to obtain crops of good quality. The general principles of brassica growing apply—thorough soil preparation with heavy dressings of manure helping to provide food and retain moisture during the growing period (see page 26). The pH of the soil should be between 6.5 and 7.5 and the site should be open but not exposed. Cauliflowers are less hardy than other brassicas and cannot withstand severe weather. They require ample food during their period of growth and, in addition to the manure dug in during the winter, a dressing of 2–3 oz per square yard of a general fertilizer should be raked into the soil before planting.

Cauliflowers are particularly susceptible to deficiencies of vital elements in the soil. A deficiency of the major elements can be corrected by following the general principles of brassica fertilization. A deficiency of the trace elements will have an equally adverse effect on the crop but, unlike a disease, mineral deficiency should not be a problem once it has been identified.

Molybdenum deficiency causes whiptail (abnormally formed leaves), and the plant may lose its growing points or fail to form curds. Making the soil neutral (pH 7) should cure the deficiency. Potassium deficiency causes yellowing and poor quality curds. This may result from an incorrect ratio of nitrogen to potassium in the soil, due to too much nitrogenous fertilization. Boron deficiency causes small, bitter curds and brown coloration. Water the soil with a solution of borax—use $\frac{1}{2}$ ounce of borax in $\frac{1}{2}$ gal of water to treat 30 square yards of soil. Be careful not to exceed the dosage because too much boron makes the soil toxic.

Cauliflower seedlings need careful handling and firm planting. They should never be short of water or they will produce small, premature heads of poor quality. Applications of up to 4 gal of water per square yard during dry periods improve the quality and yield. To maintain healthy, vigorous growth a dressing of 1 oz per square yard of sulfate of ammonia should be watered in when the young plants are well established but before the curds start to form. As with other brassicas, club-root and cabbage maggot may be troublesome and the appropriate control measures should be applied as a matter of routine.

Summer cauliflowers mature from June to August and may be raised in several ways depending on the facilities available. The easiest is to sow the seed indoors in February or March for transplanting at about the time of the last spring freeze.

Maximum yield of summer cauliflower is dependent on water supply. If the crop can be watered frequently, the spacing can be as close as 18 in by 18 in. In drier conditions, spacings of 24 in by 24 in are better.

Autumn Cauliflowers

Autumn cauliflowers are in season from September to frost and are sown outdoors in seedbeds two-and-a-half to three months before first fall frost. Their cultivation is similar to that of summer cauliflowers.

Summer cauliflower

1 Winter. Dig the soil deeply and incorporate a dressing of 15–20 lb per square yard of well-rotted manure.

2 April. Rake in a dressing of 2–3 oz per square yard of a balanced fertilizer 1–2 weeks before planting.

3 Water the seedlings before lifting them. Lift them carefully and dip the roots in calomel paste to combat club-root.

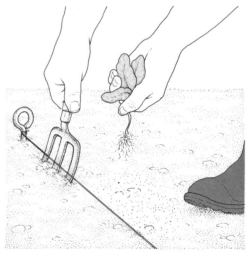

4 Plant the seedlings at 24 in intervals in rows 24 in apart on the prepared site, watered on the previous day. Water or puddle in the transplanted seedlings. Check that they are firmly planted by tugging the uppermost leaf of each.

Cauliflowers 2

A new variety of cauliflower is self-blanching. Other varieties, whether grown for summer or autumn use, require blanching. To do this tie the outer leaves up over the flower head when it is about the size of an egg. Tie the leaf tips together tightly to keep out sun, but do not blanch the leaves so close around the head that its growth is restricted. Harvest when it reaches 6–8 in in diameter.

Pests and Diseases of Brassicas

Brassicas can be attacked and damaged by a number of different pests and diseases.

Pests There are several pests that feed on the leaves of brassicas including mealy cabbage aphid, cabbage whitefly and some species of caterpillar. Mealy cabbage aphids are blue-gray sap-sucking insects. They turn the foliage yellow and can cause severe stunting. They usually occur on the undersides of leaves but may also infest Brussels sprout buttons and the hearts of cauliflowers and cabbages, making them inedible. If aphids are present spray with dimethoate, formothion or menazon. Burn old plants after cropping to kill the aphids' over-wintering eggs. Cabbage whitefly, a small white moth-like insect, is a much less damaging pest since it generally attacks only the outer leaves.

Caterpillars of the large and the small cabbage white butterfly and of the cabbage looper all eat holes in the foliage and often burrow into the hearts of cabbages. Remove them by hand as soon as the damage is seen. Alternatively, dust plants with carbaryl or spray with fenitrothion, trichlorphon or *Bacillus thuringiensis.*

The roots of brassicas may also be damaged by pests. Cabbage maggots eat the roots of seedlings and newly planted brassicas until the root system is reduced to a blackened, rotting stump, growth ceases and the foliage turns blue-green. Prevent attacks by treating seed rows and the soil around transplants with diazinon, chlorpyrifos, bromophos or azinphos-methyl. If symptoms of the trouble are seen, drench the soil with spray-strength trichlorphon. Turnip gall weevil causes galls on the roots which are often mistaken for club root disease. However, if cut in half, the weevil's small white grub can be seen. The plants' growth is not affected.

Diseases Club root is the most serious disease of brassicas. It causes the roots to become a distorted and swollen mass and, since they cannot function normally, the plants' growth is poor and stunted. Prevent attacks by buying only healthy plants, improving the drainage of heavy soils, liming very acid soils and by destroying all cruciferous weeds, which can act as hosts for the organism. Alternatively, apply PCNB to the seedbed before sowing brassicas and spray young plants with this pesticide when transplanting.

If brassicas are grown too soft, that is given too much nitrogenous fertilizer, they may be attacked by various fungi, particularly in wet seasons. Leaf spot fungi cause round brown spots on the leaves that sometimes fall away leaving holes. Gray mould fungi produce a gray-brown growth on the plants, and bacterial soft rot causes the affected parts to turn slimy with an unpleasant smell. If any of these diseases occur, remove and burn affected leaves, or the whole plant if necessary, and thin out plants that are growing too close together. Reduce the risk of attacks by limiting the use of nitrogenous fertilizers and by applying a dressing of sulfate of potash before planting.

Disorders The chief physiological disorders affecting cabbages are splitting and failure to heart. Prevent these by watering before the soil dries out completely and planting seedlings carefully in well prepared, humus-rich soil. Broccoli and cauliflowers may be affected by whiptail, caused by molybdenum deficiency; the leaves are reduced to the midrib and the heads fail to develop. Apply a solution of sodium molybdate at 1 oz in 2½ gal of water to each 10 sq yd of soil.

5 Apply bromophos or diazinon to the soil around the plants to combat cabbage root fly. Continue to water the transplants daily until they are fully established. Make sure they are never short of water because otherwise they will produce small heads.

6 May (frame-raised plants) or July (plants sown outdoors in March to April). Water in a dressing of sulphate of ammonia at 1 oz per square yard before the curds start to form.

7 In dry weather apply water at 4 gal per square yard each week. If this is not possible give a single application at the same rate, when the curds are forming or 2–3 weeks before the crop is due to mature, to improve quality and yield.

8 June to August/September. Cut the mature cauliflowers as needed. The curds are ready for harvesting when they are firm and well developed but not yet beginning to open.

Broccoli

Purple cauliflower

Purple cauliflower takes about a month longer to mature than standard varieties but is grown in the same way for summer or fall use. It is not blanched. After the large head is cut, small heads will continue to develop on side shoots for a couple of months. Pick them regularly to stimulate further young growth and to prevent flowering. If the shoots are allowed to flower the production of side-shoots stops.

Broccoli

Broccoli is a little hardier than cauliflower and easier to grow. The general principles of brassica growing, including pest and disease controls, apply to it although it will grow well in relatively poor soils.

Sowing The seed is sown indoors in February or March and the young seedlings are transplanted to the vegetable plot at about the time of the last freeze. For a later crop, seed is sown where the plants are to grow shortly after the last freeze and for a fall crop, seed is sown in a seedbed or directly in the garden about 90–100 days before the first fall frost. In all cases, the seedlings should be planted in rows 18 in apart with 18 in between the plants. Closer spacings of 12 in by 12 in may be used provided that ample water is available for irrigation.

Pests and diseases

Club root and cabbage maggot may be troublesome. Cabbage maggots can devastate seedlings and young plants. Damaged plants stop growing and wilt in warm weather. Treat seed rows and transplanting sites with diazinon or bromophos. Check attacks on established plants by drenching the soil with spray-strength trichlorphon. Club root causes plants to become stunted. Apply PCNB to the seedbed before sowing, and spray young plants with the chemical when transplanting.

Harvesting

As the large flowerheads mature, cut them off on a slant (so water will run off the stem) and then water in a light dressing of $\frac{1}{2}$ oz per square yard of a general fertilizer around the plants. This encourages the growth of side-shoots. Pick these every few days.

Late April to May

1 Water the seedlings in the flats the day before transplanting. Lift the seedlings carefully. Dip the roots in calomel paste to combat club-root.

June onward

4 Keep the plants free from weeds. In dry weather apply water at 4 gal per square yard each week or give 1 application at the same rate as the central head forms.

2 Plant the seedlings at 18 in intervals in rows 18 in apart and water them in well. Check that they are firmly planted by gently tugging the uppermost leaves.

5 When the central heads mature cut them for use. Water in a dressing of $\frac{1}{2}$ oz of a general fertilizer.

3 Apply diazinon to the soil around the plants to combat cabbage maggot. Water the transplants daily until they are fully established.

6 Cut the side-shoots of broccoli every few days as they mature to maintain a succession of spears.

Kale

The dark green, crinkly leaves and shoots of kale can be eaten in spring and fall. As it is extremely hardy it is a most useful vegetable for winter use. Kale is often said to taste bitter, but if the small tender shoots and leaves are used instead of larger coarse foliage, the flavor is very pleasant. It often succeeds where other brassicas will not, because it is tolerant of most diseases and pests, and it will grow and crop reasonably well on poor soils. It also tolerates harsher climatic conditions than other brassicas. Whether curly or plain-leaved, all popular varieties are usually sown in the garden where they are to grow. But they can also be started in flats or seedbeds and then transplanted like other brassicas.

Some types of kale are ornamental, with colored decorative leaves. These can be grown in flower beds where they fill the dual purpose of an ornamental and food crop. Perennial kales can be grown but they are of less use as a food crop.

Cultivation

Although tolerant of poor soils, kale does best in fertile conditions. It will grow in most soils, whether acid or alkaline. The soil must however, be well-drained because waterlogged conditions cause root rot. The general rules for brassica cultivation (see page 26) should be followed and the site should be open. Less shelter is needed than for other brassicas, but in areas exposed to cold winter winds some protection will be repaid by better growth. As with Brussels sprouts, firm planting is important, particularly with the tall varieties, because the crop may have to withstand winter winds.

The seed is sown directly in the garden as soon as the soil can be worked in the spring. You should then be able to start harvesting in two months. However, the more common practice—especially in the South—is to sow seed two months before first fall frost. Pick off leaves as you want them throughout the fall and even into the winter. Light freezing improves the flavor. Kale should be planted in rows 18 in apart with 12 in between the individual plants in the rows.

As with cabbage, avoid nitrogen-rich fertilizers which encourage soft growth and thus increase the risk of frost damage. Hill up around the stems to protect the plants from wind and frost.

Harvesting

Use young leaves and shoots only, pulling off and discarding yellowing or tough old leaves. Further side-shoots will be produced, and again these should be gathered when young and succulent. Pick the side-shoots from the top downward. Some varieties produce edible flowering heads.

If the plants are given some protection, they should survive the winter in all but the coldest areas so that they can be harvested again in early spring, providing a useful gap-filler before the new season's crops mature. Protect with cloches or straw.

Collards

Collards are brassicas grown primarily in the South—although they can be grown in all climate zones—as a substitute for cabbage. They have crumpled leaves that generally form a loose cluster but sometimes form a head. When young, the entire plant is cooked. When older, the tender leaves at the top of the plant are used.

Cultivation

Collards are grown like cabbage. Seeds are usually sown directly in the garden where the plants are to grow. Sow seeds for a spring crop before the last spring freeze; for a fall crop, in August. Space plants 15 in apart in rows 2 ft wide. Harvest when stalks are young and tender. The leaves can be blanched by tying them together loosely 2–3 weeks before harvesting. 'Vates' is a popular variety, tolerant of cold and 24- to 36-inch tall. Leaves can be picked after 75 days' growth. 'Georgia' is another very adaptable variety.

1 Sow seed thinly where the plants are to be grown as soon as the soil can be worked. Make the drills ¾–1 in deep. Space the drills 18 in apart.

2 Thin the plants to 12 in apart when the seedlings are large enough to be handled.

3 Hill up each plant to the base of the first leaf as a protection against frost and wind.

4 Harvest kale by picking the young shoots from the top of the plant downward. Some varieties produce edible flowering heads. Use young shoots and leaves only.

Spinach/New Zealand spinach 1

SPINACH

SUMMER
'Long Standing Round'.

WINTER
'Green Market' (hardy),
'Long Standing Prickly',
'Sigmaleaf' (bolt resistant).

NEW ZEALAND SPINACH
No named varieties available.

Spinach (*Spinacia oleracea*) is an annual plant. Highly nutritious, it is grown for the use of its leaves which are either cooked or eaten raw in salads. New Zealand spinach (*Tetragona tetragonioides*) is not botanically related to ordinary spinach but is also grown for its leaves. The roughly triangular, blunt-tipped leaves are milder in flavor than those of ordinary spinach and are therefore preferred by many gardeners.

NEW ZEALAND SPINACH

New Zealand spinach needs a good medium to light soil and an open sunny position. It is not a hardy plant and must be sown indoors in early March for planting out in May or as soon as the danger of frost is past. The seeds are very hard and it helps germination if they are soaked in water overnight before sowing. Sow three seeds together in a $\frac{1}{2}$ in drill with 1 ft between each group of seeds. Thin the seedlings when they emerge, leaving the strongest one from each group of three. New Zealand spinach has a trailing habit and takes up a lot of ground. Unlike ordinary spinach, however, it does not bolt in hot dry weather although it should be watered well during such spells to encourage growth. Hoe regularly at first to keep down weeds, but later the plants' own thick growth will control them. Pinch out the tips of well-grown plants to produce more branching and young leaves. From June to September harvest New Zealand spinach by picking a few leaves from each plant. It is a cut-and-come-again vegetable, regular picking encourages it.

Cultivation
Ordinary spinach needs a soil rich in organic matter and therefore capable of retaining water. When winter digging, add well-rotted compost and manure.

Soil and situation Spinach will not thrive on poor, dry or extremely acid soils. It grows best at a pH of 6.5–7.5. Since it is very fast growing, summer spinach can be cultivated as a catch crop between rows of taller vegetables, such as peas or beans, which provide slight shade in the summer months.

Summer spinach
For a continual supply of fresh leaves throughout the summer, sow the seed at two or three week intervals from early spring (as soon as the soil is workable) to May. Take out $\frac{1}{2}$–$\frac{3}{4}$ in drills, 12 in apart, and sow the seed very thinly.

Thinning Spinach has a much better flavor if it grows without any check and for this reason both thin sowing and early thinning are important tasks. Overcrowding in the row results in weak plants that run to seed easily. As soon as the seedlings have emerged and are large enough to handle, thin them until the individual plants are 3 in apart. As soon as these plants begin to close in on each other, thin again until they are 6 in apart. These thinnings can be eaten. Hoe between the rows very regularly to keep down weeds.

Watering Spinach must be kept well watered, especially in hot dry weather when there is a risk of bolting. Give the plants up to 4 gal per square yard each week in such conditions, even if they are still very small.

Fall spinach
Late-season sowings can be disappointing. Sow the seed in the usual way 6–8 weeks before first fall frost, but at this time it is best to choose a sunnier site. In zone 7, if you cover the plants with cloches after the first frost, they should continue growing through most or all of the winter. Leave the cloches in place as long as necessary.

In areas with mild winters, a second sowing can be made later in the fall and a third sowing can be made in late January. In this way plants can be grown virtually throughout the year without protection.

SPINACH AND SWISS CHARD VARIETIES
Melody, winner of an All-America award, is hardy. It is adaptable to either early spring or late fall sowings in northern areas, and it can also be successfully grown as a winter crop in the South in zones 8–10. Melody also has the advantage of being disease-resistant and it is vigorous. Cold Resistant Savoy is a 45-day crop, useful for overwintering in the milder zones to provide a harvest of spinach in early spring. Other varieties include Long Standing Bloomsdale and America. Swiss chard varieties include Lucullus and White King.

Summer spinach

 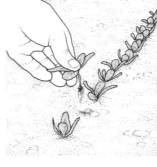 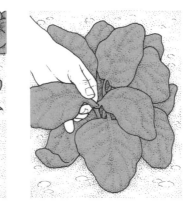

1 Winter. Incorporate well-rotted compost into the soil during winter digging.

2 March to May, every 2–3 weeks. Sow the seed thinly in $\frac{1}{2}$–$\frac{3}{4}$ in deep drills, 12 in apart. Thin to 3 in apart.

3 When the seedlings begin to touch each other, thin again to 6 in apart. These thinnings can be eaten.

Fall spinach

 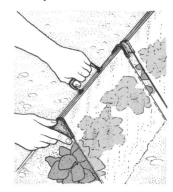

4 In dry weather apply water at a rate of up to 4 gal per square yard each week. Hoe weeds regularly.

5 Six to eight weeks after sowing, cut or pick the outside leaves by breaking away their stalks.

6 October onward. In cold areas cover the growing plants with cloches.

Spinach/Swiss Chard

Harvesting

Summer spinach is ready to pick 6–8 weeks after sowing. Up to half the foliage on each plant can be picked at a time.

Fall and winter spinach takes longer to mature and is not ready until about 10–12 weeks after sowing. Only a few leaves should be taken from each plant at any one time.

Pick the outside leaves while they are young and tender by breaking the stalk by hand. Do not tear the leaf stems away from the plant's base because this damages the plant. If spinach is harvested regularly in this way the plants are encouraged to produce more leaves and the cropping period is longer.

Storing Spinach is best consumed as soon as possible after harvesting, although it can be frozen successfully.

Pests and diseases

Proper thinning of the growing plants and vigilant watering should deter downy mildew. But if it does strike, spray the plants with zineb or a copper fungicide.

Swiss chard

Swiss chard is also known as seakale beet or silver beet. A very attractive vegetable, it has extra wide leaf stalks and midribs. The leaves are treated in the same way as ordinary spinach but the stalks and midribs may be used instead of asparagus. The midribs do not have the same texture as asparagus.

In April sow three seeds together at 15 in intervals in $\frac{1}{2}$–$\frac{3}{4}$ in deep drills that are 15 in apart. Thin the seedlings to the strongest in each group. Hoe regularly throughout the summer and water liberally, especially during dry weather. The plants should continue growing throughout the summer if you pick the leaves as they are ready. But you can make repeat sowings at any time up to mid-summer. With cloche protection in fall, growing should continue for a long time.

Swiss chard is ready to pick from June or about two months after sowing. As soon as the leaves are big enough a few can be picked at a time from each plant. Break the stalks off at the base, taking the outside ones first. Swiss chard does not keep well and should be eaten immediately.

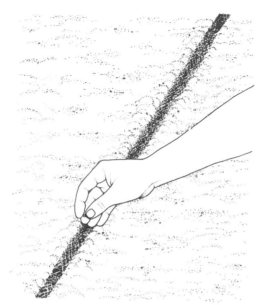

1 April to July. Sow 3–4 seeds at 9 in intervals in $\frac{1}{2}$–$\frac{3}{4}$ in deep drills, 15 in apart. Choose a soil rich in organic content and water-retentive.

2 When the seedlings are big enough to handle thin the groups, leaving 1 seedling at each station.

3 During the growing season hoe between the rows regularly.

4 Fall. Protect the plants with cloches as necessary to extend the growing season.

5 As they develop, water the growing plants liberally, up to 2–3 gal per week in dry weather.

6 June onwards. Harvest a few of the largest leaves from each plant regularly, picking them off as close to the ground as possible. Pick regularly to encourage production.

Asparagus 1

Asparagus is a perennial fern-like plant grown for its young shoots which are cut as fat, succulent spears soon after they come through the soil. Appreciated as a luxury vegetable, asparagus is expensive to buy but economical to grow because the same plants, when established and well-managed, will provide crops for 20 years or even longer. Asparagus is easy to grow and it is a beautiful plant, but it does require time and patience.

Cultivation

Plants may be raised from seed but there is a three-year delay between seed sowing and the first crop. The more usual way of starting an asparagus bed is with bought crowns, which can be one, two or three years old. For all ages the period between planting and harvesting is the same. The one-year-old is the best buy because it is cheaper and it establishes a good root system as quickly after planting as does a two- or three-year-old. Order the crowns from the grower well in advance and ask for delivery in April, which is the best planting time.

Soil and situation Asparagus will grow in most soils but a pH of 6.5–7.5 is preferable and good drainage and freedom from perennial weeds are essential. Dig a dressing of well-rotted manure or compost at 15 lb per square yard into the top foot of soil in the fall or early winter before planting. Asparagus roots tend to develop laterally so it is best to maintain the food supply in the top spit. Asparagus grows best in an open site.

The first year

Never let the crowns dry out; choose a damp day for planting and leave the crowns wrapped until the last minute.

Planting The traditional asparagus bed, which consists of three rows of crowns with access on either side, is more than 5 ft wide. However, if only a single row is planted in each trench, weed control and cutting are easier. In April dig a trench about 10 in deep and 15 in wide for each row. Then lightly fork in a balanced general fertilizer, such as 10-10-10, at 3 oz per square yard. In very nitrogen-rich soils dig in 1½ oz superphosphate and 1 oz

SOWING ASPARAGUS

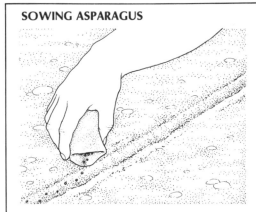

Asparagus seed can be sown outdoors in March or early April.

Sow the seed thinly in ½–¾ in deep drills, 18 in apart. When the seedlings emerge thin them until they are eventually 6 in apart. Keep the bed completely weed-free and water in dry weather. The seedlings can be transplanted to the permanent bed in March or April of the following year.

However, another year in the seedling row will mean that the seed-bearing female plants can be identified and removed before their seeds fall and germinate. In a permanent bed planted with male crowns only there is no seedhead production and constant weeding out of unwanted seedlings will not be necessary. Plant out and proceed as for one-year-old crowns.

The first year

1 Winter. Dig the ground to a depth of 1 spit and incorporate well-rotted manure or compost with a fork. Also remove perennial weeds.

2 April. Dig a trench 15 in wide and 10 in deep. Lightly rake in fertilizer at 3 oz per square yard. Make a 3 in deep ridge at the bottom of the trench.

3 April. Plant the crowns at 18 in intervals on the ridge with the roots sloping outwards. Cover the crowns with 2–3 in of soil.

4 October. Cut the fern when it has turned yellow. Apply a 2–3 in layer of manure or compost and mound up the soil several inches deep over the row.

Asparagus 2

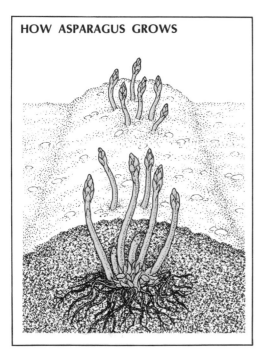

HOW ASPARAGUS GROWS

sulfate of potash. Make a ridge in the bottom of the trench and place each crown at 18 in intervals on the ridge, with the roots spread outwards over the ridge. Cover them quickly and carefully with fine soil to fill in the trench. If more than one trench is dug the rows should be 4 ft apart.

Once an asparagus bed is established its upkeep is routine. The common reasons for deterioration are lack of weeding, cutting over too long a season and disregard of the need for fern production. Hand weed regularly and never cultivate deeply or dig near a bed because asparagus roots spread out widely and are easily damaged. In the fall when the foliage turns yellow, cut it down and clear any weeds. Mound up the soil several inches deep over the row.

The second year
In late February or early March top-dress with a balanced general fertilizer, such as 10-10-10, at 3 oz per square yard.

Do not cut the foliage until it yellows in the fall. Then clear the bed and apply a 2–3 in layer of well-rotted manure or compost. Ridge up the row with soil if necessary.

Harvesting
Do not cut any spears until the third season after planting. Eventual heavy cropping depends on a slow build-up of crown size, starting with the all important first two seasons, when no cutting should be done.

The cutting season for asparagus is from the end of April to late June, and no longer. Cut all the spears when they are 5–6 in above ground, even if they vary in thickness. In the third year cut for a period of six weeks after the first shoots appear. In the fourth and subsequent years the cutting period is up to eight weeks.

A special asparagus knife is ideal for cutting, but an ordinary sharp knife used carefully will do. By the time a bed is established the crowns will be about 4 in below the soil surface.

Cut the spears obliquely about 1–2 in below the soil surface. An asparagus crown produces many small shoots at different stages of maturity and it is important to cut the spears cleanly and carefully so that the plant will continue to crop.

Aftercare
From June onwards the ferns must be allowed to grow in order to play their vital role in building up food reserves in the crown for the following year's crop. To encourage this growth apply a general, balanced fertilizer at 3 oz per square yard immediately after the last cutting.

When the ferns have turned yellow, and not before, cut them down to ground level. Burn them because they are too woody for the compost heap. Clear away any debris, such as dried leaves and stems, and tidy the bed after cutting the ferns down.

Pests and diseases
If asparagus beetle grubs damage shoots during the cutting season spray the plants with derris. If slugs are troublesome control them by the methods described in the section on pests and diseases (see page 15).

The second year

5 Late February to early March. Top-dress the bed with fertilizer at 3 oz per square yard.

6 Fall. Cut down the yellow ferns and apply manure or compost. Ridge up the row with soil if necessary.

Third and subsequent years

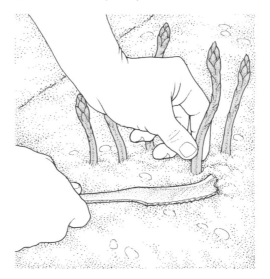

7 April to late June. Cut all the spears with a sharp knife when they are 5–6 in above soil level. Cut each spear obliquely 1–2 in below the soil surface.

8 June onward. Immediately after the last cut, apply a general, balanced fertilizer at 3 oz per square yard to the bed.

Artichokes/Cardoons

The artichoke—also called globe artichoke—is a perennial plant grown for the attractive foliage and the immature flowerheads, parts of which are edible. It grows best in California's four central coastal counties but can also be grown in zones 8–10 elsewhere. In zone 7, it succeeds only if it is rigorously protected in winter. It is sometimes grown in this zone as an annual.

Cultivation
The artichoke is simple to cultivate but it takes up a lot of space for a small yield. It is a three-year crop, discarded after the third year. Artichokes can be grown from seed but some seedlings produce inferior flowerheads so they are usually grown from "suckers."

Soil and situation An open position and a fertile soil of pH 6.5–7.5 is required for the best results, although artichokes are tolerant of most soils unless the drainage is poor. Dig the ground well in winter, incorporating manure or compost, and a couple of weeks before planting rake in a general balanced fertilizer at 3 oz to the square yard.

Planting Take suckers from the base of established plants from March to April. The ideal sucker is sturdy, short-jointed and about 8–9 in long. Remove them close to the main stem, making sure that some root is still attached. Plant the suckers in permanent rows 2½ ft apart with 2 ft between individual plants. They should be watered initially until they are established and then during dry spells. Hoe weeds throughout the summer.

Harvesting
In the first year each plant will produce 4–6 flowerheads for cutting in August. In the second and third years each plant should produce 10–12 heads and cutting can commence in July. Cut when the heads are mature and fleshy but while the scales are still shut tight. Cut the main heads first.

Cut the old stems down after harvesting and tidy the rows. Cover the rows with straw or bracken. The plants are at their best when two or three years old.

Pests and diseases
For precautions against slugs and various rodents see page 17.

The first year

1 March to April. Cut the suckers cleanly, with some root still attached, from the base of established plants.

2 Plant the suckers at 2 ft intervals in rows 2½ ft apart and water them. Keep watering until the plants are established, when the leaves stop flagging.

3 Throughout summer. Hoe regularly to keep the rows weed-free and water in dry weather.

4 August to October. Cut unripened flowerheads before any of the bud scales are purple. In November cut old stems right down and cover the rows with straw.

The second year

5 March to April. Remove the straw from the rows and top-dress with 3 oz per square yard of a general, balanced fertilizer.

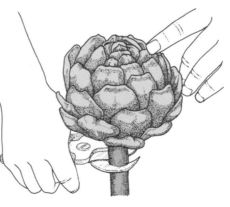

6 July to October. Cut the mature fleshy flowerheads when the scales are still shut tight. Cut the main heads first, followed by the smaller heads.

CARDOONS
Closely related to the artichoke, the cardoon is an attractive plant grown in zones 8–10 for the fleshy stems of its inner leaves, which require blanching.

Sow the seed in April in a well cultivated, moist soil. Sow groups of 3–4 seeds at 18 in intervals in rows 2½ ft apart and thin to the sturdiest seedling at each station. From late August to early September blanch cardoons. After 4–5 weeks the stems should be ready to harvest. Lift whole plants with a fork and trim the roots. Cardoons are not fully frost hardy.

Blanch cardoons by wrapping the stems of each plant in a light-proof material, such as black polyethylene. Loosely tie the covering and hoe up soil around the base of each plant.

'Lily White'.

Seakale

Seakale is a hardy perennial plant, grown as a luxury vegetable for the production of its blanched leaf stems.

Cultivation
Seakale can be produced from seed but it takes two years to produce edible shoots. Most people prefer to use "planting crowns" which can be obtained from a nursery or another gardener, or produced from root-cuttings (thongs). Seakale blanched outdoors can be left to produce more crops, provided they are well tended, in the following years.

Soil and situation Seakale needs a well-drained fertile soil of pH 6.5–7.5; the best results are obtained in deep, rich sandy loams. An open site with no competition from other crops or nearby tree roots is also necessary. Dig the ground well in winter, incorporating 15 lb per square yard of well-rotted garden compost or manure.

In spring, 1–2 weeks before planting, rake 3 oz per square yard of a balanced general fertilizer, such as Growmore, into the soil.

Planting In late March plant the crowns or "thongs" 2 in deep and 15 in apart with 18 in between the rows. Before planting rub off all but the strongest bud from each crown.

Keep the plants weed-free and water them in dry weather. Remove any flower stems.

Blanching In the autumn clean up the beds and cut down the yellowing foliage. In January force seakale outdoors by placing a light-proof plastic pot, 9 in in diameter, on top of each crown. Cover the drainage holes and place straw over each pot.

Harvesting
At the end of March or early April begin to cut, when the blanched shoots are 5–7 in long, and continue until late April.

Aftercare At the end of April finish cutting the blanched shoots. Rake in 3 oz of fertilizer per square yard and mulch the beds with well-rotted compost or manure. Keep the beds weed-free and repeat the blanching process in the following January. A well-tended seakale bed will continue to produce for about five years.

PROPAGATION FROM ROOT-CUTTINGS

Take root-cuttings (thongs) from the fleshy side roots (off the main roots) of plants lifted in the autumn. They should be about 3–6 in long and as thick as a pencil. Make a straight cut across the top (the end nearest the main root) and a sloping one at the bottom to distinguish them for planting later. Store in sand until March.

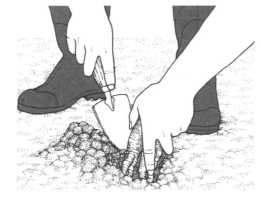

1 Late March to early April. Plant the crowns, having rubbed off all but the strongest bud from each, 2 in deep at 15 in intervals in rows 18 in apart.

2 Summer. Hoe weeds regularly and water in dry weather. Remove any flower stems that develop. In autumn clean up the bed and remove the yellowing foliage.

3 January. Completely cover the crowns with light-proof, 9 in dia., plastic pots. Cover the pots with straw.

4 End of March to early April. Scrape soil away from the blanched crowns and cut off the shoots with a sharp knife when they are 5–7 in long.

5 End of April. Stop cutting and rake in 3 oz per square yard of a general balanced fertilizer. Mulch the bed with well-rotted compost or manure.

INDOOR BLANCHING

Seakale can be produced from November onwards by blanching indoors. Lift the crowns from late September to late October and trim off the side roots. Leave the main roots trimmed to a length of about 6 in. Then pot the crowns in plastic pots (9 in in diameter) filled with rich soil such as John Innes No. 3, allowing three crowns per pot. Cover each pot with another pot of the same size, placed upside down, and keep them in complete darkness at a temperature of 10°–13°C/50°–55°F. A cellar is ideal. The seakale should be ready within 5–6 weeks. Forced roots are useless for propagation so they should be discarded and burnt afterwards.

Celery

SELF-BLANCHING
'American Green', 'Golden
Self Blanching' (white).

TRENCH CELERY
'Giant Pink', 'Giant Red',
'Giant White', 'Prizetaker'
(white).

Celery is a biennial plant grown as an annual for its blanched stems which are cooked or used for salads. There are green and yellow varieties.

Cultivation

Choose an open site with rich, well-drained soil of pH 6.5–7.5. There are two methods of growing celery. By tradition it is grown in trenches which are gradually filled in to blanch the stems. Alternatively, self-blanching varieties can be used which do not require hilling up but these are less hardy (with a correspondingly shorter growing season) than the trenched varieties. They require much less work and are especially suitable for heavy soils which are laborious to trench and where the trench may become waterlogged with consequent slug damage and rotting.

Trench method Take out a trench 15 in wide and 12 in deep in March or April. If more than one trench is required the centers of each should be 4 ft apart. Fork manure into the bottom of the trench at a rate of 15 lb (1 bucketful) per square yard and return the soil to within 3 in of ground level. The trench should then be left open until planting out time in early summer.

Sowing Use treated seed if available. In February or March (10 weeks before last spring frost) sow the seed thinly in flats in a prepared

sterile soil mixture at 13°–16°C/55°–60°F. Do not cover the seed but keep it moist. The seed germinates in 2–3 weeks. Prick out the seedlings when they have two true leaves into flats of soil mixture. Alternatively, place them singly in 3 in pots. Harden them off gradually for planting out in late May or June. Just before planting, rake in a balanced general fertilizer at the rate of 2–3 oz per square yard into the bottom of the trench and apply a diazinon drench to combat carrot rust fly.

Planting When danger of frost is past, plant out the seedlings at 9 in intervals in double-staggered rows 9 in apart in each trench. Water the plants thoroughly. When the plants are about 12 in high cut out any side-shoots at the base and loosely tie the stems just below the leaves, using raffia or soft string.

As with all leafy crops ample water is essential during the growing season. In dry weather apply 4 gal per square yard. Alternatively, 10–20 days before the final hilling up apply 4 gal per square yard. This improves the quality and size of the crop markedly.

Hilling up As the plants grow, hill up progressively at intervals of about three weeks, leaving plenty of leaf above the soil and taking care not to let soil fall into the hearts. Hill up after rain when the soil is damp, never when it is dry, because the foliage acts as an

umbrella and keeps the soil around the roots as dry or as damp as it was when hilled up.

Harvesting

Most varieties mature in about 4 months. Lift celery carefully with a trowel as they are required. The roots may penetrate very deeply and in such cases it is best to lift with a fork. Bracken or straw placed over the trench assists lifting in frosty weather.

Pests and diseases

Celery fly larvae bore into the foliage leaving brown blisters. Pinch out affected leaves and

spray with dimethoate at the first sign of damage. Slugs may be a problem, especially on heavy soils, and so put down slug pellets around the plants. Carrot rust fly may attack the roots of celery and should be combated by applying diazinon before transplanting.

Celery leaf spot can be prevented by using treated seed or spraying the plants with benomyl as soon as any spots are visible on the leaves. For early and late blight, which cause brown spots on stems and leaves, spray weekly with zineb. For later crops of celery, seed is sown in an outdoor seedbed 4–4½ months before last frost.

SELF-BLANCHING CELERY

 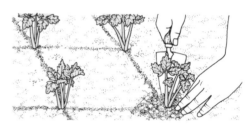

Sow the seed as for trench-grown varieties but plant out the seedlings on the flat. Prepare the bed in April by digging in well-rotted manure or compost at 15 lb per square yard. Plant out the seedlings during May in a square, not in a row, 11 in apart each way or 6 in each way for a higher yield of smaller sticks.

 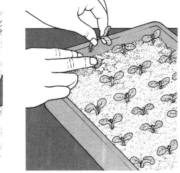  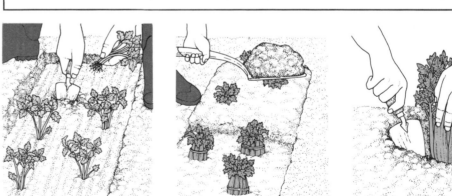 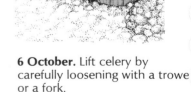

1 February or March. Dig a trench 15 in wide and 12 in deep. Fork manure into the bottom and return the soil to within 3 in of ground level.

2 March or April. Sow the seed thinly in seed compost at 13°–16°C/55°–60°F. Do not cover and keep moist. After 2–3 weeks prick the seedlings out in flats of potting soil.

3 Just before planting, rake fertilizer into the trench bottom at 2–3 oz per square yard.

4 May. Plant out the seedlings at 9 in intervals in double-staggered rows 9 in apart. Water well.

5 July. When the plants are 12 in high loosely tie the stems just below the leaves. Hill up every 3 weeks when the soil is damp to cover the leaf bases.

6 October. Lift celery by carefully loosening with a trowel or a fork.

Bean sprouts/Alfalfa

The mung bean or black gram (*Phaseolus mungo*) is not grown as an outdoor crop in the United States because it requires tropical or sub-tropical conditions. However, it can be successfully germinated indoors to produce bean sprouts. These can be eaten raw in salads or cooked and they are a valuable source of protein and vitamin C. Bean sprouts are simple and quick to grow, and they can be "harvested" all the year round.

Cultivation

The beans can be sprouted at any time of the year provided they have sufficient warmth and moisture. Light must be excluded to blanch the shoots, keeping them sweet, white and palatable.

Sowing First rinse the beans and leave them to soak in cold water for 1–2 days or until they are slightly swollen and the skins have begun to split. Line a tray, shallow bowl or other suitable container with absorbent material, such as flannel or toweling. Moisten it well and spread the soaked beans evenly and not too thickly over the surface.

Place the container in a polyethylene bag or wrap it loosely in polyethylene to provide insulation and help to retain the moisture. Do not make the bag airtight because this encourages rotting.

Keep the container in a warm place 16°–24°C/60°–75°F) and exclude light by covering it with brown paper or newspaper or by placing it in a dark cupboard.

Watering The beans should be kept constantly damp, so water them 2–3 times daily. However, do not allow them to become too wet or too warm or they will go moldy.

Harvesting

The sprouts are ready to harvest in 4–9 days depending on the temperature at which they have been grown. They should be 1½–2 in long, plump and white, with pale green leaves. Do not allow them to grow longer than this because they will become stringy, bitter and rather unpalatable.

Cut the bean sprouts with scissors or pull them up by hand. Remove the remains of the seedcoats if necessary.

ALFALFA

Alfalfa is grown commercially as a fodder crop but the seeds can be germinated indoors at any time of the year to produce shoots for eating raw in salads. They resemble cress in appearance and uncooked garden peas in taste. Sprouting is usually done by the jar method.

Put ¼ oz of the seed into a jelly jar or other similar clear glass container. Cover it with water and leave it to soak overnight.

Seal the jar with a piece of muslin fastened with a rubber band. Pour off the water through the muslin, fill the jar with fresh water and pour off again. Rinse the seed daily in this way. Keep the jar at room temperature (20°C/68°F) and in the light but out of direct sunlight.

The shoots are ready to harvest in 5–7 days, when they have almost filled the jar and are a mass of curly white stems and bright green leaves. Pull them apart in tufts to use as required.

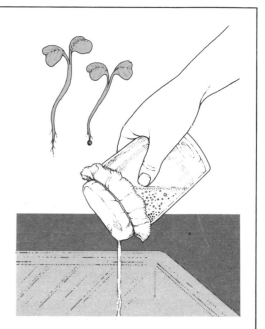

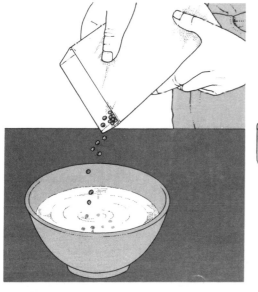

1 Soak the beans in cold water for 1–2 days or until the skins begin to split.

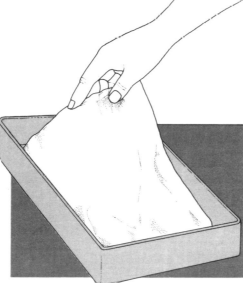

2 Line a shallow tray with absorbent material. Moisten well and sprinkle the soaked beans evenly over the surface.

3 Place the tray in a polyethylene bag and cover with newspaper. Keep in warm, dark place and water two or three times per day.

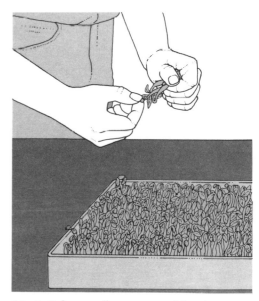

4 In 4–9 days, pull up or cut with scissors when the shoots are 1½–2 in long, plump and white. Remove any seedcoat remains.

Rhubarb

FORCING
'Timperley Early'.

MAIN CROP
'Hawke's Champagne',
'Prince Albert', 'Sutton',
'Victoria'.

Rhubarb (*Rheum rhaponticum*) is a hardy perennial grown for its delicately-flavored pink leaf-stalks, and is therefore classed as a vegetable not a fruit. The leaves contain oxalic acid and are poisonous. Rhubarb is in season from March to July, although earlier crops can be obtained in January and February by forcing plants.

Cultivation

Rhubarb grows best on a sunny site in a fairly heavy, acid soil of pH 5.0–6.0. However, it will tolerate a wide range of conditions and is likely to fail only on very waterlogged soils. The plants will stand for about 5–10 years, so the bed should be thoroughly prepared in the fall before planting.

Dig the ground deeply, removing all perennial weeds and incorporating organic manure or well-rotted garden compost at a rate of 20–30 lb per square yard. Just before planting rake in a dressing of 3–4 oz of fertilizer.

Propagation Raising rhubarb from seed is a lengthy process which often gives poor results, so either propagate it from root-cuttings or obtain offsets of a named variety from a nursery. Propagation should be from established plants at least three years old. Cut the roots into sections that have at least one eye with a sharp knife.

Planting Plant in early spring, leaving 3 ft be-tween the plants. If more than one row is required, leave 3–4 ft between the rows. The eyes should be just below the soil surface. Firm in and water if necessary during dry weather. Cut out flowering shoots as they appear.

Harvesting

Rhubarb can be harvested from April to July. Do not pull at all in the first year after planting and only lightly in the second. Hold the stalk near the base and pull up with a twisting movement. Take a few stalks from each crown as required, but always leave 3–4 leaves on each plant to avoid weakening it.

Aftercare In autumn, when harvesting is over and the foliage has died down, clean up around the plants and apply a light top dressing of a balanced general fertilizer at 2–3 oz per square yard. In late winter mulch with well-rotted compost or manure.

Pests and diseases

Stem and bulb eelworm may attack rhubarb, causing poor growth and distorted leaves. Crown rot is the only major disease, the symptoms of which are dull foliage, small stalks and dead buds. There is no cure for either of these problems so dig up and burn affected plants. Do not replant rhubarb on the same ground.

FORCING RHUBARB

Forcing the plants during the winter produces earlier crops of pinker, more tender rhubarb. It can be harvested from February to March if forced *in situ* or as early as January if forced indoors.

Outdoors In mid-January to February cover the plants to be forced with a bucket or barrel to exclude the light. Put straw or strawy manure over and around the cover for insulation. The plants should not normally need watering and the stalks will be ready in 5–6 weeks. Do not pick from the plants for at least two years after forcing to allow them to recuperate.

Indoors In October to early November dig up strong clumps and leave them on the soil surface exposed to frosty weather for 1–2 weeks. This encourages rapid growth during forcing. Then pack the roots close together in a box, cover with a thin layer of soil and water well. Invert another box and place it on top, and exclude light with newspaper or black polyethylene. Keep in a warm greenhouse or shed at 10°–13°C/50°–55°F. Water the plants occasionally to keep them moist. Pull the stalks in 4–5 weeks. Stagger the times of boxing for a constant supply.

First year

1 Early spring. Cut the roots of an established plant into sections, ensuring each has at least 1 eye.

2 Plant the sections 3 ft apart in well-prepared ground, with the eyes just below the soil surface. Rows should be 3–4 ft apart.

3 Summer. Water the plants in dry weather and cut out any flowering shoots.

4 October. Remove old foliage. Apply 2–3 oz of fertilizer to each plant.

Second and subsequent years

5 April to July. Pull stalks by grasping near the base and twisting upwards.

SOY BEANS
No named varieties available.

SHELL BEANS
'Chevrier Vert', 'Comtesse de Chambourd'.

Soybean and shell beans

Soybean and Shell beans

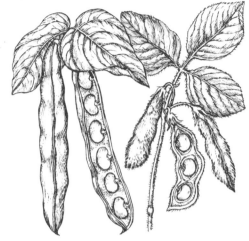

The soybean has a bushy habit and produces oval seeds that can be eaten whole with the pod, or shelled out and dried. It is a tender annual, and warm weather is needed to ripen the pods and beans. Soybeans are the most protein-rich legume in the world but they are difficult to grow successfully in temperate climates. Shell beans are the dried seeds of certain varieties of bush beans, such as French Horticultural, Great Northern, Pinto, Red and white Kidney and white Marrowfat.

Cultivation

Soybeans grow best in well-drained, fertile soils and warm, sunny situations. They do not thrive in cold, wet soils so delay sowing until the ground is warm and dry. Make sure that the soil is not acid; neutral soil (pH of 7.0) is ideal. Apply 1–2 oz per square yard of a general, balanced fertilizer and cultivate it in one or two weeks before sowing. No more fertilizer should be needed.

Sowing Sow in drills 2 in deep during May when the soil is warm. Never sow in cold, wet soil. Space the seeds 2–4 in apart in the row and leave 18 in between the rows. Water the bottom of the drill before sowing to provide sufficient moisture for germination. Mice may dig up and eat the seeds but they can be deterred by dipping the seeds in kerosene before sowing.

Growing Hoe around the plants to eliminate weeds, especially in the early stages. A mulch of peat, compost or straw will keep down later weeds, maintain a warm soil and reduce moisture loss. Water the plants regularly in dry weather and also when they are flowering to ensure a good crop.

Harvesting

Soybean pods can be picked green and eaten whole. Alternatively, like shell beans, they can be left to dry and the beans shelled out. In a fine autumn the pods may yellow and dry on the plant, but usually it is necessary to pull up the plants and dry them further.

Pests and diseases

Aphids and red spider mites may attack the plants. Spray them with malathion or derris. Bacterial blight is difficult to control and infected plants should be burnt. Maturing pods and beans may be damaged by gray mold or mildews in wet weather. Spray with zineb fungicide.

Storing Shell the beans from the dried pods. Spread them on newspaper in a cool room to complete the drying. Store in a mesh bag.

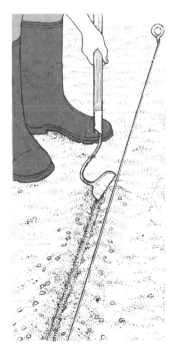

1 April. Using a hoe, take out 2 in deep drills in rows 18 in apart. Water the bottom of the drills before sowing. Dip the seeds in kerosene to deter mice.

2 Early May. When the soil is warm, sow individual seeds at 2–4 in intervals.

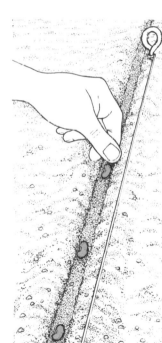

3 During summer. Mulch the growing plants. Water when the flowers appear. Hoe around the plants regularly to eliminate weeds.

4 Early fall. When the pods turn yellow, pull up the plants on a fine day when both the foliage and the pods are dry. In wet weather it may be necessary to pull up the plants and hang them up to dry indoors. Shell the beans and store.

BACTERIAL BLIGHT

Bacterial blight is a bacterial disease that causes dark, water-soaked areas on leaves and pods; the characteristic "halo" forms as a yellow edge around the dark areas. Damp, humid conditions favor the spread of bacterial blight, which usually originates from infected seed. Never save seed for next season from diseased plants. Dig up and burn any plants with bacterial blight. Fungicidal sprays are usually ineffective against bacterial diseases.

Bush beans 1

BUSH BEANS

Bush beans (also called snap beans or green beans) are tender annuals. Dwarf and climbing (pole) types are available. They grow best in warm conditions. The beans are eaten with the pods. Green podded types with either flat or cylindrical pods are most common, and there are also yellow, so-called "wax" beans and a purple bean that turns green when cooked. Two rows of dwarf beans 18 in apart should produce 10–15 lb of beans—pole beans produce 20–30 lb. Like other beans, bush beans are valuable for their vitamin and mineral content.

Cultivation

Bush beans grow best in a well-drained, fertile soil of pH 6.5–7.0. A layer of farmyard manure or compost dug in during the winter is sufficient to maintain fertility in most soils. Do not grow bush beans in shaded situations. Apply and work in a fertilizer, such as 10-10-10, at 1–2 oz per square yard a couple of weeks before sowing. Overrich soils and too much nitrogenous fertilizer encourage soft growth and excessive leaf production. No top dressing should be needed for this crop.

Sowing Do not make outdoor sowings too early. A soil temperature of at least 10°C/50°F is needed for successful and rapid germination. Be sure that all danger from frost has passed. Bush beans do not thrive in cold soils and the seeds will rot if conditions are too wet. The first dwarf bean sowings can be made outside in May in most places. Monthly sowings until July or even August give beans throughout the summer.

Pole types should be sown in mid-to-late May in cold regions.

Sow dwarf beans in rows 18 in apart. Space the seeds 2–3 in apart in 2 in drills. Water the bottom of the drill before sowing to encourage germination. Pole beans are sown in the same way but usually in hills spaced 3 ft apart.

Growing Pole beans need a support and training system because the plants grow to 6–7 ft. The usual practice is to make a tripod from three 8 ft poles lashed together at the top. Sow the beans around this in a circle and thin out to about 5 plants. Another method is to plant the beans in rows and build a tall framelike trellis of poles with 2–3 wires stretched between them. Tie strong vertical strings between the wires at about 9 in intervals. Let one or two plants climb each.

Hoe out any weeds and mulch the plants in June with peat, straw or lengths of black polyethylene. Once the seedlings are established, do not water until the flowers appear unless the weather is dry. Too much water during early growth encourages leaves to grow at the expense of the flowers.

Water the plants generously once the flowers appear; beans are particularly sensitive to moisture stress at the flower-opening and pod swelling stages and it is essential to keep them well watered at these times.

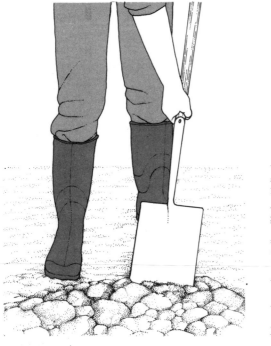

1 During winter, dig in a layer of farmyard manure or compost where the beans are to be grown.

2 Late April. Rake in general balanced fertilizer at 1–2 oz per square yard 1–2 weeks before sowing.

3 Take out a 2 in drill, spacing rows 18 in apart. Water the bottom of the drill to encourage germination.

4 May. Sow individual seeds at 2–3 in intervals in 2 in drills, 18 in apart for dwarf; 3–4 in intervals and 2 ft apart for pole.

Bush beans 2

Watering at 3–4 gal per square yard each week markedly increases pod-set, yield and quality. Syringing the flowers to "set" the pods, a traditional practice, is not effective. The organic matter dug in during the winter will help to retain moisture.

Harvesting

Regular picking is essential to maintain a continuous supply of beans. Dwarf beans produce their pods over a relatively short period (hence the successive sowings) but pole types continue to crop throughout the summer. Pick the beans while they are young and tender. Over-mature pods are stringy and show the beans bulging out the pod walls. Remove the pods carefully so as not to damage the plants; they should snap off the plants cleanly.

Pests and diseases

Aphids (green and black) may feed on the growing shoots, and red spider mites may be found on the under surfaces of leaves. These mites produce yellow dots on the upper surfaces of leaves, which eventually become bronzed and brittle. Gray mold (*Botrytis cinerea*) and mildew diseases can be problems during wet weather in the picking season. Damaged pods are soon infected and rot on the plant. Spray the plants regularly with zineb during wet or humid conditions.

Bacterial blight may attack bush beans (see page 45). It causes dark, water-soaked areas on leaves and pods, and the characteristic "halo" forms a yellow edge around the dark areas. Damp, humid conditions favor the spread of bacterial blight and fungicidal sprays are usually ineffective against it. Destroy any bush beans affected by the disease and never save seed for the next season from them. The worst insect pest is the yellow Mexican bean beetle, but this is readily controlled by dusting with rotenone.

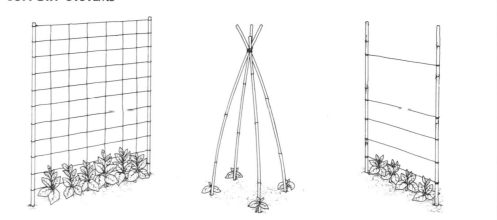

SUPPORT SYSTEMS

Pole beans must be supported on sticks, strings or nets because the plants grow up to 6–7 ft tall. Supports can be nets attached to poles, poles arranged in tripods, tied at the top, or wires stretched between poles.

5 Throughout summer. Hoe to keep down weeds and then mulch with peat, straw or black polyethylene to preserve moisture.

6 In June, mulch the plants with peat, straw or black polyethylene to keep down weeds.

7 As flowers appear, carefully apply water at a rate of 3–4 gal per week. Avoid splashing the foliage.

8 July onward. Pick the pods when they are 5–6 in long. They should snap in half easily and show no stringiness.

Runner beans 1

Runner beans are perennials that produce small root tubers, but they are usually grown as half-hardy annuals. In temperate zones they may be damaged by frost at the beginning or at the end of the season. The plants are very attractive with different varieties having white, pink or, more usually, scarlet flowers. Their tall habit and dense foliage make them a useful screen plant. A runner bean wigwam makes an attractive centerpiece in an annual flower border.

Cultivation

Runner beans should not be growing while frost is still a danger. When they are sown or planted rapid growth is required, however, and light, well-drained, fertile soils of pH 6.0–7.0 are best suited for this crop. Wet soils cause the large seeds to rot. Careful soil preparation for runner beans is rewarded with excellent growth and yields. Prepare a 2 ft wide, single spade depth trench in early spring. Fork large quantities of farmyard manure or well-rotted garden compost into the bottom of the trench before replacing the soil. These materials retain moisture during the life of the crop and encourage good growth and setting.

Situation Choose a sheltered but open, sunny site for runner beans, because winds can damage the plants and young beans. Still conditions also encourage the insects which are essential for runner bean pollination. One or two weeks before sowing, hoe in 2–3 oz per square yard of a general fertilizer such as 10-10-10.

Plant establishment There are several possible support systems for runner beans and the method of propagation varies with the system. Beans may either be sown or planted. Plants are raised in a cool greenhouse (10°C/50°F) in individual containers. Sow the seed approximately four weeks before the expected planting date. Pre-germinate the seeds first between layers of moistened kitchen toweling kept in a warm place. A germination rate of more than 80 per cent can be expected. Keep the propagation temperature down to maintain strong, sturdy growth. Harden off the plants in a cold frame or under cloches for a few days before planting. Do not plant out until all danger of frost

EARLY CROPS

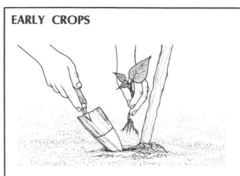

Early crops can be produced from transplanted plants raised by sowing seeds in pots in a cool greenhouse. Sow the seeds about four weeks before the expected planting date, which must be after the last frost. Make a good-sized hole with a trowel and plant a single bean plant beside each cane, pole or string. Sufficiently long shoots should be twisted around their support and the plants must be thoroughly watered at the base.

has passed. Sowing should take place outside from mid-May onwards depending on the frost incidence in the area. A soil temperature of at least 10°C/50°F is needed for germination. Cloches can be used to protect sowings made during April. Use the cloches to warm up the soil for three or four weeks before sowing and sow a single row with the beans spaced 6 in apart. Runner bean seeds should be sown 2 in deep and the positioning in the row depends on the support system.

Support systems

Runner beans are usually grown up supports. They can be trained up canes, poles, strings or nets. The plants will grow 8 ft tall, but they can be stopped by pinching out the growing point when they reach the top of the support.

Single rows of beans can be grown up any of the supports mentioned. In windy areas, a wall can provide shelter for a single row of beans. Nail or screw a batten horizontally on a wall about 8 ft above the ground. Canes or poles can then be pushed into the soil and secured to the batten with string, wire or

nails. If a second batten is fixed to the wall near the ground, a row of strings can be tied vertically at the desired interval. Seeds should be sown at 6 in intervals and the canes, poles or strings should be spaced 6 in apart. If nets are used they should be attached to wires stretched between vertical stakes.

Double row systems use 8 ft canes or poles which are crossed over and wired or tied together at the top to form an inverted V-shape. Sow the beans at 6 in intervals in the rows which should be 24 in apart. If poles are scarce or expensive, two plants can climb each support, but the yield will be reduced. Leave a 36 in path between double rows.

Canes or poles can also be made into wigwam support frameworks. Four to ten supports may be used. A 4-cane wigwam has canes at the corners of a 3 ft square. The canes or poles are wired or tied together at the top. In this case erect the wigwam and sow or plant the beans next to each cane or pole. Runner beans, when fully grown and cropping, are heavy and prone to wind damage. Make the support system used robust.

1 Early spring. Take out a trench one spit deep and 2 ft wide. Dig 1–2 bucketsful of farmyard manure or well-rotted garden compost into the bottom and re-fill with the original soil.

2 April. Rake in 2–3 oz per square yard of a balanced general fertilizer. Use cloches to warm the soil in cold seasons.

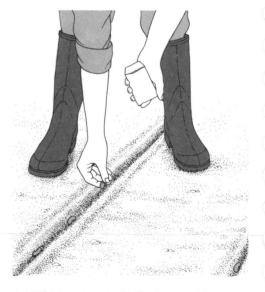

3 Mid-May. Sow individual seeds 6 in apart in 2 in deep drills. Two drills 24 in apart are sown for double row growing systems.

Runner beans 2

Growing Gently twist the plants counter-clockwise around their supports to encourage them to climb. Water runner beans only when they are in flower or cropping. Too much water early on encourages leaf growth at the expense of flowers and beans. If the plants become short of water, flowers will drop off and pods fail to develop. Bulky organic manures dug in during the soil preparations help to retain moisture around the roots. Mulch around the plants to eliminate weeds and minimize moisture loss.

Runner beans are insect pollinated and so care is needed when using insecticides. Use low persistence chemicals, such as malathion, and apply them in the evening when pollinating insects have finished working. Pinch out the growing points of beans at frequent intervals to keep the plants compact.

The first severe frost kills runner bean foliage, which can be cut down and composted if it is disease-free. Diseased foliage should be burned. Dig the small root tubers into the soil because they will add useful nitrogenous material. Clean and store the canes or poles for next season. Nets and strings should be burned after one season but plastic netting can be sterilized and used again for beans or other crops.

Harvesting
Picking of the cloched and pinched crops starts in July, with the supported crops coming in at the beginning of August. Careful and rigorous picking of pinched crops keeps down the number of soil-splashed and bent beans. Harvesting from these crops continues for about three or four weeks.

Supported crops produce beans until the first severe frost kills the plants. Pick them regularly to maintain a continuity of production. At the height of the season it is necessary to pick every other day.

Pests and diseases
Aphids and red spider mites are major pests, and gray mold (*Botrytis cinerea*) and bacterial blight may be problems in wet or humid weather. See page 47 for details of symptoms and treatment.

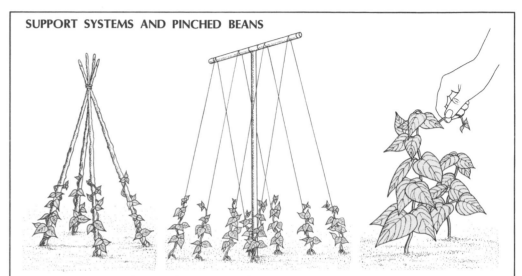

SUPPORT SYSTEMS AND PINCHED BEANS

Strings, canes or poles are the most usual supports although nets are sometimes used. Plants may be grown in single or double rows. Wigwam supports are formed by joining 4–10 canes or poles together at the top. Unsupported plants—pinched beans—have the growing point removed to produce a dwarf habit.

Supporting a double row

4 June. When the plants are 3–4 in tall erect a double row of crossed 8 ft poles. Space them 6–12 in apart, and train 1–2 plants up each. Place a horizontal pole on top for added stability.

5 June to July. Mulch around the plants once they are established. Use a 3–4 in layer of straw or peat.

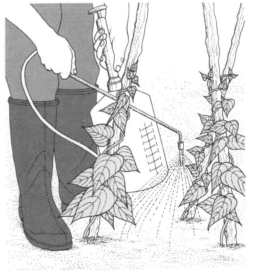

6 June to July. Spray against aphids and red spider mites if necessary. Spray late in the evening to avoid harming heavy-bodied insects, such as bees.

7 Late July to early August. Pick young, tender beans with no hint of swollen seeds through the pod wall. Regular picking, every other day if possible, encourages more runner bean pods to form.

Broad beans 1

Broad beans

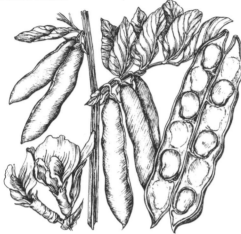

The broad bean is a hardy annual vegetable. It is a legume and is therefore grown both for its value to the soil (it enriches the soil with nitrogen which is fixed by nitrogen-fixing bacteria in the roots of the plants) and also as a rich source of protein. It can either be eaten freshly picked (like peas) or it can be dried, stored for months at a time and used in an assortment of recipes. Broad beans are slow to mature so give them as long a growing season as possible by sowing the seeds as the variety and climate will allow. The first pickings are made in July.

Cultivation

Broad beans—in common with other legumes —ideally prefer neutral or slightly alkaline soils, but grow well between pH 6.0–7.0. They tolerate relatively infertile soils but better growth and heavier yields occur on rich, fertile, well-drained soils. Cold, wet soils must be avoided especially for the over-wintered crops. However, fava broad beans can withstand cool soils and can be sown soon after last spring frost. The soil should be kept evenly moist throughout the growing season. Mulch to conserve moisture and keep down weeds. Broad beans have the largest seeds of all vegetables and they will soon rot in water-logged soils. Soil for broad beans should be given a dressing of 2–3 oz per square yard of a balanced fertilizer, such as 10-10-10, 1–2 weeks before sowing. No more fertilizer should then be needed.

Sowing Broad bean seeds are very large and there is no need to prepare a very fine seedbed. Sowing of broad beans can begin outdoors as soon as the soil is workable.

Unlike bush beans, broad beans withstand some frost. The seeds germinate well at soil temperatures of 5°C/39°F. The germination rate should be at least 80 percent. Successive sowings at monthly intervals will produce beans through the fall.

Single and double rows

Broad beans can be grown in either single or double rows. Research has shown that dwarf varieties should be sown 9 in apart with 9 in between rows. Taller varieties should be spaced 5 in apart with 18 in between rows. The seeds may be sown in a 3 in deep drill taken out with a draw hoe. Alternatively, they can be sown at the same depth in holes made with a trowel or dibble alongside a line.

Broad beans can also be sown in pots under glass in February or March and planted out

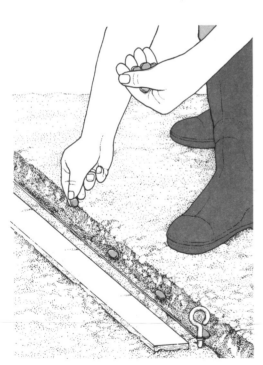

1 March or April. Make drills 18 in apart and 3 in deep. Sow single seeds 5 in apart. For dwarf varieties make the drills 9 in apart and sow the seeds at 9 in intervals. Broad bean seeds are very large so there is no need to prepare a very fine seedbed for them.

2 April. Hammer stakes into the ground at each end of the rows, leaving 3–4 ft above the ground.

3 April onward. Hoe regularly around the plants and when they are big enough run string around the stakes at 12 in intervals to provide support as they develop.

4 When the plants are in full flower pinch out 4–6 in of shoot to reduce the danger of bean aphid attack and to encourage a uniform development of pods up the plants.

Broad beans 2

as soon as the garden soil is workable. This system is useful in cold climates if you want the earliest possible crop. Hoeing for weed control is necessary until there is a good foliage cover of beans. Taller varieties need not be supported. Stakes should be hammered in at the ends or corners of the rows. Leave 3–4 ft of stake above ground and wind successive lengths of string from the stakes all around the plants. Layers of string should be attached at 12 in intervals. Keep the plants well watered during flowering and cropping, but water only in dry spells at other times in the growing period.

Watch for bean aphids which will attack the plants in May or June. They feed on the young shoot tips and their arrival usually coincides with the flowering of the beans. Remove 4–6 in of the growing tips to dis-

courage this pest and to encourage more uniform development of pods up the plant. Spray the plants with primicarb.

Harvesting

Picking begins in July and can continue, from successive spring sowings, into the fall. Broad beans are usually shelled from the pods before cooking and the stage of picking is critical. The pods should not be tough and fibrous, while the beans themselves must be young and tender. Pods can also be picked when immature (4–6 in long) and either cooked whole or sliced.

After harvesting, cut off the plant tops and dig the roots in so that the nitrogen-fixing bacteria which they contain is kept to improve the soil fertility for subsequent crops. The roots also make excellent compost, and

can be dug up and composted if their fertility value is needed for another part of the garden.

Pests and diseases

Bean aphids can be sprayed with low-persistence insecticides such as malathion, pyrethrum or derris. Spray late in the evening to minimize damage to pollinating insects such as bees. It is best to spray before the infestation takes a firm hold of the crop. Repeat the spraying weekly during the most likely months of attack. Pea and bean weevils feed on leaves, producing a scalloped pattern around the edge. Nearly all broad bean crops develop dark brown spots or blotches on the leaves and stems, although the pods are attacked only in severe outbreaks. These are the symptoms of chocolate spot fungus caused by a type of gray mold (*Botrytis*

cinerea). If you soak beans in water before sowing to help them germinate then be sure to spray with Maneb to check the spread of disease among the seeds. Poorly grown plants are attacked most severely, with damaged leaves, overcrowding and soft, lush growth contributing to the spread of the disease. It is rarely sufficiently severe to warrant chemical control measures and it is much better to avoid the disease by growing healthy plants.

Lima beans

The lima bean is also called the butter bean or butter pea. They are shelled from the 3–4 in pods and eaten fresh or dried. Pole or bush varieties are grown. Sow seed when the soil is warm, usually in early to mid June in cooler zones. Thin to 8–12 in apart and mulch well. Harvest when pods are full.

5 During flowering and cropping, water well to boost crop yield. Do not water before flowering unless the weather is very dry because too much watering during the early life of broad beans increases leafy growth at the expense of flowers and fruit.

6 June to July onward. Pick young broad beans before the pod walls become tough and fibrous. Shell them from the pods before cooking—the attachment scars of individual seeds should be green rather than black.

7 After harvesting. Cut down the stems to within 4 in of the soil immediately after picking has finished. Compost healthy stem material and dig in the stem bases and roots.

AUTUMN-SOWN BROAD BEANS

Sow broad beans in November in the usual way, using the special winter-hardy varieties available. Do not fertilize, or there will be too much growth which will suffer from winter frosts.

In February, apply a top-dressing of nitrogenous fertilizer, such as nitro-chalk, at a rate of 1–2 oz per square yard and hoe it in around the plants.

Garden peas 1

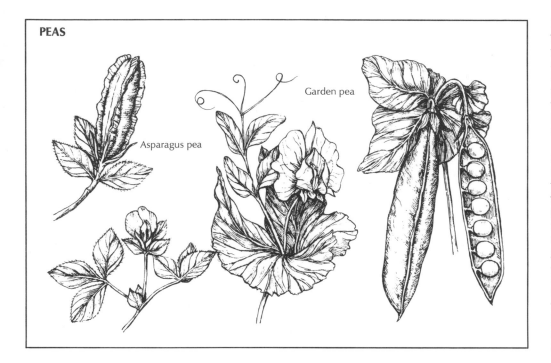

PEAS

Garden pea

Asparagus pea

Peas are treated as hardy annuals. The round-seeded types are hardier than the wrinkle-seeded types. Sugar or snow peas and the petit pois of France are closely related to garden peas. The yield depends upon the variety grown. Tall types produce two to three times as many peas as do dwarf types. Peas are usually shelled from the pods before cooking.

Cultivation

Peas must be grown on well-drained, rich, fertile soils of pH 6.0–7.0. Dig in a 2 in layer of farmyard manure or well-rotted garden compost in the winter to improve soil fertility and retain moisture. Peas grown on well-manured soils do not require any fertilizers, but crops grown on low fertility soils respond to an application of 1–2 oz per square yard of a balanced fertilizer with low nitrogen content. Incorporate the fertilizer just before sowing the peas.

Sowing Popular varieties of peas mature in 55–75 days. Successive sowings from late March to mid-May of each maturity type produce peas from about mid-June until August. A final sowing with an early variety can be made in July for picking in September or October, but don't count on success

Although pea seeds germinate at 5°C/39°F and the plants tolerate below-freezing temperatures, sowing as soon as frost is out of the ground rarely gives as much of a head-start as many gardeners think, because the plants will make slow growth if the weather continues cold and they may be killed by disease. It is better to wait for several weeks.

Peas may be sown in single rows in a V-shaped drill or broadcast in an 8–10 in wide flat-bottomed drill. Experiments have shown that the best yields can be expected from lines of three drills 5 in apart, with 18 in between each group of drills. Space the peas 5 in apart in the drill, which should be 2 in deep. If sowing in a flat-bottomed drill, first make the drill with a broad-bladed draw hoe or with a spade. The drill should also be 2 in deep. Broadcast the seeds evenly in the drill so that they are about 3 in apart each way. Rake soil back into the drill and firm it lightly

Garden peas

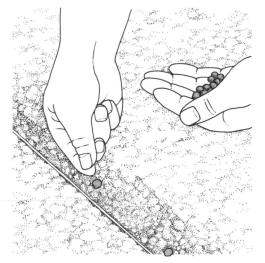

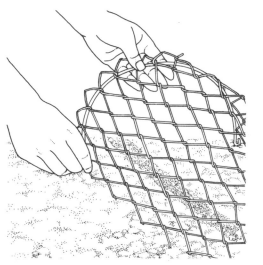

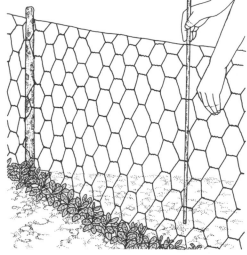

1 March until May. Use a draw hoe to make drills 2 in deep. Sow the seeds about 5 in apart in the bottom of the drill. For the distance between drills (18–48 in) check the mature height of the variety being grown.

2 March until May. Rake the soil back into the drill after sowing. Firm the soil down onto the seeds by lightly tamping with the back of the rake.

3 At the same time, put hoop-shaped, fine-meshed wire netting over the rows immediately after sowing to deter birds from digging up the seeds or eating newly emerged seedlings.

4 When the plants are 3–4 in tall erect the support system. Use a post and wire framework to support the netting up which the peas should climb.

Garden peas/Asparagus peas

with the back of the rake. The distance between rows should be the same as the eventual height of the mature crops. This varies from 18 in for the dwarf varieties to 5 ft for later varieties. These spaces can be used for catch crops of rapidly-maturing vegetables such as radishes early in the season. Birds may dig up the peas unless wire mesh guards are put over the rows immediately after sowing.

Sugar peas and petit pois are sown in the same way but they reach heights of 4 ft and 3 ft respectively.

Growing Peas can be grown without supports but growth and yields are better if the plants—especially of tall varieties— are able to climb and develop off the ground. The traditional method was to use twiggy branches pushed in alongside and within the rows. If these are difficult to find, use wire or nylon netting. Erect a post and wire framework along each row and attach an appropriate width of netting for the expected height of the peas. Put up the supports when the plants are 3–4 in tall.

Watering Never allow peas to become too dry when they are in full bloom or when the pods are swelling. Too much water before flowering reduces the yield; water only in very dry spells.

Mulching the plants with peat, straw or black polyethylene helps to reduce water loss. Mulching also keeps down weeds, and organic mulches add nutrients.

Harvesting

Picking of garden peas should begin about four weeks after full flower. Regular picking encourages more pods to develop. Pods at the base of the plant are ready first. The pods are the edible portion of sugar peas and it is vital that the peas inside them have not started to swell.

Petit pois must be harvested young or they lose their sweet, delicate flavor and become hard and unpalatable.

Cut down pea plants after harvesting and either put the roots on the compost heap or dig them into the soil in order to improve fertility.

Pests and diseases

Pea thrips attack the pods of peas. They are tiny insects up to $\frac{1}{10}$ in long which suck sap from the foliage and pods. Control thrips by spraying thoroughly with fenitrothion or malathion as soon as signs of damage are noted. Viruses such as pea mosaic virus cause stunting of plants and green or green and yellow mottling on leaves. Burn all affected plants. Aphids can infest the growing tips of pea plants. Spray with an insecticide, using primocarb, which is relatively harmless to bees, when the plants are in flower. Pea moth caterpillars can attack late pea crops. To control them, spray at dusk with fenitrothion seven days after flowering starts.

Asparagus peas

The asparagus or winged pea is quite different from other garden peas. It is half-hardy and has a bushy habit. The red flowers produce 4-winged fruits, 1–1½ in long, which are eaten whole. Asparagus peas are sometimes grown as a fodder crop.

Cultivation

Choose a light, well-drained soil in a sunny position on which to grow asparagus peas. Apply 1–2 oz per square yard of a general, balanced fertilizer two weeks before sowing.

Sowing Asparagus peas will be killed by frost, so choose a sowing date that takes this into account. Sow outside in early May when the main danger of frost is over. Space the seeds 4–6 in apart in 1 in deep drills, which should be 12 in apart. Water the bottom of the drill before sowing to encourage germination. Alternatively, the seeds can be sown in small pots indoors in early April and planted out at the end of May.

Growing Hoe weeds from around developing plants. Keep them well supplied with water from flowering time onwards. Too much water in the early stages reduces the yield. Asparagus pea plants have a tendency to sprawl and they should be supported by sticks.

Harvesting

It is important to pick the pods young, when about 1 in long, because they become tough.

5 Mid-June to August. Pick young and tender but well-filled pods. Regular harvesting encourages more pods to develop.

Asparagus peas

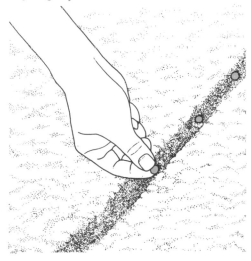

1 Early May. Sow the seed outside at 4–6 in intervals in the drill. In dry weather water the drill before sowing to aid germination. Choose a light, well-drained soil in a sunny position.

2 When 2–3 in high, add stakes to support the plants.

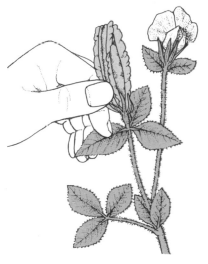

3 Late July to early August. Pick asparagus peas when they are 1 in long, otherwise they soon become stringy and tough.

Corn

This half-hardy annual grows most sweet and tender in northern gardens. It thrives on warmth—especially warm nights—and bright sunshine. Male and female flowers are produced in different places on the same plant. Male flowers grow at the top of the plant whereas the female flowers—which develop into the corn cobs—are found lower down. You can expect each plant to produce one or sometimes two cobs.

Cultivation

A light, well-drained and fertile soil of pH 5.5–7.0 is essential. Dig in a 2–3 in layer of bulky manure or garden compost during the winter. Avoid shaded sites but choose a sheltered position because the plants can be damaged by wind. Corn plants need plenty of food and water.

Apply 3–4 oz per square yard of balanced fertilizer a couple of weeks before sowing or planting and be prepared to topdress with an additional 1–2 oz per square yard in June or July.

Sowing Early sowings can be made under cloches at the end of April provided the cloches have been used to warm up the soil beforehand. Outdoor sowings should not take place until all danger of frost is past and soil temperature has reached 10°–13°C/50°–55°F. Sow 1 in deep. To assure that pollination takes place, you should plant either in two or more parallel rows or in hills. In rows, sow seeds 4–6 in apart and thin to 1 ft; the rows should be 24–30 in apart. If you use the hill method, sow 5–6 seeds together in a 1 ft circle, and space the hills 30 in apart in both directions. You may have to protect the seeds and plants against birds with fabric or by dipping the seeds in creosote.

Growing Hoe to keep down weeds but be careful not to damage the young plant stems. Keep the plants moist if dry spells occur. No watering is normally needed until the flowers (tassels) appear, when regular weekly applications of 3–4 gal per square yard (unless the weather is very wet) will improve the quality and yield. In windy positions stake the plants,

but raising the soil around the stems is usually sufficient to keep the plants upright.

Harvesting

Pollen is produced from the male flowers from July onwards and falls on to the female flowers. These soon begin to wither, and the cobs should be ready about a month later. The cobs should be firm and well filled and are ready when the silks have turned brown but before they are completely dry. Test maturity by pushing a fingernail into one of the grains. A creamy liquid indicates that the cob is ready. Twist the cobs off the plant and cook or freeze them immediately. Corn is a vegetable which freezes well. Eat frozen corn on the cob within 6–8 weeks of freezing.

All the main ears in a single planting of one variety mature within a 5–7 day period. If the plants produce second ears, these mature together in the same way at a slightly later date. Therefore, if you want to eat corn throughout the summer, you must make more than one planting. You can either (1)

use the same variety and make successive sowings at 10–14 day intervals from spring until 75–90 days before first fall frost; or (2) plant three different-maturity varieties at the same time in the spring; or (3) use a combination of both methods.

Popcorn

Popcorn ears are generally smaller and more irregular than sweetcorn ears. The kernels are usually yellow or white but may be red. All varieties take three months or more to mature. The same cultivation methods as for corn should be employed.

Popcorn is grown like sweetcorn, but both varieties are kept apart. If you plant yellow popcorn close to white sweetcorn, the sweetcorn ears will contain yellow kernels. Let the ears of popcorn remain on the stalks till the kernels are dry. Then pick, husk and store them in a dry place until the kernels fall off easily when you rub your fingers along the ears. They are then ready to be popped or bagged.

Harvesting

1 Winter. Dig a 2–3 in layer of manure or garden compost into the soil. Choose a sunny, sheltered site with a well-drained soil of pH 5.5–7.0.

2 Spring. When all danger of frost is past, sow seeds 4–6 in apart in parallel rows. Alternatively, sow in a circle on hills 30 in apart.

3 Harvesting. When the silks have withered press a fingernail into 1 of the grains underneath the protective leaves on each cob.

4 If the pressed grain exudes a creamy-white liquid harvest the cobs with a twisting, downward movement away from the plant stem.

Onions 1

ONIONS

AUTUMN-SOWN
'Express Yellow', 'Kaizuka',
'Kaizuka Extra Early', 'Yellow
Globe'.

SPRING-SOWN
'Ailsa Craig', 'Bedfordshire
Champion', 'Hygro', 'Wijbo'.

ONION SETS
'Sturon', 'Stuttgarter Giant'.

PICKLING ONIONS
'Paris Silverskin', 'The Queen'.

SALAD (SPRING) ONIONS
'White Lisbon', 'Winter Hardy'.

The onion is a biennial plant which is grown as an annual. The familiar bulbs are formed from swollen leaf bases. Salad onions (spring onions) are grown for the immature plants and should not produce bulbs.

Cultivation
Onions are easily grown from seed, and the bulb crop may also be grown from sets or transplants. Seed sowings can be made outdoors in the North in March and April, or under glass in January or February, to mature in late summer and fall. In the South, sowings made outdoors in October and over-wintered are ready the following summer. Sets planted in March to April mature in July to August. Sow salad onions in the spring for summer and fall use. For earlier salad onions, plant sets. Onion seed germinates very slowly and seedling growth is also slow.

Soil and situation The soil for onion growing should be well drained, reasonably fertile but not freshly manured. The pH should be more than 6.5. Choose a sunny but sheltered site. Soil-borne diseases can be serious, so do not grow onions on the same ground each year. This avoids most disease problems.

Double dig the land in early winter, working a 2–3 in layer of bulky organic material into the lower spit. Leave the surface rough to allow it to break down naturally during the winter. If onions are to be grown to full size, give them a fertilizer which contains about twice as much potash as nitrogen. Apply 2–3 oz per square yard of such a compound 7–10 days before sowing.

Spring-sown crops
Onion seed germinates at temperatures of 7°C/45°F and above. In cold areas it is wise to raise seedlings under glass. Sow in January or February for planting out in April or May. Sow in March under cloches, and in April in the open. The seedbed is most important. Digging in early winter should ensure that the soil is friable and breaks down easily. Work it down with a cultivator and rake it into a fine tilth, then make it firm and level. Be careful on silt or clay soils, where very fine tilths "cap" over if wet conditions are followed by drying weather (see page 8). The young seedlings can find it difficult to penetrate the capped surface. Sow the seed thinly in drills 9–12 in apart and ½ in deep. Water the drill gently if

the soil is dry. Thin to 2–3 in between seedlings as soon as they have straightened up.

During the summer onions should be kept free from weeds. Additional watering is not usually required except in very dry weather in spring or early summer when applications of 2 gal per 10 ft run may be given each week. Further feeding is unnecessary. As the bulbs approach maturity in mid-to-late August or September, their leaves begin to yellow and topple over. In wet seasons this may be delayed, and the tops should be bent over by hand to assist the ripening of the bulbs. The leaves of some plants in a row may remain standing and these bulbs often have a wide neck (bull necks). Do not attempt to keep these bulbs as they soon rot in storage.

Autumn-sown crops
Onions sown in autumn mature from May to June, earlier than crops sown in spring. The seed should be sown in the same way as for spring-sown onions. Onion seed does not germinate well above 24°C/75°F, so in hot weather germination may be erratic. Pre-germination of the seeds at lower temperatures or lowering the soil temperature of the

seedbed by frequent light waterings may be necessary in some seasons.

If the seed has been sown thinly the young onions should be left to over-winter and thinned to 1½–2 in (3 in for larger onions) in spring (March to April) as growth begins. A top dressing of 1–2 oz per square yard of a balanced fertilizer should be hoed in after thinning. Autumn-sown onions should not be transplanted because they tend to bolt.

Spring cultivation is then as for spring-sown onions.

Growing from sets
Growing from sets is probably the most convenient method of growing onions, especially in areas where the growing season is short. It is important to keep onion crops free from weeds but this is best done by hand because any digging near the roots is harmful to the bulbs. Mulch to discourage weeds and conserve moisture. Sun is essential to ripen the bulbs—usually from late July to August, when watering should have stopped. Bend the leaves over in wet seasons to help ripening. The crop is ready for harvesting when the leaves have turned yellow.

Spring-sown onions

1 Early March. Apply a balanced fertilizer at a rate of 2–3 oz per square yard 7–10 days before sowing. Rake it in and tread the soil down to produce a firm seedbed with a fine tilth.

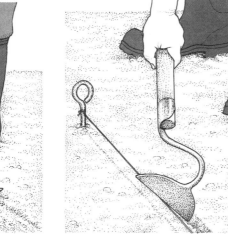

2 March to April. Draw out drills 9–12 in apart and ½ in deep. Water the drills if the soil is dry. Sow the seed thinly.

3 May. As soon as the seedlings have straightened up thin them to 1–2 in apart, or 3 in apart if large onions are required. Water the rows with diazinon solution against onion maggot.

4 May to July. Keep the developing onions free from weeds. In very dry weather water at a rate of 2 gal per 10 ft run each week.

Onions 2

If onions are to be stored successfully, care should be taken to ripen them correctly. Spoiled crops can usually be avoided by seeing that the bulbs are properly dried and stored in a well-ventilated place. Only sound bulbs should be selected for storage and it is important that the leaves are not broken off, leaving the bulb exposed. Lay the bulbs on burlap or on a raised wire netting frame in a sunny part of the garden until the leaves are brittle. Store them in wooden crates, or string and hang them in a cool, frost-free place. Remove those that have gone soft during the winter.

Less common onions

A number of other *Allium* species, grown mainly for their curiosity value or in the herb garden, are also excellent for eating and easily cultivated. The tree onion is a perennial plant which forms normal clumps of bulbs at ground level but also sends up tall stems bearing clusters of small onions instead of flowers. These may be used in cooking or to increase the stock by using them as sets. Easily grown on any well-drained soil and providing crops for several years without

complications, an alternative common name might be the "lazy gardener's onion".

The potato onion, which forms a number of mild-flavored offsets just below soil level, can do duty for shallots. All are easily grown, providing useful and unusual space-fillers in a small garden.

Pests and diseases

Female onion flies lay their eggs in the base of the leaf shafts, near the ground, in the spring. They hatch into maggots which tunnel into the developing bulbs, causing the whole plant to turn yellow and die. Young plants should be protected before the eggs are laid. Water along the rows with a diazinon solution or dust the seedlings with lindane (gamma HCH). A seed disinfectant may help.

Downy mildew can be particularly bad in wet seasons. Gray patches appear on the leaves and turn purple as the disease progresses. Eventually the leaves topple over and collapse. Spray with zineb at the first sign of trouble. The best way to protect onions against other diseases, such as pink root and smudge, is to plant in well-drained soils and rotate crops on a 4-year basis.

TRANSPLANTED ONIONS

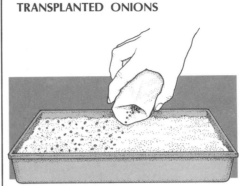 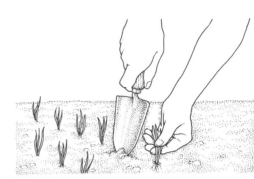

Early onions and those intended for showing should be transplanted. Sow the seed in flats during January or February in a warm, bright spot. Keep them at a temperature of 16°C/60°F. Germination is slow, but when the seedlings are large enough to handle they can be pricked out. For exhibition purposes grow each plant in a $3\frac{1}{2}$ in pot containing a proprietary potting compost. For general garden purposes prick out the onion seedlings individually into peat pots or into a seed tray, spacing them 2 in apart each way.

Gradually reduce the temperature to 10°C/50°F and harden off the plants in a cold frame or under a cloche for a few days before planting. Plant outdoors soon after the soil is workable in rows 12–15 in apart. Space the onions 2–3 in apart in the row. Plant shallowly with a trowel—deep planting hinders bulb development. Water thoroughly after planting.

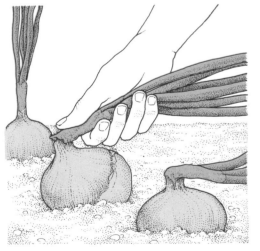

5 August to September. If the leaves have not toppled over naturally, which sometimes happens in wet weather, bend them over by hand to assist ripening. Plants which remain standing may have bull necks.

6 September. Lift the bulbs for drying and storing when the fallen tops have begun to yellow and become brittle.

Autumn-sown onions

1 August to September. Prepare the ground and sow as for spring-sown onions, but do not thin the plants.

2 March to April. Thin the young plants to $1\frac{1}{2}$–2 in apart, 3 in if large onions are required. Top-dress with 1–2 oz per square yard of balanced general fertilizer or nitro-chalk after thinning.

Onions 3

Onion sets

Sets are partly developed onion bulbs. They are stored during winter and replanted in the spring, when they grow away rapidly. Sets are particularly useful for growing onions in places with short growing seasons. Consistently higher yields are possible from sets or seedling plants. As the sets have to be bought, it is more expensive to grow onions this way. This expense can be avoided by saving some onions from the previous season's crop and drying them carefully so that they become next season's sets. The best sets are $\frac{1}{2}-\frac{3}{4}$ in in diameter and firm. It is also sensible to buy small sets of this size because they are less likely to bolt than larger bulbs and are cheaper per plant.

Planting onion sets

Plant onion sets as soon as the soil is worked into a fine tilth. Mark out rows 10 in apart with a garden line and push the sets 1 in into the ground at 2–3 in intervals, or at 4 in intervals if larger bulbs are required. There is no point in using the wider spacings sometimes recommended because the yield from a given area will be much reduced. Firm the soil around the sets.

Birds may pull up the sets and prolonged frosty weather may also lift them out of the ground. In either case, they should be replanted immediately. As a precaution against birds, excess dried leaves should be cut close to the bulb but avoid exposing the inner leaves. The remaining operations are as for spring-sown or transplanted bulb onions.

SPRING ONIONS

Spring onions, or scallions, are immature onion plants. They are grown close together and eaten as a salad vegetable when the bulb is $\frac{1}{2}$–1 in across. Many of their requirements are the same as for bulb onions. The earliest spring onions are ready in the spring from sets and transplants. Continuity through the summer is then maintained from successive sowings made at two-week intervals from March until mid-June. Spring onions are grown close together in rows 4 in apart to prevent bulbs from developing. Sow the seed reasonably thinly in $\frac{1}{2}$ in drills. The drills should be watered before sowing if the soil is dry. The plants should grow $\frac{1}{2}$–1 in apart in the rows. Pull the onions before the bases swell. It helps to water them before pulling from dry soils. Pulling is easier if rows are first well watered.

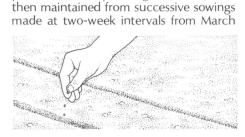

1 February to June, every 2 weeks make sowings in $\frac{1}{2}$ in deep drills 4 in apart.

2 Summer. Lift the immature onions with a fork as the bases swell.

RIPENING AND STORAGE

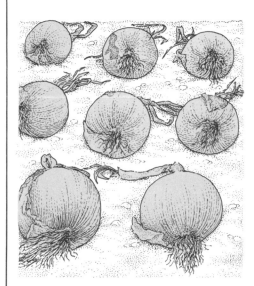

1 After digging up onions, place the bulbs outside in a shady, airy spot to dry and ripen further.

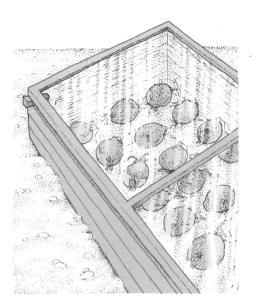

2 In wet weather arrange the bulbs in a single layer in a shed.

3 Turn the bulbs regularly to prevent diseases developing on the damp skins and wait 3–4 weeks for complete drying.

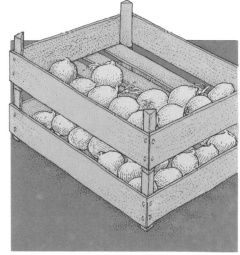

4 Store well-dried onions in trays that aid circulation and inspection, at a temperature of about 0°C/32°F.

Shallots/Garlic

Shallots have a milder flavor than bulb onions and are sometimes grown in preference to onions in smaller gardens, because they keep better and are more easily grown. They are grown from small bulbs (offsets) saved from the previous year's crop. Each newly planted bulb produces a cluster of 8–12 daughter bulbs by the end of the season.

Cultivation

Soil and fertilizer requirements are the same as for spring-sown or planted bulb onions (see page 55). Early planting is very important for shallots, so dig the land as soon as it becomes available.

Planting Save sound, firm bulbs from the previous season, or buy sets. Small bulbs of about $\frac{1}{3}$ oz weight (50 to the pound) are best to obtain maximum yield. Plant the bulbs when the soil is workable; space them 6 in apart in rows which are 8 in apart. Larger bulbs should be spaced 6 in apart with 12 in between the rows. Push the bulbs into the ground so that only the tips show above the soil surface. Alternatively, the bulbs can be planted in a shallow drill and then covered

and firmed. Shallots can also be planted outdoors in early fall and left in the ground until they are harvested in late spring.

Weeds can be a problem, especially while the crop is young. Hoe carefully around the clusters, but do not damage the developing bulbs or they will not keep. Do not water unless the weather is very dry. Shallots suffer from the same pests and diseases as do onions (see page 56).

Shallots are ready for harvesting earlier than are spring-planted onions. They should be ready in July, and the bulbs will begin to ripen about three weeks before that. Draw away the soil from around the bulbs to encourage quicker ripening.

Harvesting

Dig up the clusters of bulbs when the leaves turn yellow. Separate them into individual bulbs and, in fine weather, leave them on the soil to dry off; dry them under protection in wet weather.

Remove soil and any loose, dry leaves from the ripened bulbs before storing them in nets in a cool, but frost-free place.

Shallots

  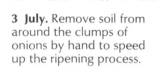

1 March. Push the bulbs into the ground so that their tops are just visible. Space them 6 in apart in rows 8 in apart.

2 April to July. Use a small onion hoe to keep the developing plants weed-free at all times. Remove any difficult weeds by hand.

3 July. Remove soil from around the clumps of onions by hand to speed up the ripening process.

GARLIC

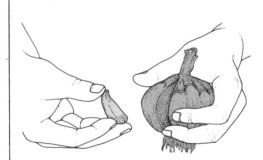

Garlic is a member of the onion family. Because of its strong flavor it is used sparingly in cooking. The plant is a perennial with long flat leaves and attractive white flowers. It can be grown in the open or in a pot or window-box. The soil must be rich, moist and well drained.

Garlic grows best in a sunny position, because high temperatures are needed to ripen the bulbs. Before planting prepare

the ground as for onion growing. Garlic seed is not readily available and so plants are usually grown from bulb segments (cloves) saved from a previous crop or bought from a food store. In the North, they are planted in March or April; in zones 8–10, in late summer or fall. Split a bulb into cloves. Plant them 1 in deep and 4 in apart with their pointed ends upward. The rows should be 6–8 in apart. Do not press the cloves into the soil because this prevents root development. Weed carefully between the bulbs with an onion hoe.

In late summer the stems and leaves begin to yellow and bend over. Loosen the bulbs gently out of the ground with a fork. Dry the bulbs in a cool, dry, shady spot. Do not handle the bulbs roughly because this may damage their necks and encourage rotting. Store garlic in string bags in a cool but frost-free shed. Cloves can be taken from bulbs as needed.

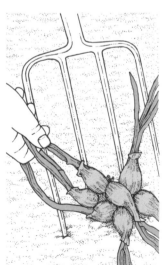 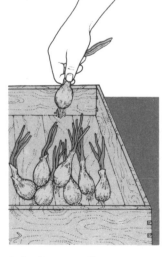 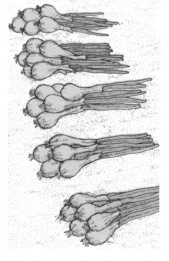

4 July onward. Lift shallots when the leaves turn yellow. Remove soil from around the roots and rub off loose leaves.

5 At the same time, save small bulbs of about $\frac{1}{3}$ oz in weight (50 to the pound) for next year's propagation material.

6 In fine weather, leave the bulbs in rows in the garden to dry out. In wet weather, dry them under protection in a well-ventilated place.

Leeks

EARLY
'Early Market', 'Lyon-Prizetaker'.

MID-SEASON
'Musselburgh',
'Walton Mammoth'.

LATE
'Royal Favorite', 'Winter
Crop' (very hardy).

Leeks are biennial plants grown as annuals. The stem-like collection of rolled leaves is eaten. Leeks have a long growing season and start to mature from late August. They are winter-hardy in mild climates and can be left in the garden for harvesting as you need them; but in cold climates, they should be dug up and stored or frozen. Leeks grow best in fertile, well-drained soils of pH 6.5–7.5. Although they will tolerate slightly more acid or alkaline conditions, they do not thrive in heavy soils which remain wet in winter. Dig the soil well because they must be planted deeply or hilled up to blanch. The ground should be dug well during the winter before planting. Incorporate a 2–3 in layer of bulky organic material or well-rotted garden compost. Do not give so much fertilizer that the plants become too lush and incapable of standing through frosty fall conditions. Apply 2–3 oz per square yard of a well-balanced fertilizer, such as 10-10-10, one or two weeks before planting.

Sowing and planting The germination and early growth of leeks are slow. The seeds need a soil temperature of at least 7°C/45°F for successful germination.

For early crops, sow in a seed tray about eight weeks before the last spring frost. Prick out into other trays when the leaves have straightened up, spacing the seedlings 2 in apart each way. Maintain a cool temperature until hardening off the plants in a cold frame during March. The plants should be planted on the mean date of the last frost.

Main crop leeks are sown outside in March to April shortly before the last frost, and can be transplanted during late May or June or left to grow where they are. Sow the seed thinly in drills ½ in deep and in rows 6 in apart.

Planting Leek plants should be planted out when pencil-thick and 6–8 in tall. Plant in rows 12 in apart. Make 2 in wide, 6 in deep holes with a dibble at 6 in intervals. After putting a seedling into the hole, do not replace the soil but fill each hole with water. This will settle sufficient soil around the roots. Alternatively, leeks can be planted on the flat or in 2 in deep trenches and blanched by progressively drawing up soil around the plants during the growing season. Hoe out any weeds. Water the plants only in very dry

conditions, when 2 gal of water per 10 ft row should be applied weekly. Mulch crops grown on dry soils. On poor soils liquid fertilizer can be used, but do not apply fertilizer to leeks late in the summer because soft growth prone to frost damage will be produced. Leeks are relatively free from pests and diseases.

Harvesting
Early varieties are ready in late August; others are ready a little later. Lift them as required using a fork. Leeks are hardy and in mild areas, they will remain usable until May.

Pests and diseases
Leeks are susceptible to the same pests and diseases that affect other members of the onion family (see page 56) but in fact they are seldom diseased.

PLANTING ON THE FLAT

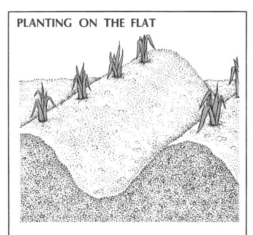

Blanched stems are produced when leeks are planted in holes, as described on the left, but longer white stems can be obtained if plants are hilled up. Plant the leeks 6 in apart in rows 12 in apart. Make holes 2–3 in deep and firm the soil around the base of each plant. Gradually draw up soil around the plants as they develop. Cardboard or paper collars may be tied around them to prevent soil getting into the plant centers.

Continue hilling up until only the tops of the leaves show above the soil. It might be necessary to add further collars to exclude earth as the leeks develop.

Sowing

1 Late March to mid-April. Prepare a seedbed. Sow the seeds thinly in ½ in deep drills 6 in apart.

2 Early May. Thin the seedlings to ½–1 in apart. Firm the soil around the bases of the remaining seedlings.

4 June until harvest. Mulch the crop with peat, black polyethylene (or similar) once the seedlings are established.

Planting

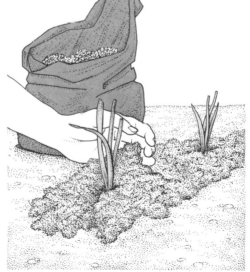

3 Late May to early June. Make 6 in deep holes, with a dibble, every 6 in in rows 12 in apart. Drop 1 plant into each. Fill with water.

5 August onward. Lift leeks as required with a fork. Trim off the roots and tips of the leaves.

Carrots

SHORT
'Amsterdam Forcing', 'Nantes', 'Paris Forcing'.

INTERMEDIATE
'Autumn King', 'Chantenay Red-cored', 'Red Intermediate'.

LONG
'St Valery', 'Scarlet Perfection'.

Carrots are hardy biennial plants grown as annuals for their tasty roots. Depending on the variety, the roots range from $3\frac{1}{2}$ to 9 in long. A 10 ft row can yield 10–12 lb, depending on the variety. All can be eaten immediately or stored or frozen for winter use.

Cultivation

Long-rooted varieties need a deep soil but short-rooted varieties are suitable for shallow soils and will grow in heavy conditions.

Soil and situation The ideal soil has a pH between 6.5 and 7.5, is well-drained, stone-free and of medium texture. It should not have been manured for at least a year before sowing. Thorough, deep winter digging is important. An application of balanced general fertilizer at 2–3 oz per square yard about a week before sowing will maintain fertility. Choose an open situation for carrots.

Watering If deprived of water carrots become woody and coarse. In dry weather apply water at a rate of 2 gal per square yard at weekly intervals. If the plants become too wet as a result of applications of water in rainy weather, the development of foliage as opposed to roots is encouraged.

Early carrots In February or March, sow short varieties under cloches or in frames in $\frac{1}{2}$–$\frac{3}{4}$ in deep drills, 6 in apart. Always sow carrot seeds very thinly and thin the seedlings to $1\frac{1}{2}$–2 in intervals when they emerge. Young carrots mature from mid-May onward.

Alternatively, sow the seed outdoors every three to four weeks from March to August. These carrots are ready from June until November. Cover the later crops with cloches from September onward.

Main crop carrots From April to June, sow intermediate or long varieties very thinly in $\frac{1}{2}$–$\frac{3}{4}$ in deep drills, with 6 in between the rows. These mature from July to September.

Hoe between the rows, and as soon as the first rough leaves appear, thin the seedlings until the distance between the plants is 2 in for short-, medium- and long-rooted varieties. Water the plants to refirm them after thinning. The thinnings from larger varieties of carrots can be eaten. Hill up soil over roots that become exposed to keep the shoulders from turning green.

Carrot rust flies are attracted by the smell of crushed foliage. The females lay eggs around the plants and the resulting larvae eat the roots. Attacks can be minimized by thinning the carrots late in the evening, removing the thinnings and watering immediately afterward.

Harvesting

Start pulling the early sowings by hand as soon as they are big enough to eat. Young tender roots are the sweetest. Gently ease up carrots for storage, with a fork, in October. Reject any that are unhealthy or damaged.

Remove the soil and foliage from carrots before storing them.

Storing Healthy carrots will last until March or April of the following year if they are stored properly in the right conditions. In many regions, they can be left in the ground and lifted as required. Protect them from severe frost with a covering of straw or similar material, but even if they are frozen into the ground they are still good to eat.

Pests and diseases

A brown discoloration of the foliage is often a symptom of carrot rust fly attack. By the time the symptom appears the infestation has already damaged the crop, so prevention is better than cure. Apply diazinon granules at sowing time. Spray greenfly with derris or malathion.

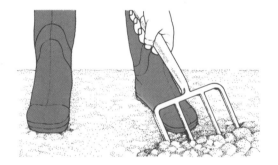

1 Winter. Dig the soil early so that a crumbly tilth develops. In spring apply fertilizer at 2–3 oz per square yard.

2 March onward. Prepare a fine tilth. Sow the seed in $\frac{1}{2}$–$\frac{3}{4}$ in deep drills 6 in apart. Cover the drills.

3 Thin the seedlings regularly after the first rough leaf appears to 2 in for short-, medium- and long-rooted varieties.

4 Water and firm the rows after thinning. Do not leave thinnings lying about. Hoe between the rows.

5 Throughout the summer. Pull early sowings by hand while they are young and tender.

6 October. Leave carrots in the ground where they have been grown but protect them from frost with a covering of straw.

7 Alternatively, dig up carrots required for indoor storing with a fork. Select healthy roots only and twist off the foliage.

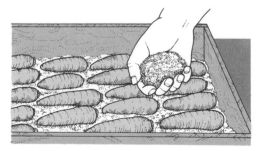

8 Pack the roots in boxes of dry sand, keeping individual roots apart, and store them in a cool frost-free place.

SHORT	LONG
'Avonresister' (canker resistant).	'Improved Hollow Crown', 'Leda', 'Offenham', 'Tender and
INTERMEDIATE	True' (canker resistant).
'White Gem'.	

Parsnips

Parsnips are hardy biennial plants grown as annuals for the production of their edible roots. They have a long growing season.

Cultivation

Parsnips need a well-drained soil of medium texture which must not have been manured for at least a year before sowing. Parsnips have a low nitrogen requirement, take care not to overmanure and do not use nitrogen-rich fertilizers. As with other root crops, parsnips are likely to develop with forked roots—caused either by soil that is freshly manured or the application of too much nitrogenous fertilizer. Also, a soil that is too rich in nitrogen or is deficient in lime encourages canker. The best soil is slightly acid or neutral (pH 6.5–7.0) and the best position is open and sunny, although parsnips will tolerate a lightly shaded spot. Avoid stony soil. Deep digging in the winter is essential because parsnips often root down to a depth of 2 ft. Dig the soil one spade deep and if the layer below is too packed for the feeding roots to penetrate easily, loosen it with a fork. Such deep digging is not really necessary for short varieties, however. One to two weeks before sowing apply a balanced fertilizer, such as 10-10-10, to the soil at 2 oz per square yard.

Sowing Parsnips are best when the roots are frozen—sow the seed in summer $2-3\frac{1}{2}$ months before first fall frost. Always use fresh seed because older parsnip seed rapidly loses its viability. Even with fresh seed, the germination rate is low. Take out $\frac{1}{2}-\frac{3}{4}$ in deep drills. Keep a 12 in distance between rows for large-rooted varieties. If the soil is dry, water the drill before sowing. Sow the seeds in groups of three or four, with 6 in spacings between groups. Small-rooted varieties should be sown 3 in apart with 8 in between rows. Parsnip seeds germinate slowly, so it is advisable to mark the rows before seedlings appear by sowing quick-germinating radishes between the stations.

In warm climates, parsnip seed is sown in winter about six weeks before last spring frost, and they are harvested in the spring. But they do not have such fine flavor as those that are frozen.

When the seedlings have their first true leaves carefully remove all but the strongest plant in each group. Weed between the seedlings by hand in the early stages. Carefully hoe between the plants later. If the shoulders of young plants are damaged, parsnip canker or other diseases are likely to infest the plants.

Never allow the soil to dry out. If the soil becomes dry and is then dampened by rain or watering, the parsnips often split. Water at a rate of 2 gal per square yard per week unless the weather makes it unnecessary.

Harvesting

Lifting may begin when the foliage begins to die down, usually in late fall or early winter. Use a fork to dig along the side of the row so as to lift without breaking the roots.

Storing Leave parsnips in the ground throughout the winter and lift the roots as required. If parsnips are dug up in the fall, store them in soil in a cold garage or outdoor pit.

Pests and diseases

Young seedlings should be protected from carrot rust fly. Sprinkle diazinon along the row when the seedlings are about 2–3 in tall.

Parsnip canker develops in the crown of the plants and causes the roots to rot. There is no chemical control—prevention is the only answer. Premature sowing, lime deficient soils and damage to roots by carrot rust fly larvae or careless hoeing are all likely to encourage the disease.

EXHIBITION PARSNIPS

For long straight roots prepare the soil well and use a crowbar to make holes 3 ft deep and 6 in in diameter. Fill these conical holes with fine soil or potting compost and sow the seed in the usual way as early as possible. Throughout the growing season weed by hand and mulch with peat or black polyethylene to retain moisture.

Water regularly, especially when dry weather is forecast, to prevent any cracking of the long roots. Lift them as near as possible to the showing date. Remove the rootlets and cut off the tops. Protect exhibition parsnips from damage by wrapping them in damp cloth.

1 June to July. Dig the soil 1 spit deep. If the layer below is compacted break it up with a fork.

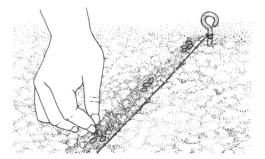

2 Apply fertilizer at 2 oz per square yard 1–2 weeks before sowing. Apply diazinon against carrot rust fly.

3 Sow 3–4 seeds at 6 in intervals (3 in for small varieties) in $\frac{1}{2}-\frac{3}{4}$ in deep drills 12 in (8 in) apart.

4 When the first true leaves appear thin the seedlings to leave the strongest plant at each station.

5 Throughout the summer. Water frequently and hoe weeds regularly, taking care not to damage the shoulders of young plants.

6 Late fall onward. When the foliage dies down lift parsnips as needed, using a fork to loosen the surrounding soil.

Turnips and Rutabagas 1

Turnips and rutabagas are biennials grown mainly for their edible roots. Rutabagas are usually grown as a crop for winter harvesting, but turnips may be eaten all summer. Cut young leaves or "turnip greens" in May.

Cultivation

Turnips and rutabagas are brassicas and have broadly similar requirements to cabbages and Brussels sprouts.

Soil and situation They thrive in light, well-drained, firm soils of pH 6.0–7.0, rich in humus and water-retentive during the growing season. Main crop turnips and rutabagas require much the same methods of cultivation, although sowing dates and plant spacings differ. Soil preparation is identical and both crops are thinned in the seed rows to the appropriate distance and not transplanted.

The roots fork if they are grown in soil that has received dressings of fresh manure and so a site well manured for a previous crop should be used if possible. The site is dug over and prepared as a seedbed. Before sowing rake in a dressing of balanced fertilizer at 3 oz per square yard to improve fertility. Then apply calomel dust to combat club-root, and diazinon to control cabbage maggot.

Watering The size and quality of both turnips and rutabagas are improved if ample water is available. If they are allowed to become dry at any stage the roots are likely to become woody and less palatable. Experimental work has shown that applications of 2 gal per square yard of water each week in dry weather increase both yield and quality, although flavor is slightly reduced.

Pests and diseases

Turnips and rutabagas like other brassicas, are attacked by cabbage maggot, and flea beetle, turnip gall weevil and aphids (with virus as a consequence) may also be troublesome. Rutabagas are less mildew-resistant than turnips.

Turnips

Turnips are fast-growing and are ready to eat 6–12 weeks after sowing. They germinate within a few days and must never become crowded in the rows. Thinning should take place as soon as possible when the first rough, true leaves appear (at about 1 in high) or the roots will not develop satisfactorily.

In the North, the main crop is sown in July or August for fall use but earlier sowings can be made from March (under cloches) through spring and early summer. Turnips can be used in 6 or 8 weeks from sowing, so when they are 1½–2 in in diameter, they are excellent for intercropping. In the middle South, turnips are main-cropped in early spring and fall, and in the deep South, they are also planted in winter.

Rutabagas

Rutabagas, or swedes, have a sweeter taste than turnips and they are mainly grown for winter use, although immature rutabagas pulled in late summer make excellent eating. They should never be allowed to develop to the huge size of field-grown crops, which are often woody and more fitted for cattle than human consumption. They are much slower to mature than turnips, taking 90–110 days to develop fully from seed, but are hardier and can be dug as required during the winter rather than stored. Cultivation is as for main crop turnips but rutabagas are sown in late June or early July in drills 15 in apart. When the seedlings are large enough to handle, thin to 9 in apart in the rows.

PESTS AND DISEASES

Pests	Means of control
Aphids (and viruses)	Systemic insecticide
Cabbage maggot	Bromophos/diazinon
Flea beetle	Derris
Gall weevil	Bromophos/diazinon

Diseases	Means of control
Brown heart	Boron (applied as borax)
Club-root	PCNB
Soft rot	Remove affected plants

EARLY BUNCHING TURNIPS

Bunched turnips are a good salad or early summer cooked vegetable. They must grow quickly with ample supplies of water. Dig the soil early in the autumn and cover the ground with cloches for 2–3 weeks before sowing the earliest crops which are protected. Prepare a fine seedbed and apply PCNB dust against club-root and bromophos or diazinon against cabbage maggot. Then sow short-leaved, early varieties from February onward, at two week intervals for a succession. Mark out the ground into a 5 in crossed pattern with a stick, making the marks ½ in deep. Sow 2–3 seeds where the marks cross. Alternatively, sow the seed thinly in ½ in drills 12 in apart. Thin out the squared system to leave one plant per station. Row crops should be thinned to 4 in apart. Hoe very carefully in the early stages and never allow the soil to dry out.

Harvesting The roots are pulled like radishes. The first sowings mature during May when the roots are 2 in in diameter.

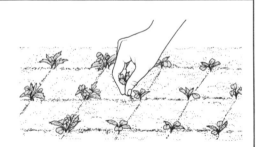

1 March. Thin grid-sown turnips to one plant per station. Thin row crops to 4 in apart at the same stage.

2 May. Pull the plants up by the leaves when the roots are 2 in in diameter.

Main crop turnips

1 July to August. Rake in 3 oz per square yard of fertilizer to the prepared seedbed and apply PCNB dust and diazinon.

2 July to August. Water the seedbed the day before sowing. Draw out drills ½–¾ in deep and 12 in apart. If the soil is dry, dribble water into the drills and allow it to drain away.

Turnips and Rutabagas 2

3 Then, sow the seed very thinly, cover, firm and gently rake over the soil.

4 Thin the seedlings to 3 in apart as soon as they produce their first rough leaves when about 1 in high. Water them if the weather is dry.

5 Dust the seedlings with derris to combat flea beetle and other pests.

6 August to September. Thin to 6 in apart as soon as the leaves of adjacent seedlings touch within the rows. Firm back the soil after thinning.

7 Keep the rows free of weeds. In dry weather water at a rate of 2 gal per square yard each week.

8 October. Lift as needed in mild areas. In cold areas lift the roots carefully in late fall when the leaves have turned yellow. Store them in boxes of sand, peat or dry soil in a frost-free shed.

RUTABAGAS SHOOTS AS GREENS

The roots of rutabagas lifted in mid-winter, if trimmed and packed closely in boxes of peat or soil and then placed in a garage or shed in semi-darkness, will sprout to produce nutritious, partly blanched growth that can be eaten like turnip tops.

TURNIP TOPS AS SPRING GREENS

In September sow the seed of winter varieties thinly in rows 3 in apart. Leave over winter without thinning. Cut the young leaves in March or April when they are 4–6 in high. If cut frequently they re-sprout several times.

Kohlrabi

Kohlrabi, like most brassicas, is grown as an annual although naturally it is a biennial. The swollen root-like stem is pleasantly and distinctively flavored and it may be eaten raw in salads, or cooked like a turnip. It is in season from May until December.

If grown well, kohlrabi can be harvested 60 days after sowing.

Cultivation
The general principles of brassica growing apply to kohlrabi (see page 26). A fertile well-drained soil of pH 6.0–7.0, rich in humus, is required. The plants must be given ample food and water and they must grow without check because otherwise the swollen stems become hard and woody. Soil requirements, seedbed preparation, and pest and disease control are the same as for turnips (see pages 62–3), but a top dressing of 1 oz per square yard of a fertilizer containing ammonium nitrate and calcium carbonate should also be applied if growth slows down.

Sowing Successive sowings of kohlrabi can be made from April through August, but because the plants do best in cool weather you should make the first sowing in early spring (before last spring frost) and a second sowing 2–3 weeks later. Make another sowing in August for a fall crop. Make $\frac{1}{2}-\frac{3}{4}$ in deep drills, 12 in apart. Sow groups of three seeds at 6 in intervals and thin to one seedling per station. Alternatively, sow the seed thinly along the drills and thin at an early stage to 4–6 in apart.

Ample water (up to 2 gal per square yard each week) should be given to a kohlrabi crop in dry weather.

Harvesting
Pull the plants as needed when the swollen stems are about the size of a tennis ball. If they are allowed to develop further than this they become woody and unpalatable.

1 April or August. Rake in 3 oz per square yard of fertilizer to the prepared seedbed and apply calomel dust, and diazinon.

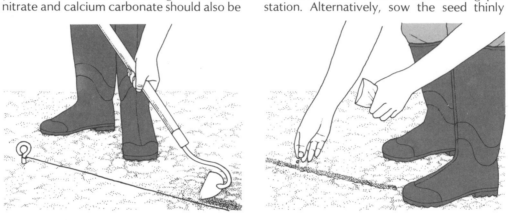

2 At the same time, water the seedbed. Draw out drills $\frac{1}{2}-\frac{3}{4}$ in deep and 12 in apart. On dry soil, dribble water into the drills and allow it to drain away.

3 Sow 3 seeds at 6 in intervals. Alternatively, sow and thin as for main crop turnips (see page 62).

4 When the first rough leaves appear and the seedlings are 1 in tall thin to 1 plant per station.

5 Thin again to 6 in apart when the leaves of adjacent seedlings touch within the rows. Firm the soil.

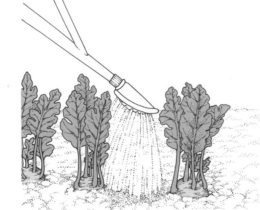

6 Water in a top dressing of 1 oz of a fertilizer containing ammonium nitrate and calcium carbonate per square yard.

7 In dry weather, water at a rate of 2 gal per square yard each week. Keep the rows free of weeds.

8 June or October. Pull up the plants as needed when the swollen stems are about the size of a tennis ball.

'Alabaster', 'Globus',
'Marble Ball'.

Celeriac

Celeriac, also known as turnip-rooted celery, is a type of common celery in which the lower part of the stem and the main roots have become swollen. This swollen portion has the typical celery flavor and is an excellent substitute for it. Celeriac can be grated raw for use in salads and it is also useful as a winter vegetable for soups.

The plants are not hilled up and they achieve their full size during the fall from sowings made in spring.

Cultivation

Celeriac needs a long growing season and responds to good growing conditions. Good-sized celeriac requires a fertile soil which has had a heavy dressing of organic manure dug in during the winter. A base dressing of 2–4 oz per square yard of a balanced fertilizer should be applied before planting.

Sowing Celeriac plants grow very slowly in the first two months from sowing. Sow the seed in March under glass at a temperature of 18°C/65°F. The seedlings should be pricked out as soon as possible and transferred into small peat blocks, pots or seed trays at a spacing of 2–2½ in square. Keep the temperature at 13°–16°C/55°–60°F throughout propagation. Alternatively, the seed may be sown in a cold frame, or under cloches, in April, or it may be sown directly in the garden on the mean date of the last spring frost.

Harden off the plants before planting out in May. Plant them at 12 in intervals in rows 15 in apart. They require firm planting and should be watered in thoroughly. Drench the base of the plants with diazinon soon after transplanting as a precaution against carrot rust fly. Never allow them to go short of water during the growing period. Heavy waterings of up to 4 gal per square yard each week in dry weather will improve the size and quality of the crop. Top-dress with 1 oz per square yard of a fertilizer containing ammonium nitrate and calcium carbonate in June or July. In poor soils weekly applications of liquid manure are beneficial. Keep the plants free of weeds. Remove dead leaves and side-shoot growths. This helps to produce a smoother swollen stem. Spray severe attacks of celery fly with dimethoate.

Harvesting

The crops are ready from September onward. In mild areas it is possible to leave celeriac in the ground until it is needed. Cover the plants with straw to prevent damage in very cold weather. Alternatively, they should be lifted and trimmed of leaves and roots before storing in boxes of peat, sand or sawdust in a frost-free building.

Pests and diseases

Celeriac can suffer from the same pests and diseases as celery (see page 42).

1 May. Harden off the seedlings by keeping them in a cold frame or under cloches for a few days.

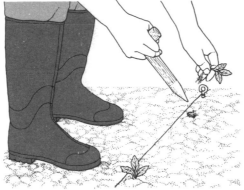

2 May. Plant them at 12 in intervals in rows 15 in apart. Water in immediately after planting. Apply a drench of diazinon to combat carrot rust fly.

3 June to July. Top-dress with a fertilizer containing ammonium nitrate and calcium carbonate at 1 oz per square yard. Water each week in dry weather.

4 During summer. Spray with dimethoate if celery fly attacks occur. Remove dead, decaying leaves and any side-shoots that appear.

5 July onward. Give weekly applications of liquid manure in poor soils.

6 September onward. Lift, trim and store the crop in a frost-free building in boxes of dry peat or sand.

7 In mild areas leave celeriac in the ground until required but protect the crop against frost damage with a covering of straw or similar material.

Beets

GLOBULAR
'Boltardy' (bolt resistant),
'Crimson Globe', 'Detroit'.

LONG
'Cheltenham Green Top',
'Dobies Purple'.

Beets are biennial plants which are grown as annuals for their edible swollen roots. They usually have red flesh and the root shape may be round or long and tapering. Beets are good for intercropping as a useful catch crop; small beets mature in about 60 days.

Cultivation

Beets are in season from May or early June through to the fall.

Soil and situation Do not grow beets on freshly manured ground. Early crops can be grown only on well-drained, fertile soils, prepared in early spring, but fall-maturing crops will tolerate heavier conditions. Beets grow best in soil with a pH of 6.5–7.5. A balanced fertilizer applied at 2–3 oz per square yard is sufficient to maintain growth. An open, shade-free site is preferable.

Sowing Beet "seeds" are actually fruits with two or three seeds contained within a cork-like pellet. They do not germinate well below 7°C/45°F, therefore warm spring weather is needed for early crops. To improve germination, soak the seeds for an hour or place them under running water before sowing.

Early crop In March, space-sow two or three seeds of round, bolt-resistant varieties at 4 in intervals under cloches or frames in rows 7 in apart. For outdoor sowing, the seeds are sown at the same spacing but from late March to early April. The plants are thinned to one per station. Station sowing can avoid thinning while the plants are under glass.

Main crop In May and June, space-sow two or three seeds of round or long varieties outdoors at 4–6 in intervals (depending on the type of beet) in rows 12 in apart. Make successional sowings to within two months of the first fall frost to provide a supply of salad-sized beets in late fall.

Watering In hot dry weather, water the plants at the rate of 2 gal per square yard each week, to maintain succulent, juicy growth. Give no more than this, however, because an excess of water may result in too much leaf at the expense of root.

Hoe around the developing roots with a short-handled hoe. Damaged roots bleed readily and are susceptible to disease so great care is needed.

Harvesting

Round varieties can be pulled as soon as they are large enough. Early sowings are ready from May to July. The main crops mature from July onward. Late crops can be lifted for use or stored for winter use.

Lift the young roots and twist off the leaves. Store sound, disease-free roots in boxes of peat, sand or sawdust in a frost-free building. Distinct white concentric rings in the flesh when the roots are cut is a sign of old age; these beets will not keep well.

Very late-sown beets are ready from October and in favorable locations this crop can be left in the ground during winter, if protected against frost with a covering of straw or similar material.

Main crop beets

1 Early May. Apply a balanced fertilizer at 2–3 oz per square yard to the prepared seedbed.

2 May or June. Soak the seeds of round or long varieties in water for an hour before sowing to improve germination.

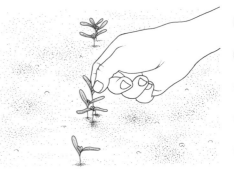

3 Space-sow 2–3 seeds at 4–6 in intervals (depending on variety) in 2 in deep rows, 12 in apart.

4 At the first true leaf stage thin to leave a single seedling at each station.

5 Hoe very carefully around the developing plants with a short-handled hoe and water at 2 gal per square yard in dry weather.

6 July or August. Gently lift beets with a fork when the roots are large enough to eat. Use immediately or store.

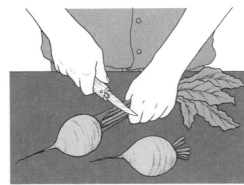

7 For storing, cut off the leaves to 3 in above each crown and remove dead or decaying leaves.

8 Arrange the beets in a box of sand. The roots should not touch. Keep the box in a cool frost-free place.

Radishes

SUMMER
'Cherry Belle', 'Wood's Early Frame',
'French Breakfast', 'Icicle',
'Red Forcing', 'Scarlet Globe'.

WINTER
'Black Spanish', 'Chinese Rose'.

Radishes are most commonly grown for use in salads but some varieties have much longer roots and these are cooked as a winter vegetable. Salad radishes have red, or red and white, skins and globular or cylindrical roots, whereas winter radishes have white, black or pink skins.

Cultivation

Both radish crops grow quickly and they are often grown as a catch crop.

Soil and situation All radishes require a fairly rich and well-drained, but not freshly manured, soil to grow well. The soil must retain enough moisture to ensure rapid uninterrupted growth but too much moisture, or fertilizer, results in excessive leaf growth. Apply 1oz per square yard of a balanced general fertilizer before each sowing.

An open situation is preferable for early and late sowings, but sowings from June to August should be made in a slight shade between other crops. Even then they may not succeed because radishes dislike hot weather.

Spring and summer radishes

The earliest salad radishes come from sowings made under cloches or frames in February and March. Successive outside sowings, without protection, can start in March and continue until August or September at two week intervals. Radishes are attacked by flea beetles and cabbage maggot. Apply diazinon to the drills before sowing as a deterrent.

Sow the seed thinly in $\frac{1}{2}-\frac{3}{4}$ in deep drills which are 4–6 in apart. Alternatively, broadcast the seed on to the prepared seedbed and rake it in lightly. When the seedlings emerge, thin, if necessary, until they are 1 in apart.

Keep the roots moist at all times. Dry, hot weather encourages hot-tasting radishes and during such periods apply water each week at the rate of 2 gal per square yard.

Winter radishes

Winter radishes are often 12 in long so a deep, friable soil is required. No fertilizer is needed when winter radishes are grown immediately after another crop, but on poor soils a general fertilizer should be raked in at a rate of 1oz per square yard before sowing. Sow winter radishes two month before first fall frost.

Take out $\frac{1}{2}-\frac{3}{4}$ in deep drills 12 in apart, and before sowing apply diazinon. Sow the seed very thinly and when the seedlings are big enough to handle thin until they are 6 in apart. Alternatively, the seed can be space-sown in groups of 3–4 at 6 in intervals and thinned to one per station.

The rapid growth of this crop means that it shades out weeds, except in the very early stages. Water in dry weather.

Harvesting

Pull spring and summer radishes when the roots are about $\frac{3}{4}$ in in diameter and they are firm and crunchy. Over-mature roots are hollow and unpalatable. The time taken to mature varies from 5 to 7 weeks at the end of the season to 3–4 weeks in midsummer.

Winter radishes are ready within about 60 days of sowing. Lift them before frost and store in boxes of dry sand for use as required. In mild areas leave them in the ground protected against frost.

EARLY SALAD RADISHES

The first sowing can be made in February. Put cloches over the ground for 3–4 weeks beforehand to dry it out. Rake the soil into a fine tilth.

Using short-topped varieties of radish broadcast the seed at $\frac{1}{4}$ oz per square yard or sow it thinly in $\frac{1}{2}-\frac{3}{4}$ in deep drills, 4–6 in apart. Water the seedbed thoroughly and keep the radishes moist throughout their life with regular applications of water.

Ventilate the crop on warm days because high temperatures under the cloche encourage leaf growth at the expense of roots.

Early salad radishes should be ready to be harvested in about eight weeks after sowing.

Spring and summer radishes

1 March. Prepare the seedbed, rake in 1oz of a balanced general fertilizer per square yard and water well.

2 March. Draw out $\frac{1}{2}-\frac{3}{4}$ in deep drills 4–6 in apart and apply diazinon. Sow the seed thinly. Cover and firm.

3 After 10–14 days. Thin the seedlings to 1 in as soon as they can be handled easily. If the weather is dry water them each week.

4 Pull the radishes as required when the roots are $\frac{3}{4}$ in in dia.

Winter radishes

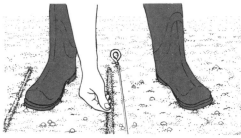

1 August or September. Space-sow the seed in groups of 3–4 at 6 in intervals in $\frac{3}{4}$ in deep drills, 12 in apart.

2 After 7–10 days. Thin the seedlings to 1 plant per station as soon as they can be handled easily. Water after thinning.

3 October. Lift the roots carefully. Twist off the leaves and store them in dry sand in a frost-free place.

'Mammoth'.

Salsify

Salsify produces long tapering roots that may reach 10 in in length.

The roots are white-skinned and the flesh is said to have a fishy or oyster-like taste. The plant is often known as vegetable oyster or oyster plant. Scorzonera is a closely related vegetable with black skin and white flesh which is not as strongly flavored as salsify. But it is rarely seen in the U.S.

The young shoots or "chards" of salsify are also blanched and eaten as salad in the spring.

Cultivation

Soil A deep, well-drained soil of pH 6.0–7.5 is necessary. If possible, it should be free of stones so that the long roots can grow without obstruction. No fresh organic matter should be dug in before growing these crops because this causes the roots to fork. Dig the ground deeply so that the roots have room to grow and rake in 2–3 oz per square yard of a balanced fertilizer, such as 10-10-10, before sowing.

Sowing Sow the seed on the mean day of the last spring frost in drills $\frac{1}{2}$ in deep and 12 in apart. Sow groups of two or three seeds at 6 in intervals along the drill. Thin to a single plant per station as soon as they are large enough to be handled.

Weeding Remove any weeds around each plant by hand. The roots are easily damaged and will "bleed" if a hoe is used carelessly. Salsify has thin, strap-like leaves that do not shade out weeds effectively, so it is important to remove all weeds regularly.

Watering Ample moisture must be available during the growing season to obtain the most succulent roots. A mulch helps to smother any weeds, conserves moisture and also reduces the risk of bolting which is likely to occur during hot, dry weather.

Harvesting

Salsify is hardy and the roots can be left in the ground to be lifted as required. Salsify is biennial and any roots left in the ground will begin to sprout in April. If hilled up in January or February, the shoots will be blanched and can be used raw in salads. If dug up in the fall, store the roots in moist sand in a cool basement or garage. When harvesting, lift carefully because the roots snap easily.

1 April. Dig the soil deeply and rake in 2–3 oz of a general balanced fertilizer per square yard.

2 Sow groups of 2–3 seeds at 6 in intervals in drills $\frac{1}{2}$ in deep and 12 in apart.

3 May. Thin the seedlings to 1 plant per station when they are large enough to handle.

4 Then, apply a 2–3 in layer of mulch. Water at the rate of 1 gal per square yard each week in dry weather.

5 Fall and winter. Leave the roots in the ground and use a fork to lift carefully as required. Avoid damaging the roots.

SALSIFY SHOOTS

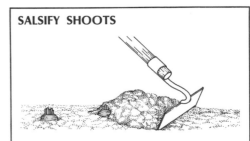

Salsify roots can be left in the ground to produce chards—edible top growth—the following spring. In the fall, cut off the old leaves, leaving about $\frac{1}{2}$–1 in exposed above the soil. Hill up the roots to a depth of about 6 in so the shoots are blanched as they develop the following spring.

In March or April, scrape away the soil and cut the blanched shoots when they are 5–6 in long. Alternatively, allow the shoots to develop naturally, without hilling up, and cut them green when they are about 6 in tall. Green shoots are allegedly less palatable than blanched shoots. Frequent cutting encourages new growth.

JERUSALEM ARTICHOKES
White and purple-skinned
varieties are available

Root artichokes

Jerusalem artichokes are perennial vegetables grown for their edible stem-tubers. They are a member of the daisy family and closely related to the common sunflower. They grow to 10 ft in good conditions and produce knobbly, irregularly-round white or purplish tubers that can be boiled, fried or used in soups. They are useful screen plants for hiding such features as compost heaps.

Cultivation

This vegetable tolerates a wide range of soil conditions but does not thrive in poorly drained or very acid soils. It grows well between pH 6.0–7.5 and crops reasonably even in relatively poor soils, although the tubers are then small and difficult to harvest. If possible grow the plants in fertile soil that has been well manured in the winter.

Planting Jerusalem artichokes are propagated by tubers purchased or saved from the previous year's crop. Choose fairly large tubers and plant them close to the mean date of the last fall frost. Jerusalem artichokes should be planted 6 in deep in rows 3 ft apart, with 12 in between each tuber in the rows.

Keep them well watered during dry spells since tuber development is reduced in dry soils. Jerusalem artichokes require supporting unless they are grown in a very sheltered site.

Hill up Jerusalem artichokes—rather like potatoes—in early summer to reduce wind rocking and encourage tuber formation close to the surface.

In poor soils from June to August apply liquid manure at 2–3 week intervals to improve tuber size.

Harvesting

Cut down the plants when frost has killed the foliage to leave about 6 in of stem above ground. Jerusalem artichokes can be left in the ground until required. Unfortunately the tubers tend to go soft and dry out when they are lifted; even so, they are often dug up and stored in sand in a cool basement. It is usually better to leave them in the ground and protect them with a covering of straw, or similar material, if severe weather is likely.

Always keep enough good-sized tubers for next year's crop but take great care to remove all tubers from the ground. Even the smallest tubers will grow again if they are left behind. The resulting plants can then be a nuisance.

Pests and diseases

Soil pests such as wireworms may cause some damage to Jerusalem artichokes. Diazinon raked into the soil before planting should control them if they are troublesome. Otherwise the crop is relatively free of problems.

Chinese artichokes

Chinese artichokes, which are grown for their white tubers, are a rarity in the United States although popular in Europe, especially in France. They are however sold by a few seedsmen. Basic culture is similar to Jerusalem artichokes, but the plants do not need hilling. Better soils are needed, however, and the addition of humus before planting and a balanced fertilizer during growth will help.

ROOT ARTICHOKES

Jerusalem

Chinese

Jerusalem artichokes

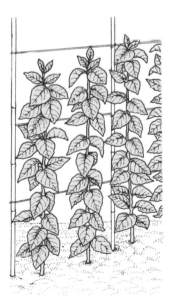

1 March or April. Plant tubers about the size of a small egg at 12 in intervals in 6 in deep holes in rows 3 ft apart.

2 May or June. Tie the plants to wires 9–12 in apart stretched between stakes about 2 ft apart.

3 At the same time, hill up Jerusalem artichokes to protect them against wind-rock and encourage tuber formation near the surface.

4 June to August. Water the plants regularly in dry weather at 2 gal per square yard. In poor soils apply liquid fertilizer every 2–3 weeks.

5 Fall. Cut top growth down leaving 6 in of stem above ground. Leave the tubers in the ground, for lifting as needed, but protect against frost.

Potatoes 1

The potato is the most widely grown vegetable in temperate zones. It is a South American perennial but it is only half-hardy in the U.S. Late frost in the spring kills the emerged leaves of a potato crop, and the first fall frosts kill the remaining foliage.

The potato is grown for its edible tubers and it is propagated from specially grown tubers ("seed") saved from the previous season. It is possible to save tubers from home-grown crops, but this is not advisable because potato plants and tubers soon become infected by debilitating virus diseases and if infected, crop yield and quality suffer. Virus-free "seed" is produced in areas where aphids that spread viruses are less of a problem. Always use certified seed.

Always use small "seed" tubers because large seed potatoes produce too many sprouts. For the maximum yield and to prevent crowded tubers being forced to the surface and "greening," small seed tubers with only two or three sprouts are ideal.

Like some other vegetables, potatoes are classified according to the time at which they mature. Earlies are ready to eat in late spring or early summer. Late varieties—the main crops—mature in the fall for winter storage. Mid-season varieties mature in October.

Cultivation

Soil and situation Potatoes tolerate a wide range of soils but they grow best in deep, fertile, well-drained soils with sufficient bulky organic manure to retain moisture in dry weather. Do not apply lime before planting potatoes because they grow best at a pH of 5.0–6.0 and alkaline conditions favor potato scab disease. Dig in 15–20 lb per square yard of well-rotted manure in the fall.

In spring, fork over the ground and rake in a general fertilizer, such as 10-10-10, at the rate of 4 oz per square yard and apply diazinon to combat wireworm and cutworm. A deep tilth is needed for hilling up. Plant in an open site but not in a frost pocket.

Planting Seed potatoes should be about 1 oz in weight, the size of a small hen's egg. Larger tubers are cut into 1½–2 oz blocks, each containing an eye. These should be planted immediately into moist soil but should be allowed to dry in a humid location if the soil is dry. Plant the tubers with the "eyes" upward in 6 in deep drills, with 12 in between early potato tubers and 16 in between mid-season and late varieties. Cover the planted drills immediately after planting. Mound up the soil 4–6 in high over each row.

Early potatoes Plant in early spring when the soil is reasonably dry and easily worked, but late enough for the plants to escape injury from frost after they appear. Plant in rows 24 in apart with 12 in between the tubers.

Mid-season and main crop Plant three to four weeks later in rows 27–30 in apart with 16 in between the tubers.

Potatoes are usually grown in ridges which are formed gradually during the season by hilling up (ridging) every two to three weeks. Cultivate and hoe between the initial mounds to provide sufficient loose soil for hilling. Use a draw hoe to pull up soil into ridges around growing plants. Cultivating and hoeing kills developing weeds.

Watering Earlies should be watered at the rate of 3–4 gal per square yard every 10–14 days to increase yield from an early stage of growth. If they are watered at the "marble" stage (when the small developing tubers are the size of a marble, approximately ½ in diameter) and not before, at the rate of 3–4 gal per square yard, they mature earlier.

Main crops should be given 4 gal per square yard at flowering time, which markedly increases yield and depresses scab.

Harvesting

Early potatoes should be ready about three months after planting, in June and July. The potatoes should be ready when the flowers are fully open. Lift as needed.

Mid-season and main crop potatoes should be lifted from August onward when the tops have died down.

Use a flat-tined fork to avoid too much damage to the tubers when lifting potatoes. Leave the tubers on the soil surface for two to three hours to dry. In wet conditions dry the tubers in a garage, a cold frame or under cloches. Make sure that all the potatoes are lifted so that no disease is carried over to the next year by overlooked tubers.

Storing Store only sound, healthy tubers.

1 Spring. Fork over the ground and rake in general balanced fertilizer at 4 oz per square yard, and apply diazinon against wireworm and cutworm.

2 March to April. Take out 6 in deep drills, 24 in apart for earlies, 27–30 in apart for later crops (according to the variety being grown).

3 At the same time, place the seed tubers in the drills at 12 in intervals for earlies, 16 in for mid-season and main crops, with the buds or "eyes" upward.

4 Use a draw hoe to cover the drills. Draw up soil from both sides to produce 4–6 in high mounds over the planted rows.

Potatoes 2

Any damaged potatoes should be used or discarded immediately. Store in a frost-free building. Boxes with raised corner posts are ideal. Keep them in the dark or cover with black polyethylene to prevent the tubers turning green. Large quantities of potatoes can be stored in pits. After lifting leave them to dry out for several hours, having removed the stems. Heap them up underneath straw to "sweat" for a couple of days before mounding up with earth.

Pests and diseases

Use virus-free seed to avoid potato virus diseases. To prevent attacks by wireworm and cutworm apply diazinon at planting. Scab is rarely a serious problem. Ample watering is a good deterrent. To control other pests, such as flea beetles and potato beetles, apply a general-purpose garden spray or dust.

Potato blight This is the worst fungal disease of the crop and it can be particularly bad in warm, humid conditions from July onward. The symptoms appear first on the leaves as yellow blotches on the upper surface. A white fungal growth may be seen underneath the leaves. The blotches turn brown and whole leaves are killed in severe attacks. Fungal spores are washed into the soil, where they can also infect the developing tubers. Regular spraying or dusting with a general-purpose garden spray (which contains fungicide such as zineb or maneb) is the only control.

5 During the summer, hoe regularly in the furrows between the ridges. Water during dry weather.

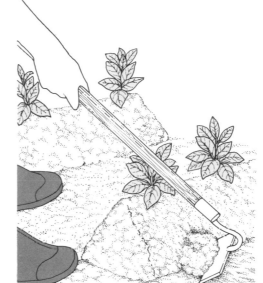

6 Hoe the soil from the furrows into ridges around the growing plants at 2–3 week intervals, until the ridges are 12–15 in high.

7 May onward. At 10 day intervals, in warm humid conditions, spray all the surfaces of the leaves with a general-purpose garden spray for control of insects and blight.

8 July. Lift early potatoes when the flowers are fully open, using a flat-tined fork to avoid excessive damage to tubers.

9 September onward. Lift mid-season and main crop potatoes when the tops have died down.

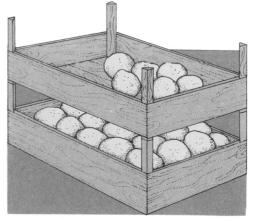

10 Store in a frost-free building in boxes with raised corner posts for easy inspection.

Potatoes 3

Place a single layer of tubers—"eyes" up-ward—in boxes or trays and keep them in a light, airy place. Begin the process in March so that sturdy shoots about $\frac{3}{4}$–1 in long will have formed prior to planting. Sprouted tubers grow quickly when planted and are particularly useful for early crops which have a relatively short growing period. It may be worth while sprouting mid-season or main crop varieties in areas where late planting is necessary because of the likelihood of frost.

Potatoes are normally grown outdoors as described on the previous pages. There are alternative systems, however, for growing out-of-season potatoes or for less intensive cultivation of this basic vegetable crop.

Out-of-season potatoes

Very early potatoes can be grown in a green-house to mature in March or April. Plant sprouted seed in a slightly heated greenhouse at a temperature of 7°–10°C/45°–50°F in Jan-uary and grow in the same way as outdoor crops. Never allow the temperature to get very high or too much foliage and few tubers will be produced. Keep the soil moist.

Growing in pots

Plant 2 or 3 sprouted tubers in large pots which are at least 12 in wide and deep, containing good garden soil.

An alternative is to grow the plants in pots. Plant 2–3 sprouted tubers in a large box or pot containing good garden soil. Keep the pots in a slightly heated greenhouse and grow as for the greenhouse crop.

Early outdoor plantings can be covered with glass cloches or polyethylene tunnels to speed development and give protection against frost. Cover the cloches with sacking when frosts are forecast.

Non-cultivation system

Potatoes can be grown without hilling up. Water the ground well before planting. In April, push sprouted tubers into the soil and

Growing under black polyethylene

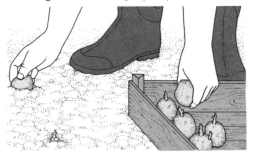

1 April. Water the ground and push sprouted tubers into the soil at the same spacings as for outdoor potatoes.

cover and mound over the drills. Cover with a black polyethylene sheet to prevent greening and weed growth, to warm the soil and to conserve moisture. Make a slit above each tuber. Bury the edges of the polyethylene by pushing them into the soil with a spade.

Slugs and wireworms thrive in the con-ditions provided by polyethylene. Control them by scattering slug pellets around the mounds.

When the shoots emerge they begin to push up through the slits in the sheet toward the light. Roll back the sheet to expose the tubers for harvesting or take them out as required through the slits.

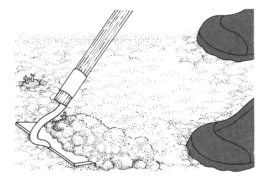

2 Cover and mound over the drills. Scatter slug pellets around the slightly mounded ridges.

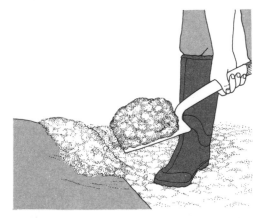

3 Cover the ridges with a 36 in wide length of black polyethylene and bury the edges to leave a 24 in wide strip exposed.

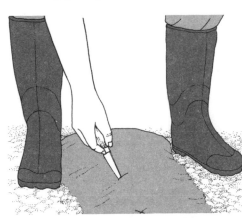

4 Make slits with a sharp knife above each tuber where the shoots have pushed against the polyethylene.

5 May. As the shoots emerge they push up through the slits in the polyethylene.

6 July. As the tubers develop, roll back the polyethylene sheeting to expose the potatoes for harvesting.

Cucumber

Cucumbers are sub-tropical plants grown for their green-skinned fruits, which are used raw in salads and made into pickles. In Great Britain, cucumbers are commonly grown in greenhouses and the varieties used produce long, cylindrical, rather slender fruits. In the US, cucumbers are almost always grown outdoors. These have shorter, thicker fruits for the most part.

American seedsmen offer two types of cucumber: slicing, or standard, varieties for use in salads and pickling varieties that are more productive and have shorter, blockier fruits. In practice, the varieties can be used interchangeably.

A recent cucumber development is the gynoecious hybrid, which produces an enormous profusion of predominantly female flowers (the female flowers are the small flowers; the large flowers are males). The result is an equally enormous profusion of fruit. In fact, there is more fruit than one family can consume, so unless it is planned to set up a small-scale pickle factory, these hybrids should either be avoided or restricted to a few plants.

Cultivation

Like most cucurbits, cucumbers grow fast and are prolific producers: therefore do not overplant. The soil should be well dug and enriched with humus and a balanced fertilizer, such as 10-10-10. If nematodes (microscopic soil insects that infest plant roots and cause a general malaise of the plants) are prevalent, the soil should be treated with a soil fumigant before cucumbers are planted; but an easier way to cope with these pests is to avoid planting cucumbers (or any other cucurbits) in the same place year after year. Growing marigolds in the vicinity of the vegetable garden also appears to discourage some nematodes.

Because of their unique flavor, cucumbers are often blamed for crossing with other cucurbits growing nearby in the same garden and altering their flavor. Actually, this happens only if seeds are saved from fruits and sown the following year. But if fresh seed from a recognized seedsman is sown every year, cucumbers can be planted alongside any other cucurbit without getting a mixture of flavors.

Planting For an extra-early crop, cucumber seeds can be sown in peat blocks indoors about four weeks before they are moved into the garden. At the time of transplanting, the seedlings should have only true leaves: larger seedlings do not transplant well. If the weather is still cold and frost threatens, cover the seedlings with cloches.

Normal practice, however, is to sow seeds directly in the garden where the plants are to grow after all danger of frost is past and the soil is warm. One or two later sowings can be made up to within about 75 days of the first fall freeze; but this is hardly necessary if the plants of the initial sowing are kept growing and producing well.

Cucumber seeds are sown $\frac{1}{2}$ in deep. They can be sown in drills 5 ft apart (if you let the plants run on the ground) or only 2 ft apart (if you train the plants up a sturdy fence of wire mesh). The alternative is to sow seeds in hills about 8 ft apart in both directions. Thin to three or four plants per hill or to 12–18 in apart in drills.

Feeding and watering About four weeks after cucumbers are thinned, side-dress them lightly with balanced fertilizer or nitrate of soda. Keep plants well watered and pull out weeds faithfully. Mulching with grass clippings, hay or black polyethylene film keeps down weeds and greatly reduces the need for watering.

Pests and diseases

Control insects, such as the spotted cucumber beetle, aphids and mites, by spraying or dusting frequently with carbaryl or rotenone after the plants are thinned. The best way to prevent attacks of mildew or mosaic is to plant cucumber varieties resistant to these diseases (if they are troublesome in the area). Diseased plants are stunted and bear puckered, yellow-mottled leaves. Destroy affected plants. Spray nonresistant varieties with a mildewcide.

Harvesting

Cucumbers can be picked when very small but have more flavor when they reach maturity. Old fruits are of poor quality and also inhibit growth and yield when left on the plant. Harvest fruits daily.

1 For early crops, sow seed indoors in peat pots about four weeks before they are to be planted out.

2 Sow outdoors in drills $\frac{1}{2}$ in deep. Space the rows 2 ft apart for supported plants, 5 ft for trailing plants.

3 Thin the seedlings to 12–18 in apart when they have produced their first true leaves.

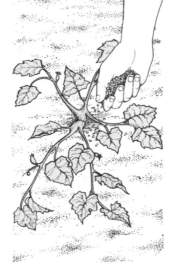

4 Four weeks after thinning, side-dress the cucumber plants lightly with balanced fertilizer.

5 Mulch the growing plants with black polyethylene, hay or grass clippings to keep down weeds.

6 Spray against insect pests with carbaryl or rotenone after the plants are thinned.

Tomatoes 1

Tomatoes are probably the most widely grown vegetable in the United States. They can be raised in all ten climate zones, although they are not reliable in zones 1 and 2. Picked when fully ripe, they are far more delicious than tomatoes found in the supermarket. Most of the varieties grown produce large, red fruits but a few have large, yellow fruits. There are also varieties that produce tiny red or yellow fruits for cocktail use.

The varieties offered by the average seed company are technically known as indeterminate, which means that the stems continue to elongate and produce new clusters of fruit throughout the late summer and fall. Determinate varieties have terminal clusters of blossoms and fruits which prevent stem growth beyond that point. Because most of the fruits ripen at the same time, determinate tomatoes are of interest primarily to commercial growers; but they are useful to home gardeners who like to can large quantities of stewed tomatoes and juice. Large tomato crops can also be turned into tomato paste.

Raising tomato plants

Tomatoes are so easily raised from seeds that there is no reason to buy plants. Sow the seeds in flats in a prepared starting mixture six to eight weeks before the last spring frost. If possible, grow the seedlings under fluorescent light; otherwise, keep them in a warm, sunny window. The seeds germinate quickly and make rapid growth. As soon as the seedlings have two true leaves, carefully move them into individual peat pots (the ideal arrangement) or into small flats about 1–1½ in apart. Keep the soil damp but not wet. Apply a balanced nutrient solution occasionally as the time for planting out approaches.

In hot climates, two sowings can be made: one in early to mid-winter for a spring crop and another in July or August for a late crop. Seed for the late crop is best started in a seedbed and moved into the garden as a succession crop.

Planting out Tomatoes are tender and should not be planted outdoors until all danger of frost has passed. If wished, however, the season can be extended a little by planting them out a week or two earlier than this and keeping them under cloches at night. In either case, before moving them into the garden, harden them off gradually by moving the flats outdoors into a sunny spot for a longer and longer time every day for about a week. They can also be hardened off in a cold frame.

Soil and planting The garden soil must be well dug and, if possible, manured before the plants are set out. Spacing for the plants depends on how they are to be trained. If you follow the common practice of tying each plant to a tall 1-inch thick stake, plant indeterminate varieties 2 ft apart in rows 24–30 in apart. If you use wire cages or tripod supports, increase spacing between plants and rows by 6–12 in. If you let the plants trail on the ground, space them 3 ft apart in rows 6 ft apart. Determinate varieties are not staked because they form more compact plants. Space them 30 in apart in rows 3 ft apart.

Tomatoes put out roots from their stems, so they can and should be planted much deeper than other vegetables. Dig the holes with a trowel about 6 in deep so the stems are covered to a depth of 2–3 in. Spindly plants should be set even deeper. Water well at planting time.

Staking Tomatoes that are allowed to sprawl on the ground require less attention during the growing season and produce more fruit than supported varieties; but they take up a lot of space. Most gardeners prefer to provide some sort of support. If you use single stakes or a tripod of stakes, start tying the plants when they reach about 15 in. Use soft twine or strips of cloth; tie it securely to the stake and loop it loosely around the plant stems under the fruit clusters. Continue tying as the plants grow. If, instead of stakes, tall, 1 ft diameter cylinders of heavy wire mesh are used, no tying is necessary.

When tomatoes are tied to single stakes, they should be pruned to prevent them from becoming so top-heavy that they fall over in

Raising tomato plants

1 Sow the seed thinly in trays 8 weeks before planting. Cover with ⅛ in of sieved compost and water before covering with glass and newspaper. Keep at 18°C/65°F.

2 Ten to twelve days after sowing, gently remove the seedlings by inserting a small dibber beneath the roots. Plant them in 3 in peat pots of potting mix.

3 Water to firm, then water little and often. Reduce the temperature to 16°C/60°F when the plants begin to shade each other. Liquid feed before planting.

4 Plant tomatoes when they are 6–9 in tall with the flowers on the first truss just opening. Water well before and after planting.

Tomatoes 2

wind or heavy rain. Some people remove all but one main stem to facilitate handling and produce fruit of maximum size; but just as big tomatoes and more of them will be produced if two stems are kept and all suckers nipped out.

This is the only way in which tomatoes—no matter how they're trained—should be pruned. Do not thin the foliage, even though it may seem excessive, because it protects the fruits from sunburning and puts more strength into the plants.

Feeding and watering About six weeks after plants are set out, give each one a small handful of balanced fertilizer, such as 10–10–10, and repeat this treatment about a month later. Keep the plants well watered until shortly before harvest starts; then reduce the supply somewhat, otherwise the fruits may crack. Remove weeds as they appear but do not hoe deeply because the roots are shallow. Maintaining a mulch of grass clippings or other organic matter at all times helps to control weeds, prevent evaporation

of the moisture and nourish the soil.

Tomatoes often drop their early blossoms if the temperature falls below 55°F. In areas that frequently experiences such low temperatures, spray the first blossom clusters when most of the flowers have opened fully (and not before) with a fruit-setting hormone such as Blossom Set. Direct the spray at the backs of the flowers and keep it off the rest of the plant as much as possible. Just dampen the flowers: don't apply enough spray to drip.

Pests and diseases

Tomatoes have several problems but the two commonest are weather-related and there is little that can be done about them. Blossom-end rot, characterized by big black, sunken spots in the base of the fruits, generally occurs when cool, wet weather during fruit development is followed by a period of hot, dry weather. Besides more careful watering during the hot, dry spell, the only thing that may prevent the rot is to spray with a dilute solution of calcium chloride.

Cracking of fruits around the stems occurs when the plants, because of warm, damp weather or an application of fertilizer, put on a sudden spurt of growth after a period of dry or cool weather. Again, the best preventive action is to keep the plants watered and fed so they grow at a more uniform pace. It also helps to select varieties that are resistant to cracking.

Probably the worst insect pest is the tomato hornworm, a large green caterpillar with a horn at the tail end. Because it is the exact color of the plants, it is not easily seen, except when the plants are defoliated. The worms have voracious appetites and can chew off the leaves of a single plant in a few days if they are not spotted and removed.

For other insects and diseases that may appear, spray or dust plants every 10 days with a general-purpose chemical.

Harvesting

If possible, allow tomatoes to ripen to a uniform bright red before picking. In very

hot weather, however, the coloring process is slower and the fruits are likely to be soft when you judge them to be fully ripe. They should, therefore, be picked in the pink stage and complete ripening indoors at 16°–21°C/60°–70°F.

In the fall, just before the first frost, pick all the paler green fruits, which are beginning to soften, and store them in a frost-free place under cover until they turn red. They can be wrapped in newspaper or not, as you wish. Note that hard, dark-green fruits rarely ripen when handled in this way. Fruits that are touched by frost are unusable.

Dwarf tomatoes

Dwarf varieties of tomato can be grown outdoors in the usual way or in large pots outdoors and indoors. In the latter case, watering is required almost every day to keep the soil moist. Indoors, the plants can be brought to harvest stage on a warm windowsill, under fluorescent light or in a greenhouse. Thus tomatoes can be grown all year.

5 Tie the plants to 1 in stakes when they reach a height of 15 in. Space plants 2 ft apart in rows 24–30 in apart.

6 About six weeks after planting, rake in a small handful of balanced fertilizer around each plant. Repeat a month later, watering well each time.

7 Pinch out side-shoots as they develop, except on bush varieties. Do not thin the foliage.

8 In cool areas, spray the first fruit clusters with a fruit-setting hormone spray. Direct the spray at the back of the flowers. Barely dampen the flowers.

Squashes 1

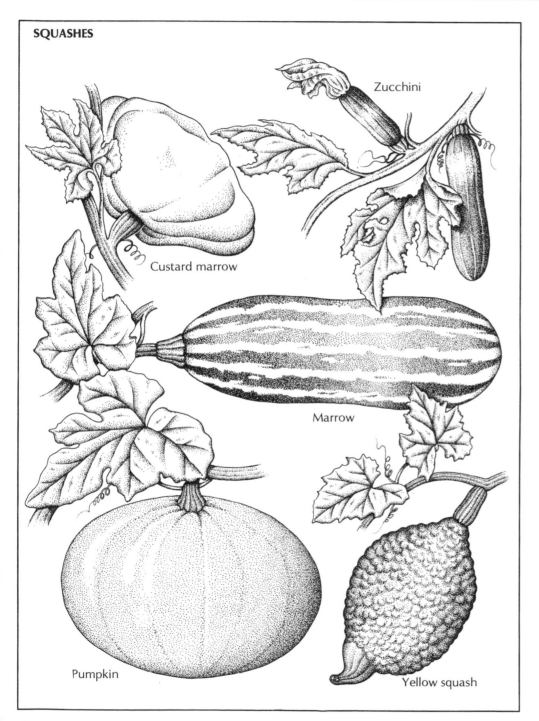

SQUASHES

Zucchini

Custard marrow

Marrow

Pumpkin

Yellow squash

Summer squash are extremely fast-growing, large, bushy plants that produce fruit in profusion, so do not overplant. Six to eight plants will usually give as much fruit as the average family can eat. Of course, the over-supply can be frozen for winter use but it does not freeze very well. Picked when very young, however, summer squash is delicious.

There are numerous varieties falling into three broad classifications: yellow squashes, which are either straight or crooked-necked and have smooth or warty rinds; zucchinis, which form long cylindrical fruits that are dark green, green-and-yellow striped, or yellow; and the patty pans, shaped like a creamy-white, flat, scalloped-edged bowl.

Cultivation

Summer squashes are very satisfying to raise because they are easy, handsome and yield abundantly about 50 days after planting. But they may suddenly die if attacked by borers, cucumber beetles, squash bugs or disease. For this reason, instead of trying to stretch out the life of one crop, it is wise to plant a succession of small crops at monthly intervals until 60 days before the first autumn freeze.

Squashes do not require exceptionally good soil but do best if you dig in an ample supply of humus and a little balanced fertilizer, such as 10-10-10. Drainage should be good; the location warm and sunny.

Planting After all danger of frost has passed, sow seeds in drills $\frac{1}{2}$ in deep and about 4–6 in apart. Thin the plants to stand 2–3 ft apart. Rows should be about 4 ft wide for the yellow squashes and zucchinis; 5–6 ft wide for patty pans. Water plants well in dry weather. The large leaves and heavy foliage tend to discourage weeds close around the plants; but when an occasional weed does appear, pull it out by hand. Cultivating without breaking the leaves is difficult.

Pests and diseases

Spraying about once a week during warm weather with methoxychlor or malathion discourages most insect pests and also helps to control bacterial wilt, which is spread by insects. Dust young plants and the surrounding soil with rotenone or carbaryl to discourage vine borers. Mildew is controllable by spraying with zineb in periods of cool, damp nights and warm, humid days. A general-purpose vegetable and fruit spray can be used instead of these separate chemicals if wished. Be sure to spray under the leaves, where the bugs hide.

Harvesting

Cut off fruits with a sharp knife while they are still small. The best zucchinis are 6–8 in long; yellow squashes, 8–10 in; and patty pans no more than 3 in across. Much larger fruits are edible as long as it is possible to penetrate the skin easily with a fingernail, but they have less flavor than the smaller ones.

Chayote or mirliton

Chayote or mirliton is also known by several other names. Botanically it is called *Sechium edule*. It is a large perennial vine producing fairly small, green or white, pear-shaped fruits that are boiled and eaten like summer squashes. Unlike squashes, to which they are related, the fruits have only a single seed.

In the warmest zones, the plants can be grown as perennials but they are more commonly treated as annuals. However, they require such a long growing season that they cannot be relied on to produce fruit north of the warmest parts of zone 7.

Cultivation

Two or more plants must be grown to assure production of fruit. The soil should be fertile and rich in humus. Apply a balanced fertilizer, such as 10-10-10, before planting and make one or more side-dressings during development. Keep the plants well watered at all times.

From zone 8 southward, plant entire fruits directly in the garden after all danger of frost has passed. Let the stem end protrude slightly above the soil. The alternative—required in zone 7—is to plant the fruits in large pots indoors and move them outside after the last frost.

Space the plants 10 ft apart. If they are allowed to sprawl on the ground, they will also need at least 10 ft on each side. To conserve space, therefore, it is better to let them grow up a sturdy wire-mesh trellis fixed between posts.

Squashes 2

1 In spring dig in ample supplies of humus and a balanced fertilizer such as 10-10-10.

2 Sow the seeds after the last frost in drills ½ in deep and 4–6 in apart in the row. Space the rows 4–6 ft apart.

3 Thin the plants to 2–3 ft apart when they have 3–4 true leaves.

4 Water the plants well in dry weather and remove any weeds that appear.

5 Spray once a week with an insecticide to combat insect pests and bacterial wilt.

Harvesting

6 Cut off fruits with a sharp knife when they are still small and tender.

Chayote

From Zone 8 southward. Plant entire fruits direct in the garden after the last frost. Let the stalks protrude.

Zone 7. Plant indoors in large pots and move the young plants outside after the last frost.

Squashes 3

Winter squash

Winter squashes take three months or more to mature so only one planting per year is possible in most parts of the country. Most varieties trail across the ground and require a great deal of space. This can be reduced somewhat, however, if you plant squashes close to corn and let them run in among the stalks. The spacing can also be reduced to a 2 ft row if the plants are trained up a sturdy fence; however, the fruits are sometimes so large and heavy that they may tear loose or drag the fence down. To solve this space problem, seedsmen are now offering more dwarf, bushy varieties; but these have smaller and fewer fruits.

The most popular winter squashes are the dark-green, fairly small acorns; the orange-brown, dumbell-shaped butternuts; and the giant dark-green or blue-gray Hubbards. An increasingly popular newer variety is the spaghetti squash, which turns yellow when ripe and may grow to great size but is picked when 10 in long. This variety has spaghetti-like strands of flesh that are boiled and served with spaghetti sauce.

Cultivation

Like summer squash, winter squash does best when the soil is enriched with humus or manure and a balanced fertilizer before planting. Apply additional balanced fertilizer when the plants are about two months old. Keep the plants well watered and pull weeds faithfully. Mulching with grass clippings, hay or black polyethylene film when the plants are young solves both the watering and weeding problems.

Planting For an early crop seeds can be sown in individual peat blocks indoors about a month before they are to be planted out. Or the seeds can be sown in the garden about two weeks later and the seedlings protected from late frosts with cloches. However, because winter squashes are usually harvested late and stored for winter use, the normal practice is to sow the seeds directly in the garden after all danger of frost has passed and the soil is warm.

Sow about ½ in deep in drills or hills (groups). Standard varieties should be thinned to 24–30 in apart in rows 7–8 ft wide. Bushier varieties are spaced 2 ft apart in rows 4–5 ft wide. By manually placing the developing stems where they are wanted, they can be prevented from smothering small plants nearby or invading lawn areas (where they do no harm but inhibit mowing).

Pests and diseases

Treat winter squash in the same way as summer squash.

Harvesting

Let winter squashes ripen fully before they are cut from the vines, but do not expose them to hard frost. If they are not ready to be picked when an early frost threatens, cover them with newspapers, plastic or anything light enough not to mash the plants. The fruits are ripe when the color is right and when the stems are pressed with a thumbnail. If the nail cannot penetrate the rind, the proper ripeness has been attained. Ripe fruits can be left in the garden for a long time (provided that they are not subjected to frost).

Pick squashes with about 1 in of stem and do not damage the rind. They can be stored for several months—perhaps until spring—in a dark, airy, slightly humid place at a temperature of 50°F/10°C. Somewhat higher temperatures will do no great harm but lower temperatures will ruin the fruits.

Pumpkin

This enormous winter vegetable, a cucurbit closely related to squashes, melons and cucumbers, is a favorite of children and gardeners who enjoy competing in pumpkin contests. But it takes so much space and has such limited culinary value that the average home gardener avoids it.

Cultivation

Pumpkins are raised like winter squashes, but require a little less sun and are therefore frequently planted—about 7 ft apart in all directions or in the middle of corn patches. They require a deep, fertile soil enriched with balanced fertilizer at planting time and again about two months later; lots of moisture; and good weed control. Mulching the soil is advisable. In addition to holding in moisture and keeping down weeds, an organic mulch helps to enrich the soil as it decomposes. Black polyethylene film has no nutritive value, but by keeping the pumpkins off the ground, it helps to prevent rot in damp weather.

If pumpkins are being grown for competition or exhibition, the need for moisture and plant food is especially important. Many competitors fertilize their plants weekly throughout the 3–4 month growing season. Use of a liquid fertilizer is recommended because a granular food is difficult to work into the soil between the many trailing stems. Water is sometimes supplied continuously by threading a cotton string through the stem of a fruit and immersing the other end in a bucket of water; but this is frowned upon by serious competitors.

Planting Sow seeds where the plants are to grow after all danger of frost has passed. Thin the plants to stand 24–30 in apart in rows 7–9 ft wide.

Pests and diseases

The same problems that beset squashes affect pumpkins and are controlled in a similar manner. To prevent ripening pumpkins from turning white or rotting where they touch the ground, slip sheets of plastic film or boards underneath. Clean straw can also be used to protect the plants.

Harvesting

Pumpkins can withstand a light frost but must be harvested before the first killing frost. Cut the stems about an inch above the fruits; take care not to bruise the rind; and store the fruits in a dark, dry, airy place at about 50°F/10°C.

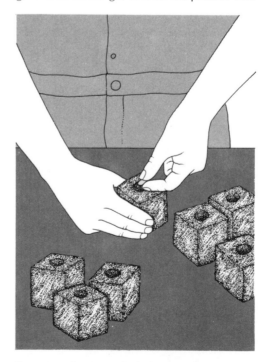

For an early crop of winter squash sow seeds in individual peat blocks indoors about a month before the young plants are due to be planted out.

Thin pumpkin seedlings to 24–30 in apart and mulch the plants well to keep down weeds and to enrich the soil. Pumpkins require plenty of moisture. Black polyethylene film mulch keeps the fruits off the ground.

Sweet potatoes/Southern peas

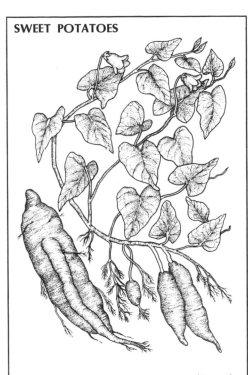

SWEET POTATOES

Sweet potatoes, or yams, are very distantly related to ordinary potatoes, but, like them, have edible tubers. It is a perennial, but is grown as an annual in the USA.

Sweet potatoes

Sweet potatoes, or yams, are relatives of the morning glory. They are fairly small vines that sprawl on the ground. The below-ground tubers are long and pointed at the ends and have a sweet yellow or orange flesh. The flesh of the best varieties, grown mainly in the South, is moist and succulent; that of more northern varieties tends to be dry and mealy.

Sweet potatoes are most successful in zones 7–10 but can be grown in zone 6. The plants generally take more than four months to produce mature fruit.

Cultivation

Do not plant sweet potatoes in the same location more than once every three years. The soil should be a well drained, sandy or clay loam with a pH of 5.2–6.7. Sweet potatoes do poorly in very heavy or very light soils. Two weeks before planting, prepare the soil well and mix in 8 oz of a low-nitrogen fertilizer, such as 5-10-10, per 50 square feet. Then form the soil into ridges 8 in high and 24–30 in wide.

Buy seedling plants from a grower of certified seed potatoes. Plants can be raised from seed but it is rather demanding.

Plant the seedlings after all danger of frost has passed. Center them in the ridges and space them 1 ft apart. Water well. Plants require about 1 in of water every week. Cultivate regularly, taking care not to disturb the roots. Side-dress with a little low-nitrogen fertilizer about half way through the growing season.

Harvesting

Dig up the potatoes when the soil is dry and can be brushed off the tubers. If the soil is damp, don't attempt to brush or wash it off. Place the tubers in a shady place—never in the sun—until the soil is dry enough to brush off. The tubers must not be cut or bruised if they are to be kept for any length of time. Before digging up the tubers, cut off the tops to allow access to the roots. It is then easy to unearth them without damaging the tubers.

Harvesting should be done before frost strikes. If this is impossible, cut the frost-blackened tops from the plants immediately. If they are allowed to remain, the tubers will be spoiled. After the tops are off, the tubers can be dug anytime within the next few days.

Sweet potatoes can be cooked and eaten immediately after digging but they can be stored for only a short time. Ideally, they should be cured. This prolongs the storage period and also improves the sweetness of the flesh. However, it is difficult for the home gardener to cure tubers well because they should be held for seven to 10 days at high temperature and high humidity (best conditions call for a 29°C/85°F temperature and 90 percent humidity). After curing, the tubers are stored at a temperature of 13°–16°C/55°–60°F in a relatively humid storeroom.

Pests and diseases

Use of plants grown from certified tubers is the best way to protect against diseases.

Southern peas

Southern peas are also known as cowpeas, field peas and table peas. Closely related to beans, they produce long, slender pods crammed with seeds that are shelled and eaten fresh like peas. They are also canned, frozen and dried. The plants are about 2 ft tall and inclined to trail. Some varieties are more compact than others.

Southern peas are, as the name indicates, most widely grown in the South but they can be grown as far north as zone 6. On average, they require about 3 months to mature. Like beans, they require warm weather.

Cultivation

Since southern peas are leguminous plants widely grown simply as a green manure crop, they do not require rich soil. But it should be well drained and contain some humus. Mix in a low-nitrogen fertilizer, such as 5-10-10 before planting. This should carry them through the growing season.

Sow the seeds in the garden after all danger of frost has passed. Sow the seeds $\frac{1}{2}$ in deep, 1–3 in apart in rows 2–3 ft wide. Do not thin the plants.

Water in dry spells. Except for keeping weeds hoed out, the plants require little attention. In fact, southern peas produce more food for less work than most other vegetables.

Harvesting

For eating fresh or for canning and freezing, the peas should be picked while the seeds are still green and have reached the desired size. For drying, leave the pods on the plants until they turn yellow or brown, then store in a cool dry place indoors.

Pests and diseases

The worst pest is the cowpea curculio. To control this, spray with toxaphene when blossoming starts and make twice-weekly applications for the next two weeks. Spray with carbaryl or malathion to control minor insects. If nematodes are present in the soil, fumigate the soil before seed sowing. Use of resistant or tolerant varieties of pea is the best way to avoid trouble from fusarium wilt and mosaic.

Watermelon

A favorite fruit on hot summer days, the watermelon is not a good vegetable for small gardens because it trails across the ground for 6–8 ft in all directions and the fruits are too large and heavy to permit growing on a trellis. If it is to be grown, put it in a sunny corner by itself.

Most favorite varieties—those producing dark green or striped white-and-green fruits up to almost 2 ft long—take too long to develop to be grown north of zone 6. But smaller varieties, such as New Hampshire Midget and Sugar Baby, require a shorter growing season and should succeed even in zone 3.

Cultivation

The soil for watermelons must be fertile and well drained. Mix in large quantities of humus and 10-10-10 fertilizer before planting. Generally, seeds are sown directly in the garden after all danger of frost has passed. For an earlier start and in colder climates, either sow seeds indoors about 4 weeks before they are planted out or sow them in the garden and keep them covered with cloches or polyethylene film. Sow the seeds or set seedlings in hills 8 ft apart and 8 ft from other vegetables. Thin to about two plants per hill.

Feeding and watering Keep the plants well watered and apply a side-dressing of balanced fertilizer or nitrate of soda when the plants start to run. Mulching the soil is advisable to keep out weeds, because these are hard to remove without damaging the vines. If a few large melons are preferred to a greater number of small ones, pick off the excess fruits when they are about 4 in across. Leave three to four fruits only per vine.

Watermelons are ripe enough to harvest when they give off a dull, muffled sound when rapped with the knuckles. When unripe, the sound is more like a metallic ring. Another sign of ripeness is the color of the rind touching the ground. If it is yellow, the fruit is ready; if white, it's not.

Pests and diseases

Watermelons are subject to the same problems that bother muskmelons and squashes, and are protected in the same way.

Peppers

Sweet peppers are in the same family as tomatoes and potatoes. They are grown for their large squarish fruits, which are usually harvested green although they can be left on the plant until they turn red.

Hot peppers (closely related to sweet peppers) produce much smaller fruits of varying shapes. All are green but turn red or yellow.

Cultivation

Peppers need similar growing conditions to tomatoes, although higher temperature and humidity is necessary. They grow in all but the very coldest areas.

Soil and situation Peppers must have well-drained, fertile soil. They need a sunny and sheltered site. They also require large amounts of moisture and the soil should be improved by the incorporation of well-rotted manure or garden compost during spring digging.

In greenhouses, peppers may be grown on the benches or in pots. Small, hot peppers can also be grown in the house on sunny windowsills or under fluorescent light.

Open ground crops should receive a base dressing of 1–2 oz per square yard of a balanced fertilizer at planting and should be fed again about six weeks later. Pot-grown plants require liquid feeding from an earlier stage and need very careful watering.

Plant raising High temperatures are needed to grow pepper plants satisfactorily and, even then, it takes 10–12 weeks from seed sowing until planting. A temperature of 21°C/70°F is needed for seed germination, reducing to 18°C/65°F for the remainder of the plant-raising period. Sow the seed thinly in a starting mixture in a seed tray and cover with a thin layer of the mixture. Water and cover with a sheet of glass and a piece of newspaper. Turn the glass daily to prevent condensation dripping on to the soil.

As soon as the seedlings appear, remove the covering; and when they are large enough to handle, prick them out into individual peat pots or plastic pots containing a good growing soil. Liquid feed to maintain growth. Alternatively, buy plants from a garden center.

Planting Plant peppers 18 in apart each way after the last spring frost. Under glass, plant in 9 in pots and space the pots 18 in apart.

Training Peppers have a bushy habit and are encouraged to branch if the growing point is removed when the plants are about 6 in tall. Support is usually unnecessary except in windy areas.

Harvesting

From August onwards peppers can be harvested. Cut the fruits as required. Green fruits turn red if left on the plant for a further two or three weeks.

Pests and diseases

Spray aphids or red spider mite on sight with a low-persistence insecticide such as derris or malathion.

Diseases are not common on peppers but gray-brown sunken areas may appear on the fruits when the plants have been grown without sufficient water. The sunken areas go soft and may become colonized by gray mold (*Botrytis cinerea*). Always keep peppers well supplied with water, especially in isolated growing systems.

1 Late February. Sow the seed thinly on moistened soil. Cover with $\frac{1}{8}$ in of soil then glass and newspaper. Turn glass daily. Keep at 21°C/70°F until growing well.

2 As soon as the seedlings are large enough to handle prick them singly into peat pots. Feed to maintain growth.

3 When the plants are 6 in tall remove the growing point on each, leaving 3–4 branches. Support the plants with canes if necessary.

4 Throughout the growing season spray aphids or red spider mite on sight with a low-persistence insecticide, such as malathion.

5 August onward. Cut the green fruits as required. Leave the fruits on the plants for a further 2–3 weeks if red fruits are desired.

Eggplants

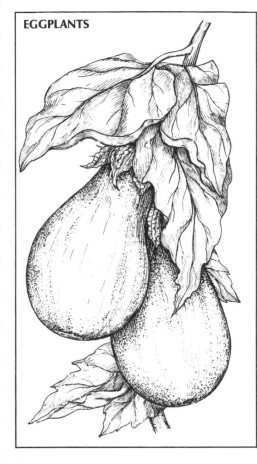

EGGPLANTS

The eggplant is a sub-tropical plant grown for its large egg-shaped fruits which give rise to its common name. The fruits are usually purple, but white-fruited types are also available.

Cultivation

Eggplants have requirements similar to tomatoes and peppers. They grow in zones 4–10. In the South, you can have two crops by sowing seed in early winter for a spring crop and in mid-season for a fall crop.

Soil and situation Eggplants must be grown in well-drained fertile soils and in a sunny, sheltered part of the garden. They should be given 1–2 oz per square yard of a balanced fertilizer before planting and should be fed again about six weeks later. Regular feeding

with a liquid fertilizer after the fruits begin to swell is helpful.

Plant raising The plant raising procedure is similar to that for peppers (see page 80) and, again, high temperatures are necessary. In early March sow the seed thinly in seed trays and keep them at a temperature of 21°C/70°F. Germination is slow and seedling growth also requires high temperatures. Prick out the seedlings into individual peat pots as soon as they can be handled. Maintain the temperature at 18°–21°C/65°–70°F and begin liquid feeding if plant growth slows down. Allow at least 8–10 weeks from seed sowing to planting.

Alternatively, purchase the plants from a grower or garden center.

Planting outside Do not plant eggplants outside until all danger of frost has passed and the soil has begun to warm up. Cover the soil with cloches for 2–3 weeks before planting and then put them back over the small eggplants to encourage establishment. Keep the cloches in place until the plants reach the glass.

Training Remove the growing point of each plant when 9–12 in high to encourage a branched habit. Eggplants are less bushy than peppers and only 3–4 branches should be allowed per plant. Space out and support the branches with string attached to overhead wires or bamboo canes.

Regular feeding and watering is necessary but "little-and-often" is the best policy to avoid the danger of waterlogging or drying out. Fruits develop readily in warm, sunny weather but good-sized eggplants are formed only if the number per plant is restricted to five or six. Remove any other flowers which then appear.

Harvesting

From August onward, cut eggplants with a sharp knife when they reach 6–8 in in length and have turned to a rich purple. Fruits that are only $\frac{1}{3}$ full size are also usable but have less flavor.

Pests and diseases

Aphids can be particularly troublesome on eggplants and the plants must be sprayed with a low-persistence insecticide.

1 Early March. Sow the seed on moistened starting mixture. Cover with $\frac{1}{8}$ in of the mixture, then with glass and newspaper. Keep at 27°C/70°F and turn the glass daily.

2 As soon as they are large enough to handle, prick out the seedlings singly into peat pots. Keep at 18°–21°C/65°–70°F. If growth slows down, water and feed.

3 When all danger of frost has passed, plant eggplants in soil previously warmed with cloches. Water in and replace the cloches until the plants reach the glass.

4 Pinch out the growing points when the plants are 9–12 in high, to encourage the growth of 3–4 strong branches. Support the plants with canes.

5 Remove all but 5–6 developing fruits on each plant, keeping them evenly spaced, and pinch out any extra flowers that form to encourage good-sized fruits.

6 August onward. When the fruits are 6–8 in long and rich purple color, cut them with a sharp knife. Smaller fruits are usable but have less flavor.

Mushrooms

The cultivated mushroom, which is commonly grown by commercial producers, is a close relative of the edible wild mushroom *Agaricus campestris*. The condition, quality and sterility of the compost on which the mushroom fungus is grown hold the key to successful mushroom cultivation, and it is extremely difficult for home gardeners to produce reliably uniform compost. A brief outline of all the stages in mushroom growing is given here, but more certain results are obtained by purchasing the proprietary bags, boxes or tubs of mushroom compost which have already been spawned. These containers must be kept in a suitable place at the recommended temperature and watered carefully to produce mushrooms. Light is not essential for growing mushrooms.

Compost making
Wheat straw from stables is the ideal material from which to prepare mushroom compost. It contains sufficient manure to cause it to ferment, give off ammonia and break down, but the straw must be watered and turned regularly at four or five day intervals. Dry straw can be used but then an artificial activator must also be added to initiate the breakdown processes. The compost may

become greasy, although this can be avoided by mixing at least 1 lb of gypsum with each hundredweight of straw. During composting the straw should change into a dark brown friable material without any smell of ammonia. The compost should be open textured and spongy, but hold only a little water rather than be waterlogged.

Commercial composting takes nearly two weeks and is followed by a week of peak heating when the compost is kept at a high temperature (60°C/140°F), to ensure that straw breakdown is complete and all harmful micro-organisms are killed. The home gardener can seldom peak heat this material, so must continue the composting process until the compost has the correct color, consistency and smell. It may take 3–4 weeks.

Spawning
The compost is then put into boxes, buckets or bags prior to spawning. Do not spawn the compost until the temperature in the middle of the container has fallen below 24°C/75°F. The propagation material for mushrooms is cereal grains or manure on which the fungus has been grown. The grains or manure are covered with a whitish fungal growth and are called "spawn". Put 9–12 in of compost

in the container and lightly firm it. Break manure spawn into golf-ball sized pieces and push them 1 in down into the compost at 10–12 in spacings each way. Sprinkle grain spawn on to the compost surface and mix it into the top 2 in. Keep the containers in a warm, dark place until the mushroom fungus begins to grow ("run"). This takes 7–10 days.

Casing
Mushrooms are produced directly on the compost surface but a covering layer (casing) is usually put on to the compost when spawn running has begun. The casing retains moisture and prevents the compost surface drying out; it also helps to supply water evenly to the developing mushrooms. A mixture of equal parts peat and lump calcium carbonate is the best casing material, and it should be thoroughly moistened before application. Put a 2 in layer over the compost.

Growing
Keep the containers at 16°–18°C/60°–65°F in a reasonably humid atmosphere. Very dry conditions cause the compost and casing to dry out, whereas prolonged dampness causes the fungus and developing mushrooms to

rot. Water carefully, giving small quantities at regular intervals rather than heavy doses irregularly. The first pin-head mushrooms should appear about three weeks after casing but it takes another 7–10 days before they are ready to harvest. At lower temperatures the mushrooms grow and fruit more slowly. After the first flush of mushrooms has been harvested there is a delay of 1–2 weeks before the next flush appears. Each crop of mushrooms produces several flushes over a 6–8 week period.

Harvesting
Twist the mushrooms off when they have reached the required stage of development. Tightly rounded button mushrooms are popular today, but the open "flats"—similar to those found in the wild during early autumn—have much more flavor. Use a sharp knife to trim off the surface of the cropping bed to remove all broken stalks and debris. Fill in any holes left from harvesting with additional casing material. After the final flush of mushrooms has been picked the compost should be emptied out and used as an organic manure in the garden. Never re-use mushroom compost because it is likely to contain harmful pests and diseases.

MUSHROOMS AT DIFFERENT STAGES OF DEVELOPMENT

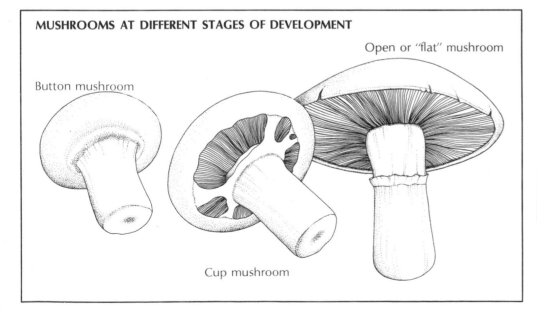

Button mushroom

Cup mushroom

Open or "flat" mushroom

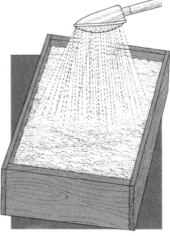

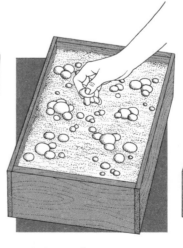

1 Water mushrooms regularly but lightly. Use the fine nozzle of a watering can to apply water.

2 Twist mushrooms away from the surface of the bed and remove any broken or damaged stalks.

3 Re-fill the holes left by removed mushrooms with casing material to ensure longer productivity.

Okra

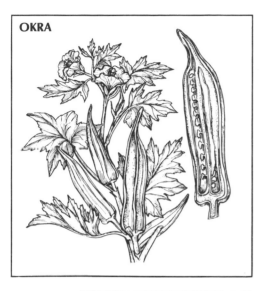

OKRA

Okra, also known as gumbo, is closely related to the garden *Hibiscus* and is grown for its long, green, finger-shaped, edible pods.

Cultivation

Okra is naturally a tropical plant, and so it grows best in the South. But it can be grown successfully as far north as zone 3 if smaller, more rapidly maturing varieties are used.

Soil and situation Okra needs a rich, loamy soil and a sunny site sheltered from wind. If necessary, improve the soil by incorporating well-rotted manure during winter digging. Crops require regular watering during the growing season.

Plant raising Fairly high temperatures are necessary to grow okra satisfactorily. A temperature of 18°–21°C/65°–70°F is necessary for seed germination and the remainder of the plant-raising period. Sow the seed thinly in the garden after all danger of frost has passed. In the South, successive sowings at monthly intervals can be made up to the middle of June. Germination is hurried by soaking the seed in water for 24 hours before sowing. Sow seeds 1 in apart in drills 24–30 in apart and thin plants to 1 ft.

The soil should have a pH of 6.0 or slightly higher. Dig in plenty of humus and 2 cups of balanced fertilizer, such as 10-20-10 or 6-12-6, for each 50 sq ft. Later, when fruit set begins, sidedress with nitrate of soda or balanced fertilizer, and make a second application of fertilizer when plant growth starts to slow down.

In windy locations, plants may require staking. Use 4 ft canes, one to a plant, and tie plants to them with soft string. Alternatively, stretch netting between posts beside the plants and tie them in as they grow.

Harvesting

The pods are ready for harvesting when they are young and tender (about 3 in long) and the seeds are still soft. Pick them from August every day or two to maintain production until frost. Do not allow the pods to mature because old pods are unpalatable.

Many gardeners remove the terminal buds on the plants after picking the first pods. This forces development of new side growth and a larger supply of pods.

Pests and diseases

Dust or spray with carbaryl at the first sign of corn earthworms and apply at 10-day intervals thereafter. This should also control brown leaf beetles (although these do no serious harm). To prevent repeated attack by fusarium and nematodes, plant okra in a different area of the garden each year.

1 After the danger of frost has passed, sow seed 1 in apart in drills 24–30 in apart. Sow in rich, loamy soil on a very sunny site. Okra needs a temperature of 18°–21°C/ 65°–70 F for germination.

2 Thin the plants to 1 ft apart when they are large enough to handle.

3 In windy locations, stake the plants. When fruits begin to set, side-dress with nitrate of soda or balanced fertilizer.

4 Harvest the pods when they are young and tender and about 3 in long. Pick them regularly from August until the first frost. Do not allow the fruits to mature as they are unpalatable when older.

Florence fennel

Florence fennel (also called finocchio or fennel) is grown for its bulb-like swollen leaf bases which taste of anise. The green-white "bulbs" can be sliced and used raw in salads or they can be cooked whole in boiling water and served with a white or cheese sauce.

The feathery leaves can be used for flavoring as a substitute for *Foeniculum vulgare* or common fennel (see page 90), of which Florence fennel is a subspecies.

Sowing indoors

1 April. Sow seed thinly in a seed tray and keep at a temperature of 16°C/60°F.

Blanching

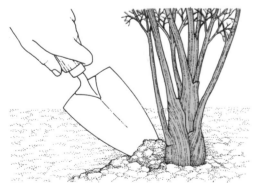

4 When the plant bases have swollen to the size of a golf ball blanch by drawing up soil around the lower parts of each stem. Continue hilling up for 4 weeks.

Cultivation

Florence fennel is grown widely in Italy because it thrives in the warm Mediterranean climate, but it is possible to grow the plant in cool temperate regions. Careful plant raising is required, however, and good-sized basal stems are produced only in warm, sunny summers. Florence fennel thrives best when given plenty of water. If it is not watered in dry weather, the stems will not be bulbous.

Pricking out

2 As soon as they can be handled prick the seedlings out singly into individual peat pots. Keep at 13°C/55°F, well-ventilated, and in good light.

5 Alternatively, blanch Florence fennel by tying cardboard collars around the base of each plant.

Soil and situation The plant grows best in well-drained, warm soils which permit early sowing or planting. Well-rotted manure or compost should be incorporated during winter digging to retain moisture and encourage the leaf bases to swell. They must swell with no obstructions, so avoid stony soils. Heavy clay soils are not suitable for this vegetable. The leaf bases are blanched at the end of the season by drawing soil up around

Transplanting

3 Four weeks later. Rake in 1–2 oz per square yard of fertilizer and transplant the seedlings at 9–12 in intervals in rows 18 in apart. Hoe and water regularly.

Harvesting

6 July onward. Four weeks after the start of blanching, when the basal stems are the size of a tennis ball, but beneath them with a sharp knife.

them and the soil must be easily cultivated for this purpose. Rapid growth is encouraged by incorporating 1–2 oz per square yard of a balanced general fertilizer before sowing or planting.

Sowing Florence fennel can be sown directly outside after last frost, although germination and growth can be slow. Use ½ in deep drills which are 18 in apart. Sow thinly and thin the seedlings to 9–12 in apart as soon as possible. Do not sow too early because the plants run immediately to flower if there is too much cold weather at the seedling stage.

Alternatively, the plants can be transplanted after sowing indoors. Sow the seed thinly in a seed tray and germinate at a temperature of 16°C/60°F. Prick the seedlings out into small, individual peat pots as soon as they can be handled. Reduce the temperature to 13°C/55°F and grow in good light with plenty of ventilation in order to produce strong, sturdy plants.

The plants should be ready for transplanting in about five weeks. Plant them at 9–12 in intervals in rows 18 in apart.

Blanching

Hoe the plants carefully to keep down weeds and keep them well watered at all times. Plants grown in dry conditions do not produce good-sized "bulbs." When the leaf bases begin to swell it is time to blanch them. Draw soil around the small bulbs when they reach the size of a golf-ball and continue the process through the summer until the Florence fennel is ready to be harvested.

Florence fennel can also be blanched by tying cardboard collars around the bases of individual plants.

Harvesting

Harvesting can begin about four weeks from the start of hilling up, by which time the "bulbs" should be slightly larger than a tennis ball. Also at this time the plants would have blanched. Harvest the entire leaf bases by cutting beneath them with a sharp knife.

Pests and diseases

Florence fennel is generally free of pest and disease trouble but it may be necessary to take precautions against slugs (see page 17).

Hamburg parsley/Horseradish

Hamburg parsley is in the carrot and parsnip family and it is a valuable, if neglected, winter vegetable. It has parsley-flavored leaves and parsnip-like roots which have a mild flavor of celery.

Cultivation

It is a hardy plant and must be sown early in the year so that it can become established and develop good-sized roots.

Sowing Sow the seed in $\frac{1}{2}$ in deep drills that are 12 in apart as early in the year as soil and weather conditions allow. Germination is slow and it is important to keep down weeds during the seedling stages. Hoe carefully around rhe plants, taking care not to damage the developing tap roots.

Thin the seedlings to 9 in apart as soon as they are large enough to handle. Water generously throughout the summer and top-dress with a nitrogenous fertilizer at 1–2 oz per square yard to maintain adequate growth.

As with celeriac, the roots continue to grow well into fall and the largest roots come from the longest growing season.

Harvesting

Lift the roots as soon as they are needed from mid-fall onward. They are frost hardy but should be heavily mulched with straw from zone 6 northward. If the roots are dug in the fall, store them in sand in a cool well-ventilated basement.

Horseradish

Horseradish is a naturally occurring perennial weed which grows in moderate climates and produces a tap root rather like a white carrot. The leaves are of no value—in fact they contain slightly poisonous compounds —but the roots are peeled and chopped for making horseradish sauce.

Cultivation

The plants grow on any type of soil with reasonable drainage, but larger roots are produced on fertile, well-drained soils. Horseradish is difficult to eradicate once it has become established because it regenerates readily from bits of root left in the soil, so that it could develop from a crop into a weed.

Planting Remove pencil-thickness roots from established plants in the fall and cut them into 6–8 in lengths. Store in sand or peat until sprouts appear in March. Make holes with a dibble at an angle of 45 degrees and plant the root-cuttings with the thickest ends uppermost. Cover with 3 in of soil, firm them in, and water if necessary. They soon begin to grow and, if competing weeds are controlled, produce lush vegetative growth which gives rise to large, fleshy roots the following fall. Cut down the foliage in the fall and lift all the roots. Keep enough pencil-thickness roots to act as propagation material for next year. The remaining roots can be stored for use as needed but they produce the best horseradish sauce if grated at once.

Hamburg parsley

1 April. Sow the seed in $\frac{1}{2}$ in deep drills which are 12 in apart. Keep down weeds by hoeing very carefully.

2 As soon as the seedlings are large enough to handle, thin them until they are 9 in apart.

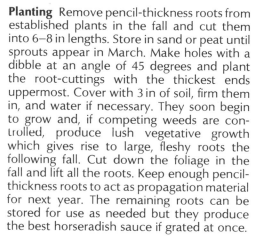

3 Throughout summer. Water the plants generously. Top-dress with 1–2 oz per square yard of a nitrogenous fertilizer.

4 Late September onward. Lift the roots as required. Cover any remaining in the ground with straw for protection against frost.

Horseradish

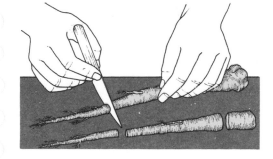

1 Autumn. Remove pencil-thickness roots from established plants and cut them into 6–8 in lengths.

2 March. With the thick ends uppermost, plant the roots at an angle of 45° in dibble-made holes.

3 Then firm them and water. Throughout summer continue to water regularly and hoe weeds.

4 October. Cut down the foliage and lift all the roots for immediate use or storing in sand in a frost-free place.

WATERCRESS
Green- or bronze-leaved. No named varieties available.

LAND CRESS
No named varieties available.

Watercress and land cress 1

Watercress is rich in iron and the plant is native to the U.S., where it grows wild in streams and ditches. The leaves, which are eaten raw, have a mustard-like flavor. Land cress, sometimes called peppergrass, has similar leaves to watercress and can be used for the same purposes. Both plants are generally free of pest and disease problems.

Watercress

Constantly running water provides the best environment for watercress. It is very important that the water is clean and uncontaminated, otherwise the leaves may cause digestive upsets when eaten. The plants can be grown without running water if they are grown in a constantly damp place.

Although watercress is completely hardy cover the plants with glass cloches or polyethylene tunnels in the winter to ensure new growth and the leaves can be harvested.

Propagation

Watercress is easily propagated from cuttings. Take healthy shoots from a purchased bunch and stand them in a glass of water.

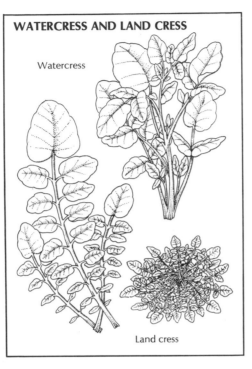

WATERCRESS AND LAND CRESS

Watercress

Land cress

Within a week or so roots will appear and the rooted cuttings can be planted in the stream or in a damp part of the garden. You can also sow seed into the chosen wet place any time during the summer. Or you can sow seed indoors or outdoors in a mixture of equal amounts of soil and peat. Keep the mixture wet until the seedlings are big enough to be transplanted.

Planting Plant the cuttings at 6 in intervals in the banks of a stream. Plant them firmly so that they are not washed away. April is the ideal time to plant, when growth should be rapid, and harvesting can begin within several months.

Not everyone is fortunate enough to have a stream in the garden but watercress can also be grown in a shaded, damp area. Dig a 24 in wide trench, 12 in deep. Put a 6 in layer of moisture-holding organic matter, such as farmyard manure or well-rotted garden compost or peat, in the bottom. Cover it with 3–4 in of soil and plant the rooted currings in April. Keep the area well watered at all times. Growth should be rapid and the plants should be clipped back to maintain a bushy habit.

Harvesting

Never allow watercress to flower because this reduces vegetative growth. Cut off flower stems as soon as they develop. Remove leaves as required but do not harvest too many leaves in the first year.

Land cress

Land or American cress grows in the absence of running water although it must have damp conditions. The plant is biennial but is grown as an annual. Land cress can be protected with cloches in the fall and winter so that harvesting can continue.

Sow the seed thinly from March onward in $\frac{1}{2}$ in deep drills which are 12 in apart. Thin the plants to 6 in apart as soon as possible. Successive sowings should be made during the summer and into the fall. Germination takes about three weeks in the spring but about half that time in midsummer. Harvesting should begin about a month after sowing. Cloche protection prolongs cropping.

Harvesting

Pick leaves from the plants as needed.

Watercress

1 March. Take healthy shoots from a bunch of watercress. Stand them in a glass of water for a week, or until roots appear.

Planting in a stream

2 April. Plant the rooted cuttings at 6 in intervals on the banks of a clean stream. Firm them in well.

Planting in a damp trench

April. Dig a trench 24 in wide and 12 in deep and place a 6 in layer of well-rotted compost in the bottom.

Then put 3–4 in of soil on top of the compost and plant the rooted cuttings 6 in apart.

Watercress and land cress 2

LAND CRESS

1 March to mid-September. Thinly sow successive batches of seed in $\frac{1}{2}$ in deep drills which are 12 in apart.

2 Three weeks later ($1\frac{1}{2}$ weeks in mid-summer) thin the seedlings to 6 in apart. Water well and often.

3 Late May onward (45 days after sowing). Pick leaves from the plants as required.

4 October onward. Cover the rows with cloches for protection against frost and to ensure further harvesting.

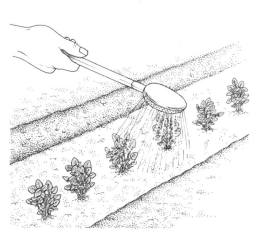

4 Keep the trench well watered throughout the growing season.

5 Clip back the plants to encourage a bushy habit, remove any flowering stems that develop.

6 September onward. Cut watercress leaves as required, but do not cut too many in the first year.

7 October onward. Cover watercress with cloches for frost protection and to ensure further harvesting.

Mustard and cress/Corn salad

Mustard and cress seedlings are used as garnishes for salads or as sandwich fillings. They are easy to grow on blotting paper or on kitchen tissue which is kept in shallow plastic dishes on the kitchen windowsill. Although the mixture is always referred to as "mustard and cress," the mustard is usually replaced by rape, which grows more evenly, is greener, and has a better flavor.

Growing
A minimum temperature of 10°C/50°F is needed for year round production so the kitchen windowsill is an ideal site. Put a layer of kitchen tissue on the bottom of a shallow plastic dish and thoroughly moisten it before broadcasting cress seed thickly and evenly over the surface. Cress seedlings are ready to eat two or three weeks after sowing, and take about 3–4 days longer to reach this stage than mustard or rape. Sow a similarly prepared dish with mustard or rape seed 3–4 days after sowing the cress.

Keep the dishes in a warm, dark place, such as an airing cupboard, until germination has occurred. Then move them on to the kitchen windowsill. Always keep the tissue watered and turn the dishes round each day so that the seedlings do not always grow the same way toward the light. Sow at weekly or two week intervals to produce mustard and cress throughout the year.

Harvesting
Cut the seedlings with scissors when they are about 2 in tall.

Pests and diseases
Mustard and cress are generally free of pests and disease troubles.

Mustard
Mustard is a brassica that forms loose heads of large, generally curled leaves that are boiled and eaten as greens. They are rich in vitamins, and can be grown in all zones.

Cultivation
Mustard likes cool weather. For a spring crop it can be sown in the garden as much as four weeks before the mean date of the last freeze. This can be followed by one or two succession sowings. For fall use, make one or two sowings, starting about two months before the first autumn freeze. The plants mature within about 45 days, and one variety, Tendergreen, can be harvested in 35 days.

The soil can be of average quality and well drained. Sow seeds in rows 1 ft apart and thin the seedlings to 6–10 in apart. Keep well watered to maintain speedy growth.

Harvest the crop while the leaves are young and tender. Take care not to let plants go to seed; otherwise the garden will be full of mustard the following year.

Corn salad
Corn salad (lamb's lettuce) is a hardy annual. The gray-green leaves of cultivated varieties can be cooked or used in salads.

Cultivation
Corn salad needs a fertile, well-drained soil. Plants benefit from a base dressing of 1–2 oz per square yard of a balanced fertilizer.

Sowing Sow in ½ in deep drills 9 in apart. Thin the seedlings to 4–6 in apart as soon as they can be handled. Alternatively, several rows can be sown 4–6 in apart so that they can be covered with glass cloches or polyethylene tunnels during late fall and winter. The first sowing can be made as soon as the soil can be worked in the spring. This is followed by one or two further sowings at 2-week intervals. For an extra-early spring crop sow seeds in later summer or early fall about 21 days before the first fall freeze. Mulch with salt hay during winter, or cover with glass.

Carefully remove weeds as soon as they can be handled. Water the plants copiously to encourage soft, plentiful growth.

Pick off the leaves as needed, but be careful not to weaken the plants too much.

Mustard and cress

1 At weekly intervals throughout the year broadcast cress seed on moistened tissue in a shallow dish. Three or four days later sow mustard or rape seed in the same way.

2 Keep the dishes in a warm, dark place until germination. Then place on a kitchen windowsill or any place with a temperature of 10°C/50°F.

3 Keep the tissue well watered and turn the dishes round daily. Cut the seedlings with scissors when they are 2 in tall, about 2–3 weeks after sowing.

Winter corn salad

1 September. Sow the seed thinly in ½ in deep drills 9 in apart.

2 Thin the seedlings to 4–6 in apart. Remove competing weeds, and water in dry spells. From late October onward give cloche protection against frost or cover with salt hay.

Harvesting

3 Winter to early spring. Pick the leaves as required, but never remove more than 2–3 leaves at a time from each plant.

Herbs 1

Most herbs are easy to grow and a selection of culinary types provides a variety of flavors to complement home-grown vegetables and enhance the flavor of everyday food. Many of them are perennial plants with invasive habits. Clean up the herb garden each spring to prevent the stronger plants from taking over, and weed it regularly by hand. Once every three or four years replant herbs using fresh stock. It is a good idea to site the herb patch as near to the kitchen as possible. Some of the herbs described on these pages also grow well in containers, provided they have good drainage.

PROPAGATING HERBS

Heel cuttings

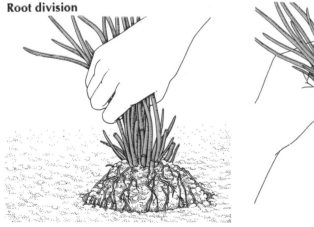

1 Strip away a young side-shoot from its parent stem so that a heel, which is a thin sliver of bark and wood, also comes away at its base.

2 Trim the tail on the heel and any leaves near it. Dip the heel cutting in rooting hormone and plant immediately, preferably in a cold frame.

Root division

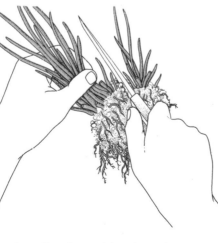

1 Lift the parent plant to be divided towards the end of the dormant season. Shake off the soil and wash the crown.

2 Cut off a piece with at least 1 developed bud. Dust the cut surfaces with fungicidal powder and replant.

Angelica (*Angelica archangelica*)

Angelica is a decorative biennial or mono-carpic herb, which can sometimes be maintained as a perennial by the prevention of seeding. It is a tall plant and can reach a height of 6 ft. It has large, indented leaves and yellow-green flowerheads which appear in late summer.

Cultivation Angelica grows best in a rich, moist but well-drained soil. It grows in semi-shade or in an open position and it is quite hardy. Angelica is best grown from seed; it can be propagated by division but this often encourages flowering. In late summer (August to September) sow the seed outside, with a cloche over the drill in cold areas. In the following March transplant the seedlings, keeping them 12 in apart. Spring sowings are also possible. Angelica needs to be kept weed-free. Remove flowerheads to maintain growth because if angelica is allowed to seed the plants die. It can be grown in a container although its height is a drawback.

Harvesting Angelica is grown for its stems which should be cut before flowering. They are candied and used for cake decoration.

Basil (*Ocimum basilicum*)

Basil is a tender plant easily killed by frost when it is grown outdoors.

Cultivation Basil should be grown in well-drained soil which has been enriched with a liberal dressing of well-rotted organic manure. The site should be warm, sheltered and sunny. The best way of plant raising is to sow the seed in a heated greenhouse during March. Keep them at a temperature of at least 16°C/60°F; the seeds germinate quite slowly. Prick off the seedlings into small, individual peat pots and maintain the temperature at 13°–16°C/55°–60°F. Harden off the plants prior to planting in early June. Space the plants 9–12 in apart each way. Do not plant out earlier because the slightest hint of frost kills basil.

Alternatively, the seed can be sown directly outside in late May. The developing seedlings should be thinned to 9–12 in apart in each direction.

Water regularly during the season and remove flower stalks as soon as they appear, to prolong vegetative growth.

Basil is killed by the first frost but plants can be lifted in September and potted into 5 in pots with a rich potting compost. Cut the plants back hard to within 2–3 in of the base, and take them indoors. Re-growth then occurs to provide young leaves for use in autumn and winter.

Harvesting Pick the leaves as required throughout the summer.

Herbs 2

Borage (*Borago officinalis*)

Chives (*Allium schoenoprasum*)

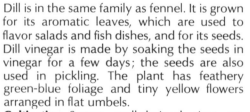

Dill (*Anethum graveolens*)

Fennel (*Foeniculum vulgare*)

This hardy annual plant grows very readily in cool, temperate climates and has a number of culinary uses. The young leaves taste of cucumber and can be added to salads or used to flavor cool summer punches. The plants have bright blue flowers, which appear from May onwards, and hairy stems and leaves. Borage grows to a height of 3 ft very quickly.

Cultivation Borage tolerates almost any site and soil although the most rapid growth occurs in fertile soils and warm, sheltered sites. Sow the seed outside in February and, as soon as they are large enough, thin the seedlings to 12 in apart in each direction.

Seeds are shed on to the ground by the plants and these germinate in the summer or the following spring.

Harvesting Pick fresh, young leaves as required. The flowers can be used to garnish salads.

This hardy perennial herb is one of the smallest and most delicately flavored members of the onion family. Chives do not have bulbs like onions but are grown for their narrow grasslike leaves which are chopped and used in savoury dishes, soups and salads.

Cultivation Chives grow well in a rich, slightly alkaline soil. They flourish in full sun but tolerate semi-shade. In March or June take out a $\frac{1}{2}$ in deep drill and sow the seeds. When the seedlings are large enough to handle, thin them out until they are about 6 in apart. Do not cut any of the leaves during the early stages of growth. Later, cut off any flowers and, to ensure a continual supply of leaves throughout the summer, cut back the leaves to 2–3 in several times during the growing season. Water chives regularly and give them a little fertilizer in October and March. The clumps should be divided every two or three years and replanted 6 in apart. They can also be grown indoors in pots.

Harvesting Cut off the leaves with sharp scissors above soil level as required.

Dill is in the same family as fennel. It is grown for its aromatic leaves, which are used to flavor salads and fish dishes, and for its seeds. Dill vinegar is made by soaking the seeds in vinegar for a few days; the seeds are also used in pickling. The plant has feathery green-blue foliage and tiny yellow flowers arranged in flat umbels.

Cultivation Sunny, well-drained sites are ideal but the plants must never be short of water or the growth becomes weak and straggly. Sow dill directly into the permanent bed because the plants do not tolerate disturbance. Sow successively from April to June for a continual supply of young leaves to harvest.

Thin the seedlings to 12 in apart as soon as possible. Seeds which fall on to the soil germinate in the next season and produce large numbers of self-sown seedlings.

Harvesting Pick fresh leaves as required when the plants are 8 in tall. Harvest the seeds at the end of the season when they are dark brown in color and the plants have turned purplish-brown. The young leaves can be cut and dried for winter use.

Fennel is an attractive perennial herb which can grow to 6 ft or more in height. It has feathery, blue-tinged foliage and yellow flowers and it is grown for its young shoots and seeds which can be used in sweet and savoury dishes. Fennel can be grown in pots or as a border plant.

Cultivation Fennel tolerates a variety of conditions but it grows best in a moist, well-drained and slightly acid soil. It needs full sun but it is quite hardy in winter. In February sow the seed in a $\frac{1}{2}$ in deep drill. Thin the seedlings to 12–15 in apart or remove all but the strongest if only one plant is required. Keep the plants weed-free.

Established fennel can be propagated by division. Divide or raise fennel from seed every three or four years to keep vigorous young stock.

Harvesting Pick fresh leaves regularly throughout the summer to maintain a constant supply. Allow the seeds to ripen fully and dry on the stem. In autumn, shake them off the stem and store in a warm, dry place.

Herbs 3

Tarragon (*Artemisia dracunculus*)

Marjoram (*Origanum majorana*)

Mint (*Mentha spicata*)

Parsley (*Petroselinum crispum*)

Tarragon is a perennial shrub which can grow to a height of 3 ft and it spreads, as does mint, by underground runners. Tarragon has widely-spaced leaves and clusters of white flowers.

Cultivation Tarragon grows well in poor soil but it must be well-drained. It should be grown in full sun. It is very seldom grown from seed and plants are usually acquired by root division, or less often from cuttings. Plant in spring when there is no longer any danger of frost. Leave a distance of 24 in between plants if more than one is being grown. Keep tarragon weed-free.

Renew tarragon every three or four years by lifting and replanting a few of the vigorous runners. Discard the older portions of the plant. Tarragon can be grown in suitably large containers.

Harvesting Cut the young leaves as needed in July. They may still be suitable in October. Cut the leaves for drying in June to July.

Sweet marjoram is a half-hardy annual. It is grown from seed each year although some forms are perennial. Pot marjoram (*Origanum onites*) is a hardy dwarf shrub which, as the name suggests, can be grown indoors in pots when it will continue to produce leaves for use during the winter.

Cultivation Sweet marjoram can be sown out of doors in mid-May in a warm, sunny site. Thin the plants to 12 in apart each way as soon as they can be handled. Alternatively, sow the seed in seed trays or pans under glass at a temperature of 16°C/60°F in early April. Prick out the seedlings into small individual peat pots and gradually harden off the plants before planting them outside in late May, when the danger of frost is over. Water the plants generously and keep down the weeds, especially in the early stages.

Pot marjoram (*Origanum onites*) is best propagated from heel cuttings taken in May or June. Otherwise, divide established plants in March and pot the plants. Keep them on the patio in summer and take them indoors in winter. Pot marjoram is deciduous and likely to lose its leaves if left outside in the cold months. Cut the plants back hard in March; new growth then appears from the base.

Harvesting Sweet marjoram can be used fresh, or the leaves can be removed and dried for winter use. Cut the shoots when they are about 8 in tall.

Common mint or spearmint (*M. spicata*) is the most popular kind of this hardy perennial herb. Apple or Bowles' mint (*M. × villosa alopecuroides*) is also common and it is considered by some people to have a more subtle and therefore preferable flavor.

Cultivation Mint grows anywhere if the soil is well dug and moist. It does equally well in a sunny or semi-shaded position. Since it is such an invasive plant underground it is advisable to restrict the roots by planting in a bottomless container sunk into the ground. Keep mint free of weeds and pinch out the flower buds when they appear to encourage maximum leaf-growth. Divide the roots each March and replant if possible in a fresh position. Otherwise, incorporate well-rotted compost or manure and a handful of bone-meal into the soil.

Mint is readily grown in pots or containers but should be kept clipped to maintain vigorous young growth.

Harvesting Pick fresh young leaves as required from May until the autumn. If dried leaves are required gather these before the plants begin to flower.

Pests and diseases If mint is attacked by the rust (*Puccinia menthae*), dig up all the roots and burn them. It is best to acquire new stock from a healthy source.

Parsley is a biennial plant which is best grown as an annual, although it will over-winter successfully and provide leaves for winter use if cloched. There are several varieties available, some with flat leaves, but the curly-leaved variety is most often grown.

Cultivation A rich, slightly alkaline, soil is ideal for parsley but poorer soils can be used if they are enriched with some well-rotted compost. Moisture is very important for successful parsley growing, and the plant grows best in a semi-shaded position. If parsley is grown in a sunny place it needs to be watered regularly.

The seed is sown in March. Germination, which is sometimes erratic, may take 6–8 weeks outdoors. This process can be speeded up by sowing the seed indoors in pots. When the seedlings are large enough to handle thin them out until they are 4 in apart. Weed regularly by hand when the seedlings are small and apply a liquid feed occasionally to increase leaf production. In the second year cut off the flower stalks to delay the plants' production of seed.

Throughout the winter parsley can be grown indoors, or in the greenhouse, in suitable containers for continual harvesting.

Harvesting Pick parsley fresh as required.

Pests and diseases Seedlings can be attacked by carrot fly. Before sowing sprinkle bromo-phos in the seed drill as a deterrent.

Rosemary (*Rosmarinus officinalis*)   **Sage** (*Salvia officinalis*)   **Sweet bay** (*Laurus nobilis*)   **Thyme** (*Thymus vulgaris*)

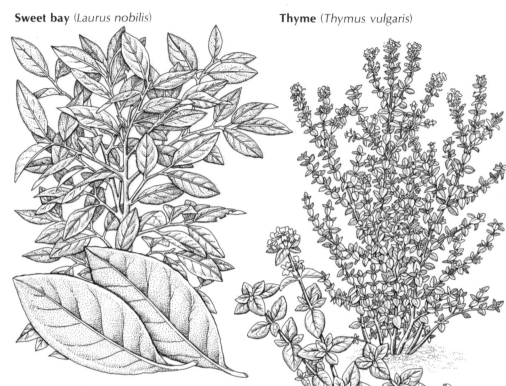

Rosemary is a perennial shrub which is very attractive when in flower. The leaves are needle-shaped and gray-green in color and the flowers, which appear from March to September, are pale to deep blue.

Cultivation Rosemary grows in any well-drained soil. It does best in a sunny sheltered spot although it may be grown in partial shade. Rosemary can be grown from seed sown in May and June but because seed is difficult to obtain and germination can be very slow, it is best to grow it from heel cuttings taken in early summer. Prune rosemary regularly to prevent straggly growth and to encourage a bushy habit.

Rosemary does well as a pot plant but it should be kept indoors during the coldest part of the winter.

Harvesting Pick fresh leaves and flowers as required but cut shoots for drying in the summer months only.

Sage is a small evergreen shrub 1½–2 ft high. The species most commonly grown, *Salvia officinalis*, may be grown from seed or propagated from heel cuttings.

Cultivation Sage tolerates any well-drained soil but grows best on a chalky loam. It requires a sheltered site in full sun. Sage shrubs grow well in any kind of container. Sow the seed under glass in March. Plant out the seedlings 12–15 in apart when there is no longer any danger of frost. Keep them weed-free and trim regularly when they are fully grown. Cut sage back lightly after flowering is over in July. Renew the shrubs every three or four years.

Harvesting Pick the leaves as required; they are best just before flowering. Cut leaves for drying in the active growing season.

Sweet bay is an attractive evergreen tree grown for its aromatic leaves. It can be grown in containers or in open soil. In some parts of the world it reaches a height of up to 50 ft.

Cultivation Sweet bay grows best in a dryish, well-drained soil which may be acid or alkaline. It grows well in full sun but a sheltered site is preferable because in severe winters the foliage, and occasionally the shoots, may be damaged. Buy a young, well-established tree from a nursery or propagate in late summer or early autumn (August to September) from cuttings of ripe shoots. Protect young trees in harsh weather to prevent the leaves turning brown. Sweet bay grows well in containers and makes a good ornamental tree because it can be clipped into shape and growth is restricted by the pot.

Place pot-grown trees indoors or in a frost-free shed during the winter months.

Harvesting Pick the young leaves as required and dry them slowly in the dark to make sure the color is retained.

Common culinary thyme is a small perennial bush about 10 in high. It has a beautiful scent and is a useful bee-plant.

Cultivation Thyme prefers a light, well-drained, neutral soil. Common thyme grows best in full sun although it is hardy. However, various other thymes grown mainly for ornament may require some winter protection.

Seed sown outdoors in March germinates fairly readily and the resulting seedlings should be thinned until they are about 12 in apart. Keep the thyme patch weed-free and trim the plants after flowering to encourage compact growth.

The plants should be renewed every three or four years. Propagate thyme by root division or heel cuttings. Common thyme grows well in containers.

Harvesting Pick the leaves for drying or immediate use before the plants flower.

Climate zones

The most important aspects of climate the gardener must consider when planning a new garden are temperature, rainfall and wind. Of these, temperature is the most crucial. Food plants can survive drought conditions and gales but they may fail to produce crops or even be killed by untimely low or high temperatures.

Broad climatic divisions are a useful basis for judging the general viability of a specific crop but local conditions must also be carefully considered.

Zones of hardiness

The map of hardiness in North America (right) was devised by the United States Department of Agriculture. It defines zones of consistent average, annual, minimum temperatures.

Throughout this book, the information on individual plants includes the zones in which they are hardy or half-hardy.

The zone map shows the expected minimum temperatures in most of the horticulturally important areas of the United States (excluding Alaska and Hawaii) and Canada. The ten hardiness zones are appropriate for general reference. Most seed and fruit plant catalogs will refer to the various zones by number when describing the hardiness and adaptability of the plants they offer, or proper planting dates for various crops. The minimum winter temperature in your zone will influence how much gardening you can expect to do in the colder months, and how much protection will be required if you expect to have vegetables during the winter.

Too high a temperature can stop plants from growing, but in the North it is only in greenhouses that this is likely to be a problem. Outdoors, plants which wilt during the day, because they give off more moisture through the leaves than they can take up through the roots, will revive at night. Tomatoes and potatoes, for example, prefer a cooler temperature at night than in the daytime and strawberries develop their best flavor in temperatures of about 10°C/50°F.

The most obvious way of mitigating the cold is to grow crops under glass—greenhouses, frames or cloches. But even in heated greenhouses, winter growth will be slow.

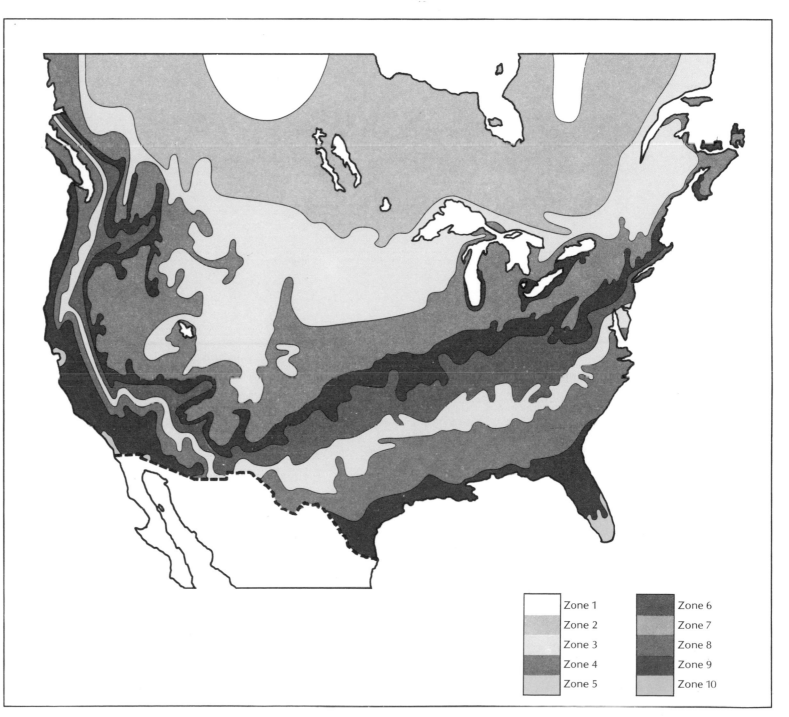

Zone 1	Zone 6
Zone 2	Zone 7
Zone 3	Zone 8
Zone 4	Zone 9
Zone 5	Zone 10

Month-by-month guide 1

This calendar is applicable to gardeners in Zone 6, where the mean date of the last spring freeze falls approximately on April 20 and the mean date of the first fall freeze is approximately October 20. (For the actual dates of the last and first freezes in your area, write to your state agricultural extension service or the US Weather Bureau.) The freeze dates determine when to plant vegetables outdoors.

In colder climate zones, plant later and harvest earlier than this calendar indicates. In warmer zones, plant earlier and harvest later. For example, in the coldest parts of Zone 3, the mean date of the last spring freeze is June 10 and of the first fall freeze, September 10. By contrast, in southernmost Florida, killing frosts are unknown, so planting just about the year round is possible.

Only the more important crops are dealt with in this month-by-month guide. For full details of cultivation, see under the specific vegetables.

JANUARY
Harvesting
Indoors Force witloof chicory and rhubarb.
Routine tasks
Plan the vegetable garden and order seeds from catalogs. Lime garden.
Check vegetables in storage.

FEBRUARY
Sowing
Indoors Sow celery seeds for early crop.
Routine tasks
Start cleaning up trash in garden.
Apply lime.
Clean seed-starting flats.
Turn over and fertilize soil in coldframe.
Harvesting
Indoors Force witloof chicory and rhubarb.
Harvest lettuce raised indoors from seed sown in fall.

MARCH
Sowing
Indoors Sow seeds of broccoli, early cabbage, cauliflower, eggplant, lettuce, parsley, peppers, tomatoes.
Routine tasks
Finish garden clean-up. Apply lime.

Harvesting
Indoors Force witloof chicory and rhubarb. Harvest lettuce grown indoors.

APRIL
Sowing
Indoors Sow seeds of cucumbers.
Coldframe Sow seeds of cucumbers.
Outdoors Sow seeds of beets, broccoli, carrots, celery, lettuce, peas, radishes, spinach, turnips.
Planting
Plant asparagus and rhubarb roots.
Plant onion sets or seedlings.
Set out broccoli, cabbage, cauliflower, celery, lettuce and parsley seedlings started earlier.
Routine tasks
Plow and fertilize garden one or two weeks before planting.
Sidedress rhubarb and asparagus.
Coldframe Sow seeds of above vegetables about two weeks later than indoors.

MAY
Sowing
Outdoors Sow seeds of all tender plants such as beans, corn, cucumbers, squash.
Make succession sowings of beets, carrots, early lettuce, peas, radishes, spinach, turnips.
Planting
Set out seedling cucumbers, eggplants, peppers, tomatoes.
Routine tasks
Thin seedlings of outdoor-sown crops as necessary.
Sidedress and hill up potatoes.
Provide support for peas.
Begin hoeing out weeds or apply mulch.
Harvesting
Radishes, spinach, turnips, early lettuce, rhubarb, first asparagus spears, spring onions.

JUNE
Sowing
Make succession sowings of snap beans, corn, radishes, beets, carrots, turnips. Sow Seed for fall celery crop.
Routine tasks
Stake tomatoes.
Remove flowering shoots on rhubarb.
Hoe and mulch crops.
Remove harvested crops and plant a follow-up.

Month-by-month guide 2

Harvesting
Radishes, spinach, turnips, lettuce, rhubarb, asparagus, beets, carrots, broccoli, early cabbage, spring onions.

JULY
Sowing
Make succession sowings of snap beans, corn, beets, carrots, turnips.
Routine tasks
Water faithfully when weather is dry.
Hoe out weeds and continue mulching if using grass clippings.
Tie up tomatoes.
Remove harvested crops and plant a follow-up.
Harvesting
Bush beans, beets, broccoli, cauliflower, carrots, celery, corn, cucumbers, lettuce, onions, peas, early potatoes, radishes, rhubarb, summer squash, turnips.
Make last cutting of asparagus before July 4.

AUGUST
Sowing
For a fall crop, sow beets, broccoli, cabbage, carrots, cauliflower, corn, radishes, spinach turnips, summer squash.

Planting
Set out cabbage and cauliflower plants if started in a seedbed.
Routine tasks
Continue watering and weeding.
Tie up tomatoes.
Remove harvested crops and plant a follow-up.
Harvesting
Practically everything in the garden except winter squash.

SEPTEMBER
Sowing
Last chance for turnips and fast-developing lettuce. Sow radish seeds, too.
Routine tasks
Start cleaning up garden as last crops are harvested.
Water in dry spells.
Keep down weeds.
Cut down asparagus foliage at end of month.
If garden is pretty well cleared out, sow winter rye as a cover crop.
Be prepared for an early touch of frost.
Harvesting
Winter squash and everything that is still

growing in garden. There is usually much more than is imagined to be picked.

OCTOBER
Sowing
Make one final sowing of radishes.
Indoors Sow lettuce for indoor crop.
Routine tasks
Be ready for a killing frost. When it comes, small plants such as lettuce can be protected under cloches, polyethylene film or suitable boxes. Most other produce, such as tomatoes, should be picked.
Continue to clear-up generally.
Mound up soil in asparagus rows.
Cut down rhubarb.
Sow winter rye as cover crop.
Plow garden or plant cover crop.
Harvesting
Lettuce, turnips, summer and winter squash, cabbage, carrots, beets, celery, radishes, pole beans, broccoli, cauliflower, corn, peppers, eggplants, tomatoes, spinach, potatoes.
Pick and store green tomatoes in a warm place to ripen just prior to frost.
Pot up a few plants of parsley and chives and bring indoors for winter use.

Dig up and store roots of witloof chicory and rhubarb for forcing.

NOVEMBER
Sowing
Indoors Lettuce for indoor crop.
Routine tasks
Final clean-up of garden.
Lime garden.
Harvesting
If weather continues mild, vegetables under cloches and polyethylene will continue to develop slowly for late harvest.
Carrots, beets and other root crops can still be dug up for use.

DECEMBER
Sowing
Indoors Lettuce.
Routine tasks
Check stored produce and do so every few weeks throughout winter.
Clean, oil and store garden tools.
Lime garden.
Harvesting
Indoors Force witloof chicory and rhubarb.
Outdoors Carrots, turnips and other root crops.

Index/Acknowledgements

The Royal Horticultural Society and the Publishers can accept no liability either for failure to control pests, diseases or weeds by any crop protection methods or for any consequences of their use. We specifically draw our readers' attention to the necessity of carefully reading and accurately following the manufacturer's instructions on any product.

Acknowledgements
The author is grateful for the facilities provided at Wye College during the preparation of this book, and also wishes to thank Frances Biggs for her invaluable help and advice.

Artists: Janet Blakeley, Lindsay Blow, Linda Broad, Charles Chambers, Pamela Dowson, Eric Howley, Edwina Keene, Alan Male, Sandra Pond, Ed Roberts, Stonecastle Graphics, Rod Sutterby, Lorna Turpin, West One Arts, John Woodcock.

Most of the artwork in this book has been based on photographs specially commissioned from the Harry Smith Horticultural Photographic Collection.